Truth and Vision in Katherine Anne Porter's Fiction

Darlene Harbour Unrue

"My stories are fragments of a larger plan," Katherine Anne Porter once wrote. And on another occasion she praised a critic who perceived that all her work, from the very beginning, was part of an "unbroken progression, all related."

In *Truth and Vision in Katherine Anne Porter's Fiction*, Darlene Unrue examines the encompassing themes that underlie Porter's shorter fiction and that combined to create the haunting events of her complex metaphorical novel, *Ship of Fools*. Porter believed that men and women are compelled toward discovering the truth about their existence, but that the nature of our world makes those truths difficult to discern. In her writing, Unrue finds, Porter explored not only this basic human need to confront the truth, but also the bewilderment and suffering that are so often the results of failing to fulfill that need.

Often in Porter's fiction the movement toward truth is obstructed by the hollow beliefs and illusions that abound in the world—by the seductions of ideology and dogmatic religion, by romantic love or the vision of a golden past. Clinging to such illusions, using them to lend a fa' coherence to their lives, Porter's chara ters are led away from the hard realiza- tion that truth requires accepting the existence of the unknowable at the center

knowable lies

views, letters, and intricate fabric of aces Porter's pur- the creation of a , from fragments le an honest vi-

is an associate e University of

Truth and Vision
in Katherine Anne Porter's Fiction

Truth and Vision
in Katherine Anne Porter's
Fiction

Darlene Harbour Unrue

The University of Georgia Press

Athens

© 1985 by the University of Georgia Press
Athens, Georgia 30602
All rights reserved

Designed by Kathi L. Dailey
Set in 11 on 13 Linotron 202 Electra

The paper in this book meets the guidelines for
permanence and durability of the Committee on
Production Guidelines for Book Longevity of the
Council on Library Resources.

Printed in the United States of America

89 88 87 86 85   5 4 3 2 1

Library of Congress Cataloging in Publication Data

Unrue, Darlene Harbour.
Truth and vision in Katherine Anne Porter's fiction.

Bibliography: p.
Includes index.
1. Porter, Katherine Anne, 1890–1980—Criticism and
interpretation.   I. Title.
PS3531.O752Z83   1985   813'.52   84-23925
ISBN 0-8203-0768-8 (alk. paper)

To my mother and father,
Hazel Turner Harbour and Earl Thomas Harbour

Contents

Preface • ix

Acknowledgments • xi

Introduction • 1

Chapter One. The Inner Darkness • 12

Chapter Two. Systems and Patterns • 60

Chapter Three. Ideals • 106

Chapter Four. Reconciliations • 146

Chapter Five. Ship of Fools • 161

Chapter Six. Style and Theme • 218

Notes • 221

Bibliography • 245

Index • 257

Preface

I began working on a critical study of Katherine Anne Porter's fiction late in 1975, and I met Porter herself the following spring in Brownwood, Texas, near her birthplace at Indian Creek. I have spent the intervening years reading the available criticism and biography, examining her letters and papers, and tracing her movements in Mexico. The book's thesis is the same as it was in 1976, when Porter read and approved of the sections on "The Grave," which from the outset illustrated the direction of my work. My research into her personal papers and correspondence confirmed and refined the theme.

Throughout the work I have not attempted to make distinctions among the short stories, long stories, and short novels—categories Porter suggested when she rejected *nouvelle* as a description of anything she wrote. But the labels are cumbersome, and I generally chose to follow the lead of the editors of her collected fictional works, placing everything but the essays, the poems, and *Ship of Fools* under the rubric *stories*. I have cited within the text the page numbers of quotations from *The Collected Essays and Occasional Writings* (designated CE) and *The Collected Stories* (CS); whenever it is clear that the quotation is from *The Collected Stories*, only numbers appear in parentheses. In chapter 5, the parenthetic numbers refer to pages in the first edition of *Ship of Fools*.

Porter's letters have not yet been collected, and very few have been published. The main depository of her papers and letters is the McKeldin Library at the University of Maryland, College Park, Maryland. The Beinecke Rare Book and Manuscript Library at Yale University also has many of her letters in the collections of others, and the Harry Ransom Humanities Research Center of the University of Texas at Austin has some important Porter letters, manuscripts, and miscellaneous materials. Other libraries and collections have been identified in individual citations.

The first problem in a thematic study like this one is that of determining where to discuss stories that contain more than one of the contributing canonical themes. In each chapter I have acknowledged all the stories that are thematically related but have reserved the major exegesis of a given story for the chapter or chapters that identify its controlling themes. The only exception has been *Ship of Fools*, which contains all the themes that are developed in the stories and which I treat in a chapter to itself.

Acknowledgments

I n the course of the long development of this book I have accumulated numerous intellectual debts. In the beginning I was aided immeasurably by administrators and faculty of Howard Payne University in Brownwood, Texas; President Roger L. Brooks introduced me to Katherine Anne Porter, Dean George C. Pittman provided a forum of Porter scholars on whom to try my thesis, and Professors Charlotte Laughlin and William Crider made possible Miss Porter's reading and commenting upon my work.

I am immediately grateful to the University of Nevada for a year's sabbatical; to the University Research Council, which underwrote much of the cost of my research in Mexico; and especially to Marjorie Barrick and the Barrick Foundation, which provided funds for travel and study crucial to the academic integrity of my work.

I am indebted as well to numerous libraries and their staffs: to the McKeldin Library at the University of Maryland, College Park, for permission to use the materials in the Katherine Anne Porter Papers, and to Donald Farren, Mary Boccaccio, and Charlotte Brown for particular help; to the Beinecke Rare Book and Manuscript Library at Yale University for permission to use Katherine Anne Porter's letters and papers in the collections of other persons, and especially to David E. Schoonover, curator of the American Literature Collection; to the Harry Ransom Humanities Research Center at the University of Texas at Austin for permission to use and cite Porter materials in their manuscript collections; to the University Research Library, Department of

Special Collections, University of California, Los Angeles, with particular thanks to Brooke Whiting and James Davis; to Howard B. Gotlieb and the Mugar Memorial Library at Boston University for supplying Porter materials held there and for permission to use materials in the Carleton Beals Collection; and to the Cornell University Library, the Newberry Library, and the Princeton University Library for use of Porter correspondence in their collections.

For sustaining help I am especially grateful to members of the library staff of the James R. Dickinson Library at the University of Nevada, Las Vegas, to Elmer Curley, Harold Erickson, Robert Ball, Corryn Crosby-Brown, Myoung-ja Lee Kwon, Joan Rozzi, Dotty Edelman, and Chester Davis, whose knowledge of Mexican popular music solved a critical problem. I thank also Harold G. Morehouse, director of libraries at the University of Nevada, Reno.

My research in Mexico yielded extraordinary results, for which I am indebted to a great many people. Colleagues from the University of Nevada—Thomas C. Wright, Costandína Titus, and my husband, John Calvin Unrue—traveled to Mexico with me to combine their own research and insights with mine and to pursue indefatigably an important aspect of my study. I owe much to generous people in Mexico who spent long hours with us and contributed their memories and knowledge to the filling in of the historical picture of Anglo-Americans and Mexicans who were Katherine Anne Porter's companions during her years there. I thank Mabel and George Rickards, who knew Carleton Beals, William Spratling, William Niven, and many other archaeologists and artists active in the revolutionary movement; Carol Reynoso, of the *Anglo-American Directory,* who led me to many survivors and heirs of the expatriate community; to Edgar Skidmore, who arrived in Mexico City during Obregón's presidency and remembered Eugene Pressly, Edward Weston, and Diego Rivera; to Katherine Skidmore Blair, whose knowledge of her mother-in-law, Antonieta Rivas de Blair, shed significant light on the inner structure of the Mexican renaissance; to Winifred Hill and her daughter, Janet Coerr, who vividly recalled artists and intellectuals, including Rivera, who routinely gathered at their home on Sunday mornings; to Joe Nash, travel editor of the Mexico City *News;* to the research staff of *Uno Mas Uno;* to Señora Soledad Guzmán, who was Katherine Anne Porter's landlady; and to Dr. Felipe García Beraza, director de actividades culturales, Instituto Mexicano-Norteamericano de Relaciones Culturales. I was especially honored by meetings with Pablo O'Higgins, who studied with Diego Rivera, and renowned architect and painter Juan O'Gorman, who shared memories, opinions, and hospitality with us. Both have since died.

Colleagues here and elsewhere have contributed expertise and encouragement over the years, and I have valued especially the help of John Irsfeld, Margaret Lyneis, Evan Blythin, Richard Harp, Michael McCollum, Linda McCollum, Donald Schmiedel, Gerald Rubin, and Hart Wegner. I thank also Arnold J. Bauer of the University of California, Davis, and John A. Britton of Francis Marion College, who generously shared his knowledge of Carleton Beals with me. The careful reading of the manuscript by Joan Givner of the University of Regina was particularly valuable, and Thomas F. Walsh, Georgetown University, provided many helpful suggestions about the Mexican material in the book. I also acknowledge with gratitude the work of student researchers Lorna McNeil, Jacklyn McNally, Richard McNally, and Kathy Baker, and secretaries Susan Buffington and Evelyn Wilson.

I owe a special debt to Isabel Bayley, Katherine Anne Porter's literary trustee; to Robert Penn Warren, who graciously allowed me to read and quote from his correspondence with Porter; to Carolyn Kennedy Beals, who directed me to information about her late husband; to the heirs of Henry Miller, who allowed me to quote from a letter Miller had written to Porter in 1934; to Malcolm Cowley, who gave me permission to quote from Porter's letters to him; to Paul Porter, Katherine Anne Porter's nephew; and to Russell Lynes, whose brother was Porter's friend and photographer. A portion of the material in chapter 3 was first published in *American Literature* as "Diego Rivera and Katherine Anne Porter's 'The Martyr'" (October 1984), and I thank the editors for permission to reprint this.

I wish to thank the editorial staff of the University of Georgia Press, and I owe special thanks to Charles East, the editor of the book, whose keen interest in Katherine Anne Porter and his competence are reflected in the thoroughness with which he has overseen the progress of the book.

The debt I owe my husband, John Calvin Unrue, is inestimable. His wisdom and inspiration, as well as his considerable literary judgment, lie close to the heart of my work.

Introduction

I n 1930 Katherine Anne Porter was known to only a small group of admiring American readers. However, the publication in that year of her first book, *Flowering Judas and Other Stories*, widened her following and began to fix her high position among twentieth-century American writers. The 1930s reviews of *Flowering Judas* were unanimously praise-filled, one reviewer saying that "all [the stories] are exquisitely done . . . in a language transcendently beautiful" and another declaring that "Miss Porter should demand much work of her talent" for "there is nothing quite like it."[1] In subsequent years, *Pale Horse, Pale Rider: Three Short Novels* (1939), *The Leaning Tower and Other Stories* (1944), and *The Days Before* (1952) received only slightly less critical acclaim. Porter's "range and versatility" and exquisite style were commonly cited by reviewers while only a very few faults were noted.[2] With the publication of *The Days Before* she was praised also for her critical prowess and her ability to charm an audience with "living lovely prose."[3] Porter's reputation did not waver until the appearance of *Ship of Fools* (1962), which provoked a critical controversy that has not yet been completely settled.[4]

The Modern Library edition of *Flowering Judas and Other Stories* (a reprinting of the 1935 edition) appeared in 1940 almost simultaneously with the first major critical article to be written about Porter's fiction, Lodwick Hartley's "Katherine Anne Porter" in the *Sewanee Review*. Taking as his departure Porter's statement that her "one aim . . . [has been] to tell a straight story and to give a true testimony," Hartley examined the stories and short novels against that standard. Although he praised Porter's "consummate mastery of detail," he focused equally on what he regarded as the failures in the stories and in Porter's artistic method, namely her "structural and emotional limitations" and her tendency "to become distinctively effeminate." He concluded, nevertheless, that "among her Southern contemporaries in short prose fiction Miss Porter has few peers."

Two years later "Irony with a Center," the classic article by Robert Penn Warren, appeared in the *Kenyon Review*. Warren lamented that Porter's fiction, despite "widespread critical adulation," had not found a popular audience. He accounted for this phenomenon by her refusal to compromise, a stance consistent with her protracted method of composition, and by an unintentional disservice of reviewers who in abstracting her fiction into phrases like "beautiful style" and "English of a purity and precision almost unique in contemporary American fiction" had chilled and "put off" potential readers. Warren dissected passages in "Flowering Judas," "Noon Wine," "The Cracked Looking-Glass," and "Old Mortality" to illustrate the evocative power of the prose. In the vivid phrasing and imagery Warren found paradox, a tension between contradictions that he regarded as the essence of both Porter's style and her world view.

Since then, numerous articles, masters' theses, and doctoral dissertations have been devoted to some portion of Porter's works or life, and in 1957 the first critical book on Porter appeared, Mooney's *The Fiction and Criticism of Katherine Anne Porter*. It was followed by West's *Katherine Anne Porter* (1963); Nance's *Katherine Anne Porter and the Art of Rejection* (1964); Hendrick's *Katherine Anne Porter* (1965); Emmons's *Katherine Anne Porter: The Regional Stories* (1967); Krishnamurthi's *Katherine Anne Porter: A Study* (1971); Liberman's *Katherine Anne Porter's Fiction* (1971); Hardy's *Katherine Anne Porter* (1973); and DeMouy's *Katherine Anne Porter's Women: The Eye of Her Fiction* (1983). In 1969, in response to what they saw as a need for a substantial Porter criticism, Lodwick Hartley and George Core offered an alternative to a unified, book-length study, *Katherine Anne Porter: A Critical Symposium*, a collection of critical and biographical essays that they hoped would "give the reader a valuable comprehensive view."

Ten years later another such anthology, *Katherine Anne Porter: A Collection of Critical Essays*, edited by Robert Penn Warren, appeared in Prentice-Hall's Twentieth Century Views series.

The numerous critical essays that have been published since Hartley's first one in 1940 have been either explications of individual stories or thematic analyses of groups of stories that seemed to offer an opportunity for discerning a coherent unity within the available canon. The essays are uneven in value, but over the years a few insightful articles have added to the general understanding of Porter's fiction.[5]

The self-evident truth that a writer's life and works are bound together inseparably is especially apparent in Porter's fiction, for it is clear that she drew heavily upon her own life for the inspiration of her art.[6] In some instances she herself verified the kernel of real-life experience that was the genesis of a work, as she does in her essay " 'Noon Wine': The Sources" and in "Why She Selected 'Flowering Judas' " in Whit Burnett's *This Is My Best*. That relationship between life and art has been a difficult ground of exploration because before 1982 biographical accounts of Porter were, to say the least, unreliable. She, too, often contributed to the confusion by contradicting herself from one interview to another and by destroying or keeping private those proofs or documents that would have clarified the details of her long life and made some of the comparisons between experience and the artistic rendering of it more readily available. Two masters' theses have dealt with Porter's life in particular parts of the United States, and Bonelyn Lugg's and Drewey Gunn's doctoral dissertations have centered in part on Porter's experiences in Mexico. The interviews Porter gave throughout her life are useful, of course, and Enrique Hank Lopez created a kind of autobiography by weaving together excerpts from Porter's taped "memories" of her earlier life with comments she made elsewhere on the same subjects. Many of the gaps were filled with the appearance in 1982 of Joan Givner's carefully researched biography of Porter, *Katherine Anne Porter: A Life*.

Considered altogether, the available body of Porter scholarship has not provided a clear and thorough answer to questions about Porter's world view and about the relationships among her stories and her novel. The need for such a study has been apparent for at least a decade, but only since Porter's papers were deposited at the University of Maryland has a thorough criticism become a possibility.

Although critics have given much attention to Porter's themes and methods, they have failed to see the proper unity among her works. An early reviewer voiced chagrin that there were no "threads of continuity between the stories," and others have resorted to such superficial categorizing as "Mexican stories" or "Miranda stories."[7] And yet Porter herself seemed to have no doubt about her work's unity. In 1940 she insisted that everything she had written and everything she would write were part of a large design. In the preface to the Modern Library edition of *Flowering Judas and Other Stories*, she says of that collection of her stories: "They are fragments of a much larger plan which I am still engaged in carrying out, and they are what I was then able to achieve in the way of order and form and statement in a period of grotesque dislocations in a whole society when the world was heaving in the sickness of a millennial change" (CE, 457).[8] Nearly twenty-five years later she wrote to Caroline Gordon: "Your perception that all my work from first to *now* (not last I hope) is an unbroken progression, all related, was a marvelous stroke of perception and critical understanding."[9]

Porter could not have reached that sense of her own work's unity until she had the advantage of some years' perspective. She needed a body of stories she could examine and some unwritten ones she could contemplate before she in fact could see the pattern in her own work. But what was "the larger plan" and how is her work related in "an unbroken progression"?

Some critics have tried to answer those questions. Among the first to try was Edmund Wilson, who insisted that Porter's stories were not "illustrations of anything that is reducible to a moral law, or a political or social analysis, or even a principle of human behavior." Wilson consequently sorted Porter's stories into three "fairly distinct groups": "stories of family life in working-class or middle-class households," "pictures of foreign parts," and "stories about women."[10] Later critics were to complicate the categories, with the most ingenious analysis presented by William Nance in *Katherine Anne Porter and the Art of Rejection*. Nance sets forth the thesis that in Porter's work "the principle of rejection is the dynamic core of a clearly defined pattern of behavior with accompanying motifs." By "rejection" he seems to mean "escape," and in order to develop his thesis he divides Porter's stories into Alpha stories and Beta stories, or stories with an autobiographical protagonist and stories with a protagonist removed from the auto-biographical center. He describes the rejection theme as "a pattern of forces which may or may not coincide with the explicit thematic inten-tion of a given story, yet always governs its dominant emotional ef-fect."[11] A different integrating theme is proposed by Jane DeMouy in *Katherine Anne Porter's Women*. Conceding that "Noon Wine" and "The Leaning Tower," among the major works, fall outside her critical frame, DeMouy identifies in Porter's works a unifying protagonist, an archetypal female who is torn between her need for love and her desire for personal identity.

The interpretation of Porter's plan that stirred the widest interest was presented in 1960 by James William Johnson. He determined that even without the then still-awaited *Ship of Fools* it was possible to see a pattern in the published work and to guess that the novel would be Porter's "summarizing 'testimony.'" Johnson defined the "essence" of her fiction in terms of themes, symbols, and what he called the "un-derlying philosophical logos." The six themes are "the individual with-in his heritage, the relationship of past to present in the mind"; "cultur-al displacement"; "unhappy marriages and the self-delusion attendant upon them"; "the death of love and the survival of individual integ-rity"; "man's slavery to his own nature and subjugation to a human fate which dooms him to suffering and disappointment"; and finally a theme that he calls "an amalgam of all Miss Porter's themes." Johnson says that symbols and a lucid style combine with the recurrent themes to propagate "a fictional point of view which is amazingly consistent and complete." He explains Porter's world view by the following "logos":

> A child is born into a world seemingly ordered and reasonable but it is in fact chaotic, ridiculous, and doubt-ridden ("The Old Order"). He learns at an early age that he is an atomistic creature, often unloved ("The Down-ward Path"), and that the delightful spectacle of life masks fear, hatred, and bitterness ("The Circus"). He discovers that life and love must end in death ("The Grave," "The Fig Tree"). He must inevitably reject his heritage as

lies and his family as hostile aliens ("Old Mortality"); but when he tries to substitute something else in their place, he is driven back by his own weaknesses to what he has been conditioned to ("María Concepción," "Magic"). If he makes the break with the past and tries to replace the lost old love with a new, he is doomed to despair ("Pale Horse, Pale Rider"). If he tries to substitute another heritage for his own, he finds it full of evil ("The Leaning Tower"); or he discovers that he has lost his power to love through denying his own tradition ("Flowering Judas"). There is nothing for him to cling to but his desperate belief in his own courage and integrity ("Theft") and what little of love and certainty he has in life ("The Cracked Looking-Glass"). But life is senselessly cruel ("He"), full of frustration and contention ("Rope," "That Tree," "A Day's Work"); and it ends in annihilation and the extinction of all hope ("The Jilting of Granny Weatherall"). Such is Miss Porter's fictional philosophy.[12]

Although the themes as Johnson defines them are not obviously related to one another, he does make an important point. He notes that Porter has had an "artistic preoccupation with 'truth.' " He sees her "truth," however, as "the truth of feeling and behavior rather than ideas." Johnson says that Porter's notion of truth accounts for her emphasis on people "rather than humanity or concepts." Porter's characters and events indeed seem real rather than allegorical, but a closer look at her "preoccupation with truth" will reveal that in her fiction the facts of accurate observation, or accurate memory, lead naturally and inevitably to philosophical truths that are unified within a large design.

Porter's concept of truth leads to her world view and eventually to the thematic unity of her fiction. Her concept begins with the premise that truth can be both subjective and elusive. In her essay "St. Augustine and the Bullfight" she wrote, "What is truth? I often ask myself. Who knows?" (CE, 93). And later, in a letter to Donald Sutherland, she said, "None of us, not one man or woman in the whole world, since we got up on our hind legs and started looking for the Truth, has ever been sure he has found it. No matter what they say, and no matter how much blood they are willing to shed in defense of their belief. I intend to go on looking for my little fragment, though, with my entire sensory and intellectual being, coming up once in awhile with some finding or other . . . what else did anyone ever do?"[13] Her use of the word *fragment* here is noteworthy in light of her description in 1940 of her stories as "fragments of a much larger plan"; by analogy, the larger plan is truth.

Porter believed that humans are compelled toward the discovery of truth. She herself expressed this compulsion when she reportedly told her father, "I want to go and see the world. I want to know the world like I know the palm of my hand."[14] Indeed, "truth" and "knowing" are nearly synonymous terms in Porter's world view and are related to the idea of "order." The truth of her universe is broad, like the natural laws or "discipline" Emerson defines in "Nature," his manifesto on Transcendentalism. For Porter, knowing comes from apprehending such universal laws within oneself and within nature. One "sees" meaning in life through a sense of order that is founded on general principles, and thus Porter's world view encompasses both absolute and subjective truth. Porter departed from Emerson, Thoreau, and Whitman among Transcendentalists, and moved closer to Hawthorne and Melville in her preoccupation with human frailty, human limitation, and the human capacity for evil, all of which she considered fundamental laws within the natural universe.

She regarded the movement toward truth as arduous and never complete, and it moreover was filled with illusion. In fact, she saw some elements of truth to be beyond human understanding and simply to be accepted as unfathomable. She wrote, "There is at the heart of the universe a riddle no man can solve, and in the end, God may be the answer."[15] Failure to accept the "unknowable" leads humans to discern a "reason" for every phenomenon and an "answer" to every question. Those reasons and answers were for Porter common illusions. The truth that is available lies in human nature. To know oneself requires confronting all parts of elemental self, including, for want of a better word, the darkness. We must accept, Porter says, all of life, both instinct and intellect, body and spirit, and the past and the present. Such modes of thought have obvious links not only to American Transcendentalism but also to Augustinian Christianity, to Freudian psychology (although she would reject as distortions some twentieth-century interpretations of it), and to a pervasive humanism.

The subjective sense of order is a highly significant concept in Porter's doctrine. The two most likely shapers of that sense are art and religion. In 1942 she wrote, "I agree with Mr. E. M. Forster that there are only two possibilities for any real order: in art and in religion." She said that "only the work of saints and artists gives us any reason to believe that the human race is worth belonging to."[16] However, in Porter's opinion the pure religion of saints was rare.

She was particularly sensitive to the possibilities that art offered for providing a proper sense of order. Like her contemporaries William Carlos Williams and Wallace Stevens, among others, she saw a world essentially chaotic and a human compulsion to find order, or meaning, in it. "So much depends," says Williams, on being able to distinguish recognizable forms in the mire of allness, and Porter seems to agree. She told Donald Sutherland, "Chaos *is*—we are in it."[17] And she elaborated to Barbara Thompson a few years later: "There seems to be a kind of order in the universe, in the movement of the stars and the turning of the earth and the changing of the seasons, and even in the cycle of human life. But human life itself is almost pure chaos." She also told Thompson, "The work of the artist—the only thing he's good for—is to take these handfuls of confusion and disparate things, things that seem to be irreconcilable, and put them together in a frame to give them some kind of shape and meaning. Even if it's only his view of a meaning."[18] She was invoking a metaphor she had used earlier when she wrote about "admirable attempts to get a little meaning and order into our view of our destiny, in the same spirit which moves the artist to labor with his little handful of chaos, bringing it to coherence within a frame."[19]

Her idea was that art should frame life, that is, interpret it within limits understandable to the finite human mind. It should not "imitate the shapelessness of life," she told Sutherland.[20] And she described her own effort to make order with art. In "St. Augustine and the Bullfight" she says, "My own habit of writing fiction has provided a wholesome exercise to my natural, incurable tendency to try to wrangle the sprawling mess of our existence in this bloody world into some kind of shape: almost any shape will do, just so it is recognizably made with human hands, one small proof the more of the validity and reality of the human imagination" (CE, 93). She defined literary art as "the business of setting human events to rights and giving them meanings that, in fact, they do not possess, or not obviously" (CE, 94). Although Porter believed that art should bring order, like Stevens's jar in Tennessee, unlike Stevens she was unwilling to put her faith in art alone.

If art and religion are primary aids for finding order, what are the particular obstacles? One must begin with art and religion themselves, for there is an illusory order to unnatural art and perverted religion. Unnatural art is either dogmatic or insincere, and Porter warns against the artist's elevating "his weaknesses into dogma" and against his accepting somebody else's idea of order as his own, in short denying spontaneity to the artistic spirit by imposing on it a codified system of either his own construction or that of someone else. [21] She refers to our being "lulled or exalted or outraged into a brief acceptance" of Homer's or Sophocles's or Dante's or Chaucer's or Shakespeare's "version of things." [22] Again in the spirit of her Transcendental forebears she reminds us that art at its best can only inspire us to continue our own search for Truth. Providing that inspiration is the province of the artist, who, like Whitman's bard or Stevens's poet, stands armed with imagination in the vanguard of the human mass.

Systematized art is not very different from systematized religion, except the latter has a capacity for malice that the former lacks. Religion that becomes a set of laws becomes an end unto itself and serves only self-satisfied and vainglorious men and women. Praising Forster's rejection of "belief in Belief" and declaring that when T. S. Eliot embraced the church his critical powers failed, she explained her sense of the value and dangers of religion:

> Grant that the idea of God is the most splendid single act of the creative human imagination, and that all his multiple faces and attributes correspond to some need and satisfy some deep desire in mankind; still, for the Inquirers, it is impossible not to conclude that this mystical concept has been harnessed rudely to machinery of the most mundane sort, and has been made to serve the ends of an organization which, ruling under divine guidance, has ruled very little better, and in some respects, worse, than certain rather mediocre but frankly manmade systems of government. And it has often lent its support to the worst evils in secular government, fighting consistently on the side of heavy artillery. And it has seemed at times

not to know the difference between Good and Evil, but to get them hopelessly confused with legalistic right and wrong; justifying the most cynical
expedients of worldly government by a high morality; and committing the
most savage crimes against human life for the love of God. [23]

Porter speaks often of distrusting systems of government, either economic or theocratic. Even the most nobly inspired revolutions in art,
religion, or politics eventually become corrupt, she implied in her
fiction, for it is very difficult to keep alive the first honorable intentions
of a movement. She came to share with existentialists the notion that
the rising phoenix carries the tinder for its own ashes, and with Yeats
the belief that only the millenium's beginning, in which the old shib-
boleths are destroyed, is truly glorious. The spirit of freedom and
change in time defers to its own impulse of self-preservation and becomes itself a rigid shell of an idea.

For Porter, however, it was not only systems that offered the appeal
of superficial order. So also are people lured by visible patterns. Like
Faulkner's Benjy Compson at the end of *The Sound and the Fury*, they
embrace a spatial, mechanical order in the external world as a substitute for both inner and universal order. It is an illusion, Porter
shows, that ensures despair as its failure is discovered.

Porter saw other kinds of illusions to which persons cling. Often
these are ideals that seem in themselves to be truths, and they are
clutched as obsessively as if they were the end-all of human life. For
some, it is the illusion of romantic love or the illusion of the perfect
past, ideals, Porter assures us, not grounded in the reality of chaotic
human life.

Each of Katherine Anne Porter's stories and her novel fall within this
design, which Robert Penn Warren summarized precisely as simply
two propositions: "the necessity for moral definition, and the difficulty
of moral definition."[24] Each of her stories and her novel are about
confronting and accepting the totality of life, including one's own
nature and the Unknowable, or the bewilderment and suffering that
come from failing to do so; or about the deception of systems and the
illusion of ideals which we embrace as we attempt to find truth. Some
of this suffering is imposed by human limitation and some is the result

of the duplicity of the propagators of systems and hollow ideals. The greatest affirmations in her work are found in her statements about the power of love that gives a glimpse of the Unknowable, or God, as she says, and in the vision of truth that emerges in our small acceptances of the multiple nature of ourselves and the universe.

Chapter One

The Inner Darkness

K atherine Anne Porter subscribed to the duality of nature, its bipartite spirit and body, goodness and evil, but like others in her time she also believed that it was the opposite of spirit or goodness that was most difficult for human beings to accept. She explains the difficulty as a phenomenon particularly relevant to the nineteenth and twentieth centuries and to a specific part of the world. She says, "At once the difficulty, and the hope, of our special time in this world of Western Europe and America is that we have been brought up for many generations in the belief, however tacit, that all humanity was almost unanimously engaged in going forward, naturally to better things and to higher reaches." She traces the belief to "the eighteenth century at least when the Encyclopedists seized upon the Platonic theory that the highest pleasure of mankind was the pursuit of the good, the true, and the beautiful." Consequently, "progress," she says, "in precisely the sense of perpetual, gradual amelioration of the hard human lot, has been taught popularly not just as theory of possibility but as an article of faith and the groundwork of a whole political doctrine."[1] The implication of her theory is that humans choose to see only the superficially good and beautiful and thus ignore an important part of universal truth. "Darkness," in the sense of the irrational as well as the destructive, seems the appropriate label, for it encompasses all those unenlightened aspects of life associated with the physical and the instinctual. Porter believed that humans dread knowing this element of truth about themselves; they choose to believe that, unlike Dr. Jekyll, they have overcome their base selves. She later referred to this human propensity in her essay on Circe, of whom she writes: "Her unique power as goddess was that she could reveal to men the truth about themselves by showing to each man himself in his true shape according to his inmost nature. For this she was rightly dreaded and feared; her very name was a word of terror" (CE, 133).

Porter believed that in the quest for truth the place to begin is oneself, and specifically the dark and primitive self. On the one hand, that which is primitive can be appealing in its simplicity, and world-weary, system-weary Inquirers often turn to it for a glimpse of elemental reality. Porter praised the artwork of children, whom she called "true primitives."[2] And she said of D. H. Lawrence that he had gone to Mexico "in the hope of finding there, among alien people and their mysterious cult, what he had failed to find in his own race or within himself: a center and a meaning to life."[3]

The reasons Porter herself went to Mexico are varied. She told Barbara Thompson that she went there in 1920, when everyone else was going to Europe, because she felt she "had business there."[4] A part of her business must have been to fulfill the lure of primitivism. She described to Monroe Wheeler the first attraction she had to Mexico: "Early in 1920, February or March, I met Adolfo Best-Maugard in New York, where he had come as a young painter with a system of design he had invented himself based on ancient Mexico designs from buried cities, mostly Mayan. Though Aztec and other tribes contributed motifs." She says, "I found it fascinating, Best and I spent long days talking about this."[5] She continues to describe plans she had with Best-Maugard for writing a textbook on the subject and also the plans they had for a Mexican ballet that was to be offered to Pavlova and that was to incorporate primitive Mexican dances set against a stylized version of Xochimilco, the most famous of the ancient floating gardens in the valley of Mexico.

Best-Maugard's and Porter's interest in primitive art forms coincided with a revival of the primitive that was very much a part of the revolution going on in Mexico, the revolution which Porter "ran smack into," as she told Thompson, for she did go to Mexico before the year 1920 was out. Although many revolutionary movements in Mexico from the early nineteenth century had sought the abolition of caste distinction, it was not until the constitution of 1917, adopted under the regime of Venustiano Carranza, that communal lands officially were restored to the Indians at the same time that the expropriation of church property was reinforced. The interest in primitive art was an outgrowth of the reforms that were designed to restore Mexico to the Mexicans, true Mexicans being the Indians, not Europeans or Creoles. As the caste system was to be replaced with a more democratic system, there were attempts to scrape away the European influences that began with the Conquistadores and to get to unadulterated origins.[6] Best-Maugard's method of painting, described as a system of seven primitive forms, was consistent with the *indiginista* philosophy in Mexico, set into motion perhaps by Francisco Madero and furthered by Alvaro Obregón, who took over the Mexican government in 1920, the year of Porter's arrival.

As welcome as many of Obregón's reforms were, his government did not exist uncontested. There were attempted insurrections and resistance from both the church and foreign interests, and the revolution continued to one degree or another for many years, through not only the Obregón regime but the Calles, Rodriquez, and Cárdenas regimes as well.[7]

The attempt at the leveling of the social classes in Mexico was tied to political change. One has only to see many of the murals painted during the twenties to see the coalition between primitive art and politics. The great Indian figures in the larger-than-life frescoes are seen first as noble inhabitants of a prelapsarian world, then as victims of the European conquerors, and later as productive happy workers with modern machines.[8] The aesthetic movement included an awesome attempt to excavate the ancient past of Mexico and bring it into harmony with twentieth-century socialistic aims. The murals symbolize many of the revolution's ideals: to instill pride in the pre-Columbian past, to "forget" the intervening Europeanization, with its repellent caste system and theocracy, and to equalize the people. It was natural that an important part of the movement in art should be an interest in Mexico's archaeological ruins.

Archaeological interest in Mexico was not new in 1920. In the first several centuries after the Conquest the pyramids in the Valley of Mexico had steadily attracted the attention of certain friars, European travelers, and academicians—persons like Bernardino de Sahagún, Giovanni Francesco Gemelli, and Alexander von Humboldt. There was a stirring of excitement in 1790 when a major artifact was discovered quite by accident as workers were carrying out the viceroy's orders to make repairs in the plaza in front of the cathedral and unearthed the great Aztec stone calendar. Another important relic was disinterred in 1823 when the Englishman William Bullock, with the Mexican government's permission, dug up the massive twelve-ton basalt statue of Coatlicue, the terrible-visaged Mexican goddess of the earth. Over the next half century, a relatively small number of scholars and scientists, mostly European, traveled to Mexico to study the artifacts and historical documents and in some instances to try to put together the history of ancient Mexico.[9]

The strife of civil wars overshadowed any widespread interest in the buried history of Mexico, although Maximilian tried to stimulate such an interest when he organized in 1864 the first scientific commission to study Mexican antiquities, with a particular emphasis on the ruins of Teotihuacán. At his execution in 1867, however, the work done by the commission was dispersed in Europe and North America, and further significant archaeological speculation in Mexico was delayed until Joseph Desire Charnay and Augustus and Alice Le Plongeon conducted excavations at Tula, Teotihuacán, and Chichen Itza in the 1870s and 1880s.

The first native Mexican to appreciate Charnay's and the Le Plongeons's excavations, generally considered the first real digs in the Mexican valley, was Leopoldo Batres, whose half-sister was the teenage wife of the aged Díaz and who was made the official inspector and protector of Mexico's archaeological monuments. With Díaz's exile, Batres lost his title and his reputation, and he was succeeded by Manuel Gamio, who had been educated at Columbia University and whom Madero named director of the archaeological section of the national museum, as well as inspector of monuments. Although exploration of the ruins and excavations continued, it was not until 1917 and the establishment of a representative democratic federal republic that sufficient peace was restored to make searching into Mexico's past a comfortable prospect. With the new liberal constitution, Gamio, as head of the Department of Anthropology at the Museo Nacional, was able to find the needed support for a thorough study from social, aesthetic, and scientific perspectives of not only the ruins of Teotihuacán but of the surrounding valley.[10]

Porter was drawn formally into the established interest in Mexico's primitive past. She met Gamio and William Niven, an aging American archaeologist who had been exploring the Mexican valley since 1889, soon after she arrived in Mexico in 1920. She describes in notes under the heading "Gamio and the Cafe" an incident at a luncheon meeting with "an enormously distinguished Mexican anthropologist," and she mentions in another page of random notes dated November 9 and 10 that she "spent [the] morning in W. A. Nivens shop of Aztec curios he has dug out of a buried city."[11] A few years later Porter was among those who with the approval of President Obregón gathered an exhibit of Mexican popular arts and crafts for showing in the United States, and she wrote the book, *Outline of Mexican Popular Arts and Crafts* (1922), that was to accompany the ill-fated exhibit.[12] In her acknowledgment in the book she describes her research into the subject as "a richly rewarded adventure among intelligences and devotions."[13] With the intelligence and devotion of primitivism, however, is the reasonless attachment to unseen forces, natural in their simplicity and equally natural in their destructiveness. Porter's writings in this period indicate that she indeed was aware of the complex nature of primitivism.

Against this backdrop and out of these experiences emerges Porter's first published story, "María Concepción." The source of the story, Porter told Hank Lopez, was an account Niven gave her of one María, who was married to his foreman, Juan. María's murdering of Juan's teenage sweetheart, the villagers' refusal to provide the authorities with incriminating evidence against María, and María's taking over the dead woman's child at the same time she again takes up her marriage with Juan are found in Porter's fictional version of the anecdote. Porter wrote the story the following year, when she had returned to New York, and it was published in the *Century*.[14] Although she had written essays and newspaper articles, had retold some children's stories, and had ghostwritten *My Chinese Marriage*, she always thought of "María Concepción" as her first published story because it was her first published original piece of fiction.

"María Concepción" is set in the early years of the primitive revival, before excavations had the blessing and encouragement of the Mexican government; the only archaeologist in the story is a foreign one, British or American, and the Indians in the story have not yet understood the value of disinterring the relics of their ancient past. The story begins with the name of the title character, an obviously Roman Catholic name, and for half the story the focus remains on the character María Concepción as the narrator describes her movements and thoughts. At the end of the first paragraph, however, there is an arresting sentence: "Juan and his chief would be waiting for their food in the damp trenches of the buried city." The word "chief" suggests a tribal relationship, and "buried city" suggests an ancient, dead social unit. At this early point in the story the topic of primitivism has been asserted, and an important thematic statement has been made.

María Concepción is not what she appears to be at first glimpse, an ordinary Mexican woman with a Christian name. She has other significant traits: "*Instinctive* serenity" softens her eyes, and she walks with the ease of the "*primitive* woman carrying an unborn child" (italics mine). Thus, María Concepción's primitivism is established, even though the narrator says that María Concepción has "no faith" in the charms of Lupe, the medicine woman, and is a "good Christian" with a reputation among the neighbors as "an energetic religious woman." Although she also has followed the church's requirements for marriage and has been married in the church, she confirms her link to primitive ways by superstitiously concluding that if she does not satisfy her desire for a crust of honey she will mark her unborn child. Of course, when María Concepción goes toward the hut of the beekeeper, María Rosa, she discovers her husband, Juan, cavorting among the beehives with María Rosa.

It is only after the shocked María Concepción moves on toward Juan's chief that the chief is revealed to be an archaeologist for whom Juan works and the buried city to be an excavation site. The archaeologist Givens obviously is modeled on Niven, who also collaborated with Porter on the *Outline*.[15] Her essay "The Charmed Life," written in 1942, is a reminiscence of her association with an unnamed aged archaeologist, who is surely Niven and who shares some traits with the fictional Givens: both are solitary men, without women to cook for them, and both have had a trusting relationship with their Indian diggers.[16] Only a few weeks after Porter records having visited Niven's curio shop, she wrote to her family, "I have dug out with my own hands skeletons and idols and pots and fragments of wall and roof many feet under ground, and all of them scorched and blackened."[17] She could have been describing Niven's digs between Texcoco and Tlalnepantla, just north of Mexico City, where he had come across pits which contained artifacts like those described in "María Concepción" and which led him to the discovery of ancient walled cities deep below the ground's surface.[18]

As the essay illustrates, Porter's Givens also shares with Niven an almost fanatic zeal. Givens is depicted sympathetically as one who shows "unearthly delight" in finding "small clay heads and bits of pottery and fragments of painted walls," for which the Indians believe there is "no good use on earth, being all broken and encrusted with clay" (CS, 6). The Indians who work for Givens, "helping him to uncover the lost city of their ancestors," humor him but are puzzled by his enthusiasm. They, on the other hand, make better pots, "perfectly stout and new," which they take to town and peddle "to foreigners for real money." Ironically, Givens the foreigner has more interest in their past than do the natives. "He would fairly roar for joy at times, waving a shattered pot or a human skull above his head, shouting for his photographer to come and make a picture of this!" (7). The mingling of primitivism and civilization already has been seen in María Concepción, and now it is seen in Givens, whose appreciation of the primitive past is primarily intellectual and aesthetic, and not a natural part of him. He is civilized man who can understand only certain aspects of primitivism. He cannot, for example, kill the fowl María Concepción brings for his lunch, saying to her, "Good God, woman, you do have nerve. . . . I can't do that. It gives me the creeps." The narrative voice makes the point that Givens "liked his Indians best when he could feel a fatherly indulgence for their primitive childish ways" (7).

The meaning of the sentence at the end of the first paragraph begins to emerge more clearly. Juan's and his chief's "waiting for their food in the damp trenches of the buried city" suggests the anticipations of the excavators who are supported by the *indigenista* interest. In the eyes of the leaders of the cultural revolution, the Indians were waiting for the spiritual nourishment that awareness of their rich past would provide. The foreign archaeologists, mostly British and American, waited likewise for nourishment at the same sites, but for them, as academics and scientists, it was only intellectual nourishment. The statement, subtle and simple, illustrates at once the heart of Porter's style, apparent in this very early story. It is a perfectly accurate and literal statement within the context, but larger meanings accrue to it as ironies and both topical and universal themes develop in the story.

The theme of primitivism enlarges as the action of the story continues. When Juan and María Rosa leave the village to join the war, María Concepción does not weep, and neither does she weep when her newborn baby dies. She rejects old Lupe's charms and instead goes regularly to the church, lighting candles, praying, and taking communion. Juan and María Rosa return from the war one day, she "burdened with a child daily expected." After Givens once again saves Juan from an unpleasant fate for his misdeeds, this time from death for desertion, María Rosa gives birth to a boy. The proud Juan celebrates with the village men in the "Death and Resurrection" pulque shop, and then he drunkenly and "unaccountably" goes to his own home, where he tries unsuccessfully to beat María Concepción. María Concepción vents the grief that has consumed her all this time, and instead of going to the market as she sets out to do, she instinctively goes to María Rosa's hut and slaughters her with the big knife she always carries at her belt.

When she returns to Juan, they go through a series of rituals that are modeled ironically on Christian ones. After she throws away the knife, she crawls toward him "as he had seen her crawl many times toward the shrine at Guadalupe Villa." Unlike his former carefree self, he assumes control of the tragic event, offers pity and protection to María Concepción, all the while cursing his circumstances under his breath. He lights a candle, not to pray but to see to wash the bloodstained knife. She washes her clothes and, like Pilate, her hands. When she sits before a *brasero* and cooks Juan's food, the blaze lights her face and darkens it by turns. Her primitive self has battled with her civilized self, and the reader knows which is in power by the "yellow phosphorescence" that glimmers "behind the dark iris," an image of an immemorial ferocity. Juan feels that María Concepción has "become invaluable" and he cannot "tell why."

In the sharing of blood knowledge, they enact the parody of a catechism. He questions her and she answers "whispering," and he instructs "her over and over until she . . . [has] her lesson by heart" (16). As Juan and María Concepción go with other villagers to María Rosa's death hut, the paradoxes and the intertwined relationship between the primitive and the civilized continues. The gendarmes from the village who announce the murder and investigate it are agents of civilization but also are "mixed-bloods themselves with Indian sympathies." Moreover, in death, María Rosa, the pagan purveyor of honey, bears the image of a Christian martyr. Her body is flanked by candles and shows evidence of wounds, thorn pricks and cuts of sharp stones, Christ-like and Stephen-like.

María Concepción is made peaceful by the revenge she has carried out, and ironically she is able to rationalize her deed even within Catholic dogma. She feels no guilt for having killed María Rosa but thinks to herself that "María Rosa had eaten too much honey and had had too much love. Now she must sit in hell, crying over her sins and her hard death forever and ever" (17).

The story illustrates several important points about the power of primitive urges. Somewhere beyond consciousness María Concepción has acted out a myth of revenge as old as time itself. It is no accident that María Rosa and María Concepción share the same first name; superficially they represent two dimensions of the civilized ideal, passion and purity. They are Mary of the Rose and Mary of the Conception. But the sharing of a name symbolizes a more profound sharing of the bond of racial myth. Like other aspects of their story, the Catholicism is shallow and serves to suggest through irony an elemental truth about the relative powers of primitivism and civilization. It is indeed ironic that the name shared by these two women who act out the ancient myth should be the name of the mother of the Christian god.

Pure instinct allows the villagers to participate in the enactment, protecting María Concepción under a code far different from that of civil law or church law, which in Mexico often have been the same. Lupe, with less of a veneer with which to contend, bows to the primitive law immediately and recognizes the "justice" of María Rosa's death. Although she knows that María Concepción has killed María Rosa, she tells the gendarmes nothing, pleading age and infirmity. She is said to be the dead woman's "godmother," language suggesting a church-appointed obligation, and yet when we see Lupe's primitive ways, we must ask, "What 'god'?" She seems to have no part in Roman Catholicism, she with her charms and "charred owl bones, the singed rabbit fur, the cat entrails, the messes and ointments [she] sold . . . to the ailing of the village" (4). She, in fact, appeals to the primitive within each of her listeners. When she describes the footfalls of the murderer as "like the tread of an evil spirit" and breaks forth "in a swelling oracular tone," the Indians stir "uneasily," as if they half expect her "to produce the evil spirit among them at once" (18). Lupe's god is clearly a pagan god, of myth perhaps, and in this sense she is the mentor not only to María Rosa but also to the whole village, and, Porter would say, to us all.

In spite of the Indians' failure to understand intellectually the importance of their own past as it is revealed in the discovered artifacts of their ancient cities, they have established their identity with that past in far more dramatic ways. The story "María Concepción" thus is about the instinctual, mythic life that binds and about the primitive that is stronger than all the centuries' layering of Catholicism and Western civilization. It is also about racial consciousness and tribal memory that link humans with one another more firmly than alien systems ever can. Several specific myths in fact are implicit in the story of Juan, María Concepción, and María Rosa, the most obvious one the Adam and Eve myth. The story begins in an Edenic atmosphere of sunshine, innocence, and contentment. María Concepción is more naive than innocent; she has completely forgotten that she had carnal knowledge of Juan before their marriage, but she is ignorant of all Juan's many infidelities. Her naiveté is delineated in her view of María Rosa, whom she regards as "a pretty, shy child only fifteen years old." Only appearing innocent, María Rosa is symbolically a temptress, a keeper of bees and a gatherer of honey, itself a symbol of the pleasures of life. Juan is certainly not innocent in the sense of goodness, but he is innocent in his ignorance. He is not deliberately malicious in his infidelities but simply is carrying out an acceptable masculine tradition of infidelity, apparently a legacy of the patriarchal European conquerors. Even Givens does not take Juan's transgressions against the marriage vows very seriously, only twitting him "with the right shade of condescension" and telling "comic stories of Juan's escapades, of how often he had saved him in the past five years" (7–8). There is an implied feminist statement here that Porter will take up more seriously in other stories, but it is appropriate that it should be here. "María Concepción" is a story set in the early stage of the cultural revolution, and feminism was as much a part of the revolution as were indigenism and socialism. María Concepción directs her anger toward María Rosa until the time comes for her to destroy the temptress, to symbolically banish her, and to restore order to the garden. Our last vision of María Concepción, having taken María Rosa's baby for her own, is a tableau of Madonna and child, she with "a strange, wakeful happiness" (21). Porter's poem "Measures for Song and Dance," which she wrote in 1950, explores a similar Edenic triangle, except that the figures are named not Juan, María Concepción, and María Rosa, but Adam and Eve and Lilith.[19]

Juan, like Adam, who succumbed to the Archetypal Temptress, has lost his "innocence" in the process of the experience which has become an initiation. He has idled away his youthful years indulgently, swaggering gaudily in his masculine pride and sexuality. The last glimpse of the "innocent" Juan is provided when he walks with his "redeemer" Givens, who in securing Juan's freedom from imprisonment is "giving" him the possibility for something more valuable than either of them knows. Juan "was walking in the early sunshine, smelling the good smells of ripening cactus-figs, peaches, and melons, of pungent berries dangling from the pepper-trees, and the smoke of his cigarette under his nose. He was on his way to civilian life with his patient chief. His situation was ineffably perfect, and he swallowed it whole" (12). The perfection is an illusion his gullibility permits, as "swallowed it whole" suggests; it is also significant that this is the last time Givens is seen in the story. What Juan is embarking upon must be undertaken alone, and during the tragedy Juan never thinks to call upon Givens for protection or salvation.

When Juan celebrates in the "Death and Resurrection" pulque shop, he begins a symbolic journey that follows the archetypal Life of Man through death and rebirth. From the pulque shop he drunkenly reels to his old home, where he collapses. He awakes to see María Concepción "looming colossally tall to his betrayed eyes." Juan says, "God's name! . . . here I am facing my death!" (14). In facing that death "with such horror that the hair of his head seemed to be lifting itself away from him," he symbolically dies and then begins his own process of resurrection. Having lost his shallow masculine pose, he wishes "to repent openly, not as a man but as a very small child." Finally, when the dreadful ordeal with the gendarmes is over, Juan feels nothing "except a vast blind hurt like a covered wound" (21). He enters their hut, strips his body of its finery just as his life has been stripped of its gaiety and he of his innocence. "With a long groaning sigh of relief," he falls "straight back on the floor, almost instantly asleep, his arms flung up and outward," an image of the crucifix with its symbolic link to death and resurrection.

Another myth implicit in the Juan, María Concepción, María Rosa story is that of the scapegoat. As in ancient custom, María Rosa becomes the village scapegoat. She probably has done nothing worse than many village people, certainly nothing worse than Juan, but she becomes the object of their passionate rejection. One villager speaks for them all: "María Rosa was not [a woman of good reputation]." María Rosa is further thought of by María Concepción as "the beaten dead" who "had thrown away her share of strength" in the villagers, lying "forfeited among them" (12). She is the ancient sacrificial victim to their own guilts and sins, and the restorative effect of the "offering" is confirmed when the departing gendarmes wish them all "Good health!" (20).

"María Concepción" is about pure primitivism in a way that none other of Porter's stories is. Even Porter's language here, always so uncluttered and pure, seems especially simple. As Lodwick Hartley accurately observed in his early critical article, the story "is aglow with the primary colors of primitive art designs." It is a story built upon oppositions and ironies, the most apparent being the ironic theme of the disparity between the present appearance and the primitive reality. It is overall a successful story, but if there is any weakness in it, it is, as Allen Tate observed in his review of *Flowering Judas and Other Stories*, that, unlike the other stories in the volume, "María Concepción" seems to reveal an "uncertainty of purpose."[20] Such uncertainty may arise from the multiplicity of threads woven into the story, which in spite of its surface simplicity is deceptively complex and rich. But it also may arise from the inconclusiveness at the end of the story. There is no true reconciliation because Juan has no true understanding of his experience, or even the peace that passes such understanding. If he feels relief after the dreadful ordeal, he also has felt "his veins fill up with bitterness, with black unendurable melancholy." His last direct thoughts reported by the narrator are, "Oh, Jesus! What bad luck overtakes a man!" (20). They serve as a further ironic reminder of the difference between the experiences of this primitive man and the Christian god whom he supposedly emulates, the god whose last words transcended self-concern and remain a model for civilized Christian charity.

"María Concepción" anticipates some of the obstacles of the cultural revolution that was to restore peace and dignity to the Indians, and it represents a hesitant voicing of some of Porter's own reservations about the probable success of the revolution after she had lived in its midst for the better part of two years. A sketch she wrote in 1921, however, shows an earlier stage of her interest in primitivism at the same time that it shows an earlier stage of her own idealistic hope for the fulfillment of the aims of the revolution. As such, it has a clear link to both "María Concepción" and "Hacienda," published ten years after

"María Concepción." The kind of primitivism in "Hacienda" is far different from that which the revolution idealized and which Porter depicts in the sketch. But it is primitivism that has been anticipated in "María Conceptión."

The sketch, "The Children of Xochitl," exists in typescript among Porter's papers at the University of Maryland and is a longer version of a sketch that appeared anonymously in the *Christian Science Monitor* 3 May 1921, under the title "Xochimilco."[21] The published sketch is ostensibly a description of a visit Porter made with friends to the village of Xochimilco, where they meandered through canals on a flower-bedecked *canoa* and captured certain images of the Indians in their pastoral, primitive existence. Having had an interest in Xochimilco even before she had seen it, as she and Best-Maugard planned the ballet for Pavlova early in 1920, she describes the Xochimilco Indians in her sketch as "a splendid remnant of the Aztec race." The picture she paints of their simple daily acts of bathing children, washing clothes, and cooking food against an Edenic background of abundant flowers is a picture unmarred by ordinary human failings like greed or contentiousness. The Indians live and work in love and harmony, the boatmen steering carefully, running their crafts almost into the canal's banks to make room for one another, and shouting cheerfully, "Have a care, comrade." Among other implicit statements, the sketch presents a picture also of the realization of the revolution's political ideal, a worker's Utopia.

There is an important difference between the unpublished sketch and the version that appeared in the *Monitor*. The longer version is introduced by the narrator's describing her group's visit to a church that is being restored and that is dedicated to the Virgin Mary. A village patriarch tells them that Xochitl, whom the narrator identifies as the legendary Aztec goddess of the earth, is also patroness of this church and is especially generous with her favors. Nothing is said about Mary's favors, and the omission implies a weaker link between the Indians and the civilized goddess. The patriarch says, "Xochitl feeds us!" Thus the goddess who feeds the Indians is their mother, they her children. As the title of the unpublished sketch suggests and as the opening anecdote more explicitly states, the Indians are more directly related to the Aztec goddess than they are to the Christian Mary, to whom the church is dedicated. But what is also clear in the sketch is that both the primitive and the civilized live together harmoniously, even if unequally.

The curious blend of the new and the ancient religions anticipates "María Concepción" and is treated also in Porter's essay "The Fiesta of Guadalupe," published a year after "María Concepción." "María Concepción" depicts an ironic but natural usurpation of the new religion by the primitive one, and the essay written the following year explores the irony still further. Porter notes that "Indians all over Mexico" gathered "at the feet of Mary Guadalupe for the greatest *fiesta* of the year, which celebrates the initiation of Mexico into the mystic company of the Church, with a saint and a miracle all her own, not transplanted from Spain." Porter's presence at the fiesta allowed her to see a curiosity among Catholic celebrations: "I picked my way through the crowd looking for the dancers, that curious survival of the ancient Dionysian rites, which in turn were brought over from an unknown time. The dance and blood sacrifice were inextricably tangled in the worship of men, and the sight of men dancing in a religious ecstasy links one's imagination, for the moment, with all the lives that have been."[22]

Both versions of "Hacienda," the short one published in 1932 in the *Virginia Quarterly Review* ("Hacienda" I) and the long one first published in 1934 ("Hacienda" II), contain elements of primitivism. On the surface "Hacienda" I is a fictionalized version of Porter's visit to the Hacienda Tetlapajac in July 1931, about a month before she sailed for Europe. Some of her friends had arranged for her to visit the pulque hacienda where Sergei Eisenstein, the renowned Russian director, was filming what eventually would be called *Que Viva Mexico*. She apparently already knew Eisenstein, and although she may not have seen him during this visit, she gathered impressions of the hacienda and the filming that would become the materials for "Hacienda."[23] Adding to the documentary atmosphere of the first version of "Hacienda" is Porter's technique of referring to most of the characters by no more than initials. Eisenstein is only "the famous director"; the business manager is "K——"; the assistant cameraman is "A——"; and the hacendado is

"Don J—." Neither the wife of "Don J—" nor the main cameraman is named. Only Justino and Vicente, the peasant actors in the film, are fully named, and thus their story, set within the larger and more intricately detailed framing story, seems to have been intended to receive the reader's closest attention. However, Porter's technique apparently was misunderstood, for the general interpretation of the early version of "Hacienda" has been that she had only thinly veiled her depictions of Eisenstein; his collaborator, Grigori Alexandrov; his Swedish-born cameraman, Eduard Tissé; the hacienda owner, don Julio Saldívar, and his wife; the business manager, Hunter Kimbrough; the art director, Adolfo Best-Maugard, and the others in the background. When the expanded version of "Hacienda" appeared, Porter included a disclaiming note that "all characters and situations in this story are entirely fictional and do not portray an actual person."[24]

If she intended the story of Justino and Vicente to stand in relief, an examination of it should clarify her theme in the first version of the story. Indeed, the tragedy of Justino, his sister, and Vicente, sketched in roughly in bold strokes, helps identify Porter's changing use of primitivism. Examining the story as it is developed in the later version illustrates the refinement of Porter's theme and her own altered attitude toward her materials. The most obvious representatives of the primitive in both versions of the story are the numerous Indians on the hacienda; the most memorable primitive image, the pulque myth illustrated in the fresco in the vat room. The story of Justino, his killing his sister and being captured by his friend Vicente, is a link to "María Concepción" in its hint at unconscious motivation. One speaker or another emphasizes that "Justino did not do it on purpose" or "nobody blames him." More to the point are the remarks of the mule car driver that "the family" is "unlucky," that "this is the second child to be killed by a brother." We are reminded of the Cain and Abel myth and see the "family" as the human family. Justino thus may have been acting out an ancient myth of incest, and Vicente may have been fulfilling his own preordained mythological role.[25] Two years separate the two versions of "Hacienda." Within that time Porter gained the necessary distance from the experience to be able to complete the task of making it into art; her own disillusionment about the fulfillment of the aims of the cultural revolution also must have increased, for "Hacienda" II expresses a more deeply bitter and futile attitude than does the first version. The archetypal consciousness hinted at in the Justino and Vicente story of the first version is elaborated in the second version. Incest is almost named as a motive in Carlos Montaña's *corrido* about Justino and Rosalita (this is the only time the sister is named), who betrayed "the heart's core of her impassioned brother." Added to this strong allusion is the suggestion that Vicente, Justino's friend who captured him, acted out of unconscious homosexuality. Andreyev points to both the unconsciousness and the motive when he says, "Imagine a man's friend betraying him so, and with a woman, and a sister! He was furious. He did not know what he was doing, maybe" (167).

The contrasts among the triangular relationships in "María Concepción" and "Hacienda" afford some insights into Porter's use of one aspect of primitivism to reveal the failure of the cultural and political revolution. In "María Concepción" the primitive force that is unleashed is violent and destructive but nevertheless natural. María Concepción drives the temptress out of the garden, and the villagers join in the opportunity to have a scapegoat at the same time that they protect María Concepción. The story of Justino, Rosalita, and Vicente seems also grounded in that part of irrationality that has a mythological source, but unlike María Concepción, Justino will not be protected. Although some characters understand the instinct that prompted Justino's destructive act, don Genaro will be unwilling to pay unscrupulous government officials in order to save the boy.

Porter's uses of primitivism as an artistic motif in "The Children of Xochitl," "María Concepción," and both versions of "Hacienda" are part of a sequentially developed theme of decaying idealism. The primitive archetypes are seen in their pastoral simplicity in Porter's sketch "The Children of Xochitl" and in their violence and destructiveness in "María Concepción." But in the final version of "Hacienda" the primitive is seen in its most ignoble form. The primitive goddess of the earth, so powerful in Porter's unpublished sketch as she exists harmoniously with the Christian Queen of Heaven, has dissolved into the unconscious in "María Concepción," usurped in the visible world by Roman Catholicism and manifest only in the primitivism that governs the actions of the descendants of her "children." By "Hacienda" she is reduced to an unnamed "half-goddess" in the "faded fresco." Ironically, in the last story she exists again harmoniously with María Santísima, but now in ineffectuality rather than in splendor. During the twenties when Porter was traveling back and forth between Mexico and the United States, she was particularly interested in unconsciousness and primitivism as a theme, writing in 1928 to Josephine Herbst, "I believe we exist on half a dozen planes in at least six dimensions and inhabit all periods of time at once, by way of memory, racial experience, dreams that are another channel of memory."[26] Many of her stories during this decade illustrate that interest.

With Porter's departure from Mexico in 1931 and the publication of her final version of "Hacienda" in 1934, she abandoned for the most part her use of the primitive as a symbol of unseen forces. Although as late as 1935 she was planning a story about bloodlust and a scapegoat, she never finished it, and the only other evocation of the primitive occurs in "The Last Leaf," published the year following the last version of "Hacienda."[27] The focus in "The Last Leaf" is on the aged Aunt Nannie, the black woman who is the closest Miranda comes in her childhood experiences to a primitive being like the Indians Porter met in Mexico. The story provides necessary background to the sixth story in the series, "The Fig Tree."

Aunt Nannie is seen here at the end of her life. In the past she always had conformed to civilized folks' view of her, always having "worn black wool dresses, or black and white figured calico with starchy white aprons and a white ruffled mobcap, or a black taffety for Sundays." But as she approaches her death, she reverts to backwards succeeding stages of primitivism. She becomes first "an aged Bantu woman . . . breathing the free air." She then wraps a blue bandanna around her head and smokes a pipe, and as her sight fails, "the eyelids crinkled and drew in, so that her face was like an eyeless mask" (349). She is looking inwardly at her unenlightened racial past, the mask symbolizing an article of primordial ritual. Thus Porter, once out of Mexico and away from the cultural revolution that had been based in part on a return to primitivism, was able to use the primitive for a purpose different from that in "María Concepción" and "Hacienda," where she at last shows primitivism decaying along with all the other ideals of the revolution. The well of primitivism that Aunt Nannie taps is once again natural and therefore noble.

In both "María Concepción" and "Hacienda" Porter has presented the primitive that contains forces beyond conscious understanding. Other reasonless areas of the darkness include lust, cruelty, bloodlust, and hate, and when humans look into this pit within self, the view is terrifying. Porter's story "The Circus" is about that experience, and it is related to a literary tradition that illustrates the confrontation with a dark self, sometimes an alter ego, a tradition which includes such works as Henry James's "The Jolly Corner."

"The Circus" is the fourth story in the seven stories Porter finally called collectively "The Old Order." Like all the others in the series, it is about the early stages of initiation of Porter's autobiographical character Miranda. The first three stories—"The Source," "The Journey," and "The Witness"—are about the family's past and thus about Miranda's past and play an important part later in Miranda's understanding. But "The Circus" is the first story that is about Miranda's acquisition of knowledge about herself, although the knowledge is absorbed at such a deep level of consciousness that Miranda would never be able to articulate what it is that she "knows." The story begins with the family—indeed a great array of family—sitting on planks in a circus tent waiting for the circus to begin. This array of family (a part of the occasion is a family reunion) is a visual summary of the first three stories, all about the family's heritage, and a transition to the fourth story, which narrows the focus to Miranda. Miranda is the youngest family member present, and her being there at all is the result of the whole family's prevailing on Grandmother, whose permission apparently was required and who never before had allowed even herself to be persuaded to attend. Grandmother "had never approved of circuses, and though she would not deny she had been amused somewhat, still there had been sights and sounds in this one which she maintained were. . .not particularly edifying to the young" (346–47). Miranda's attendance is an event, and she is "fearfully excited," a phrase that suggests her intuition of something potentially terrifying.

The first dark truth that Miranda confronts is sexual and beyond her reason. When she peeps "down between the wide crevices of the piled-up plank seats," she is "astonished to see odd-looking, roughly dressed little boys peeping up from the dust below . . . , staring up quietly." She looks "squarely into the eyes of one, who returned her a look so peculiar she gazed and gazed, trying to understand it." It is nothing "good," she sees, but something dark and troublesome. The little boy's "bold grinning stare" has no "friendliness in it" (344). The scene is reminiscent of Joyce's story "An Encounter," in which young boys meet a strange old man with bottle-green eyes and are troubled without knowing why.

The circus begins before Miranda has time to ponder her own encounter, and the exploding brass band, the rushing sound, color, and smell, the flaring lights, and the "roar of laughter like rage" create panic in her. She sees a "creature in a blousy white overall with ruffles at the neck and ankles, with bone-white skull and chalk-white face, with tufted eye brows far apart in the middle of his forehead, the lids in a black sharp angle, a long scarlet mouth stretching back into sunken cheeks, turned up at the corners in a perpetual bitter grimace of pain." Then the "cruel mouth" blows "sneering kisses," and Miranda covers her eyes and screams, "the tears pouring over her cheeks and chin" (345).

Grandmother's intuition has been right, and intuition it must have been since this is Grandmother's first circus, too. In fact the circus has sights and sounds more terrifying than anything young Miranda can understand. She has looked into the darkness, and she has "seen" that of which she has been unaware: sexual lust, without the edifying effects of love; cruelty in the clown's painted mouth; bloodlust in the crowd's savage delight in the spectacle; and death, implied in the image of the clown's "bone-white skull and chalk-white face." The circus, or the carnival, is a traditional symbol of nightmare in literature, and it derives from a literary convention that is especially appropriate in the context not only of "The Circus" but also of all of "The Old Order." As if the terrifying experience and Miranda's reaction to it, which forces her father to direct Dicey, "Get her out of here at once," were not sufficient, a still larger experience awaits her, one that throws the earlier one into another perspective. When the disgruntled Dicey seizes

Miranda and makes her way out through a flap in the tent, a dwarf is standing at the entrance, "wearing a little woolly beard, a pointed cap, tight red breeches, long shoes with turned-up toes" and carrying "a thin white wand." He shares with the clown an inhuman appearance, and as things nonhuman they represent external threats to Miranda. But her own relationship to the dwarf is implied in his making "a horrid grimace at her, *imitating her own face*" (italics mine), which causes her to strike out at him, "screaming." The more horrifying truth occurs when she sees his "haughty remote displeasure" and recognizes it as "a true grown-up look" which she knows well. Now she is "chilled . . . with a new kind of fear: she had not believed he was really human" (345). The chilling knowledge she has subconsciously absorbed is that all the darkness she has glimpsed is human darkness, not darkness external to humanity. She has not yet made the leap that she is like grown-ups, and so it is knowledge that must lie dormant until she is able to use it in the light of greater maturity. It is understandable that Miranda is afraid of the dark that night, because darkness has contained the awesome truths she has encountered that day at the circus.

The convention Porter has used appropriately is that of the grotesque, the figure that stands, sometimes symbolically, at the gateway to knowledge. The hag of folklore is an early example of the grotesque and represents what Eino Railo has described as a "Dweller of the Threshold," a name he thinks probably derived from Bulwer-Lytton's *Zanoni* (1842). Before the pilgrim traveling toward knowledge can reach the realm of the "Beyond," he or she has to struggle with the grotesque "Dweller," who is "evil and horror personified." To withstand a confrontation with the grotesque Dweller, one has to be fearless and absolutely pure.[28]

Although the precursor of the grotesque lies in ancient folk literature, the grotesque character is a late development of Gothic fiction. Some modern writers like Henry James, who was a significant influence on Porter, occasionally use the grotesque to foreshadow an important step in a character's search for knowledge or to define a horrifying revelation.[29] In James's early fiction, which is more closely related to the romance, the grotesque may be a real, if inhuman, character; in his late fiction, the grotesque functions more metaphorically. In Porter's "The Circus" the grotesque is a real character but not at all a transmundane one, as, for example, is James's grotesque dwarf in "The Last of the Valerii" (1874); James's dwarf is an excavator, a subterranean genius, "an earthly gnome of the underworld." Porter's dwarf is realistic as a part of the circus but his literary function is the same as that of James's dwarf: he signals an awakening to a dark truth. Porter uses other grotesque characters in the short stories and in *Ship of Fools*. Old Lupe, for example, in "María Concepción," with her great age and medicine charms, comes close to the grotesque hag of folklore, and she participates to some degree in the events that lead to Juan's initiation.

The dark knowledge of human life which Miranda almost apprehends includes profane love, or sexual lust, cruelty, and death. Although its central theme is something else, Porter's story "Virgin Violeta" is about a young girl's confrontation with unadorned sexual lust, as "unfriendly" as the little boy's stare at Miranda in "The Circus." But more terrifying is Miranda's sense of the crowd's enjoyment of the mortal danger of the high-wire walker. Human cruelty and the capacity for hate are important and related elements in the darkness. Cruelty in Porter's fiction is exhibited in many ways. Sometimes it is borne in ignorance, out of failing to understand human suffering; at other times it is borne in insensitivity, out of failing even to care whether others suffer, as in "The Downward Path to Wisdom." Perhaps its most overt expression is found in "He" and "Holiday," stories that contain demented or deformed persons who have the potential to function like grotesques as agents of knowledge but who do not because others fail to regard them in the proper light.

"He" is about a poor-white backwoods family, the Whipples, into whose midst is born a simpleminded son. Mrs. Whipple is "forever saying" to neighbors that she loves this son "better than . . . the other two children put together" and, for that matter, better than even "her husband and her mother" (49). The name they gave this son is never known, because he is always called "He," not only by the family but by the neighbors as well, his name ironically capitalized like that of the Deity. He does not seem like a complete person to any of them, and so

they treat him like less than one. Because he cannot articulate thoughts
and feelings and because he appears physically strong, he is secretly
treated like an animal. He does not get hurt, he does not whine for food,
and he eats "squatting in the corner." In bad weather they give his
blanket to Emly, presuming that he does not mind the cold any more
than he minds bee stings. "It's just because He ain't got sense enough to
be scared of anything," says Mr. Whipple.

When Mrs. Whipple decides to butcher one of the suckling pigs in
honor of her brother's visit, she sends Him to "get the little pig away from
his ma." After He snatches the pig and gallops "back and . . . over the
fence with the sow raging at His heels," Mrs. Whipple takes the pig and
slices "its throat with one stroke" (52). Symbolically killing Him, she
sees the pig as "too fat and soft and pitiful looking," a description really of
Him ("rolls of fat" cover him "like an overcoat"). But she is insensitive to
his subconscious identification with the pig and to his reaction when He
sees the blood: He gives "a great jolting breath" and runs away. Mrs.
Whipple's thoughts illuminate her cruelty and are far different from the
hypocritical protestations of concern she utters to the neighbors. "He'll
forget and eat plenty, just the same. . . . He'd eat it all if I didn't stop
Him. He'd eat up every mouthful from the other two if I'd let Him" (52).
And later, when He won't come to the dining table where the pig sits
"roasted to a crackling . . . full of dressing" and with "a pickled peach
in his mouth," Mrs. Whipple explains his absence to her brother and
his family as timidity.

Because He is not provided as many clothes as the other two children ("He sits around the fire a lot"), during the winter He becomes ill.
The doctor who comes warns them that He needs more warmth and
good food, which the Whipples supply lest the neighbors accuse them
of not doing "everything for Him." Oblivious to his limping and apparent pain, they make him run a cotton planter during the season and
later send him to bring in a dangerous bull. When one day He slips on
ice while doing chores, his failing body gives way, his legs swell, and
He begins having "fits." He finally is taken to the County Home for the
remainder of what surely will be a short life. We may say that He was
killed by cruelty and hate as deftly as the suckling pig was slaughtered.

On the way to the asylum, when He begins to cry, the guilt-ridden Mrs. Whipple reads his tears as accusations against her.

"Holiday" was not published until long after "He," but it may have been written at nearly the same time.[30] It, too, is about a farm family with a retarded family member, but unlike the Whipples, the Müllers are disciplined and prosperous. The unnamed narrator, who comes to their farm for a respite from her work, wrongly assumes that Ottilie, the slow-witted servant girl, is hired help from a nearby village. The Müllers' cruelty lies in their refusal to include Ottilie in the family circle and to extend love to her. The narrator's reaction to this knowledge is the heart of the story and leads to her awareness at the story's end.

The capacity for hatred is related to cruelty, and Porter once conceded that it was "a more powerful and effective motivation than love."[31] It may be the precursor of a destructive act, as is Thompson's instinctive hatred of Hatch in "Noon Wine" and as is Hatch's hatred of humanity. It is a real and active force, sometimes inexplicable and sometimes traceable, but it always must be reckoned with. Its presence is notable in "Rope," the story of a senseless confrontation between a vacationing husband and wife.[32] In "The Necessary Enemy" Porter explains the kind of hatred that is illustrated in the fictional dialogue of her little story. In order to illustrate her points about romantic love and hate, she describes the feelings of a hypothetical young wife, "frank, charming, fresh-hearted . . . who married for love." Her hatred is "real as her love is real, but her hatred has the advantage at present because it works on a blind instinctual level, it is lawless." In the same essay Porter declares that "hate needs no instruction [unlike love, which has to be "learned, and learned again and again"], but waits only to be provoked . . . hate, the unspoken word, the unacknowledged presence in the house, that faint smell of brimstone among the roses" (CE, 184). Among Porter's papers is a handwritten page, perhaps notes for a scene in a story, made about or during a Mexican party which included Carleton Beals among others. At the end of the page is an account of a brief exchange, real or imagined, between Porter and some other guest, unnamed:

"I'm getting frightfull [*sic*] fat" whatever shall I do about it
"Oh," said KA, "Hate everybody as I do, and hate will keep you thin!"
"But K.A. you know that I do hate everybody, and I'm getting fat on it."[33]

Hate as an active and self-nourishing force is explored more extensively in "The Downward Path to Wisdom" than it is elsewhere in Porter's fiction.[34] In this story Porter shows that hatred is not created by external circumstances but rather is tapped by external events, one of which is the withholding of love. In "Marriage Is Belonging" she describes the importance of love to children. She says that they "lie flat on their noses at first in what appears to be a drunken slumber, then flat on their backs kicking and screaming, demanding impossibilities in a foreign language. They are . . . one seething cauldron of primitive appetites and needs; and what do they really need? . . . They need love, first; without it everything worth saving is lost or damaged in them" (CE, 190).[35]

Thus, an important link between cruelty and hatred is designated: the cruelty of withholding love can light the spark of hatred in the unloved. In "The Downward Path to Wisdom" the point is made effectively and dramatically by the charm and sweetness of four-year-old Stephen, whose character is available through his viewpoint, a technique that Porter took from James and which she used also in the Miranda stories. She told Warren that in her mind James's child-characters were "almost the best in fiction, an extraordinary understanding of the young mind and nature, the situation of the child in an alien adult world."[36] By unfolding events from Stephen's viewpoint she allows the reader to know Stephen's innocence and potential for goodness, and thus makes the "loss" of Stephen all the more tragic and horrifying.

The theme is developed by the imagery which shows that Stephen never transcends his animal nature because he is never redeemed by love. He is described from three different perspectives in animal images that suggest a "seething cauldron of primitive appetites." The narrative voice first says that he wriggles "bare toes" in a "white fur rug" while he eats peanuts, and when Papa lifts him into the bed he sinks "between his parents like a bear cub in a warm litter" (CS, 369). A jarring note is introduced when Papa observes, "He crunches like a horse," and then asks, "Bright-looking specimen, isn't he?" His cruel descriptions of his son as "dumb as an ox" and "staring like an owl" lead him to conclude, "We'd be better off if we never . . . had him." Mama's descriptive imagery is animal imagery, too, but it at least appears to be loving. She says, "He's a dear lamb," "sweet as clover," in response to which her little son nuzzles "softly in the pit of her arm." Note, however, that Mama wants Stephen put out of the bed because "he's spilling shells all over me," and she is insensitive to the effect Papa's cruel words might have had on the little boy, telling him, "Run along, my darling. . . . Run along" (370).[37]

The chain of hate and cruelty continues. Stephen is fearful and hurt although he does not know why. He rejects breakfast because it is "hateful" stuff, and when he lets the cereal "run in white rivulets down his pajamas," Marjory the maid calls him a "dirty little old boy." His hatred already stirred, he tells Marjory, "You're dirty yourself," to which she responds, "Just like your Papa, *mean.*" After these words, he takes "up his yellow bowl full of cream and oatmeal and sugar with both hands and . . . [brings] it down with a crash on the table. It . . . [bursts] and some of the wreck . . . [lies] in chunks and some of it . . . [runs] all over everything. He . . . [feels] better" (371).

The betrayal of Stephen will continue. When his parents get into a bitter and violent quarrel, he is taken by Marjory to Grandma, who promises him "a good time" and "some of Grandma's nice fresh bread with good strawberries on it." For a while he is cared for by Grandma, Old Janet (a servant), and Uncle David, and he starts to school. But there are danger signals at Grandma's house that Stephen senses without understanding. He is still the little animal that has not been salvaged by love, and his instinct warns him of dangers. Although Grandma's sitting room is "full of flowers and dark red curtains and big soft chairs" and the windows are open, it is "still dark in there somehow; dark, and a place he did not know or trust." Moreover, Old Janet wears what Stephen sees as "a dead cat slung around her neck, its sharp ears bent over under her baggy chin," and she smells "like wet chicken feathers." Clearly it is a place fraught with dangers for little animals.

His instinctive fears are well founded, for all the grown-ups eventually do reject him. When he takes all the balloons Uncle David has been parceling out to him and when he takes a lemon from the pantry to make lemonade for himself and his friend Frances, he is called a thief and accused of telling fibs. When Grandma says, "You're going home. Mama is coming for you in a few minutes," Stephen is frightened by Grandma's face, for there is "something wrong with her smile." Stephen indeed is banished for seemingly minor crimes: " 'He went in the icebox and left it open,' Janet told Grandma, 'and he got into the lump sugar and spilt it all over the floor. Lumps everywhere under foot. He dribbled water all over the clean kitchen floor, and he baptized the rose bush blaspheming. And he took your Spode teapot' " (383). Uncle David's balloons, which have printing on them, obviously are intended to be given away for advertising.

They have banished him without giving him love, and as Porter says, "Everything worth saving is lost or damaged in him." Even Mama's cuddling him and calling him "darling" and "my baby" cannot stop the tide of hate that has been loosed. As he and Mama drive away, Stephen sings "his new secret," an "inside song so Mama would not hear": "I hate Papa, I hate Mama, I hate Grandma, I hate Uncle David, I hate Old Janet, I hate Marjory, I hate Papa, I hate Mama" (387). It is "a comfortable, sleepy song."

Hate begets hate. Papa's cruelty and hate have evoked a response in Stephen, but neither is Mama blameless. She comes to get Stephen only after David tells her to come and get him—"and keep him." When David tells her, "It's simply in the blood," he is referring to Stephen's father, whom apparently Mama ran away to marry against her family's wishes. It is not Stephen's transgressions that are in the blood but rather hate that is "in the blood" of humanity. And hate is rampant among them. Uncle David hates Papa and Mama, and while Papa no doubt reciprocates, Mama's hate for Uncle David is apparent. She says to Grandma, "You know David was a coward and a bully and a self-righteous little beast all his life," and as she leaves she smiles at David "with both rows of teeth." Papa's capacity for cruelty and hatred is already known, and Mama already has said to Papa, "I hate you when you say that." Grandma poses the unanswerable question when she laments, "All this hate, hate—what is it for?" (386). Porter's answer in "The Necessary Enemy" and in "Marriage Is Belonging" is that hate has a real source in human nature, and in "The Downward Path to Wisdom" she shows the damage that is done when hate is not tempered with love. Like his namesake, Stephen is a martyr to human cruelty.

The cruelty of Stephen's family as well as the cruelty of the Whipples and the Müllers is the cold cruelty of withholding love and human compassion. Miranda glimpsed this cruelty at the circus, but there were other black, less penetrable, corners of the darkness that were perhaps even more terrifying. The fiendish enjoyment of the crowd in watching the clown flirt with death suggested something to Miranda that had she been able to give a name she might have called the "bloodlust." It is a primitive and destructive force within humans, and it has been seen in María Rosa's murder and sacrifice and in both Mrs. Whipple's slaughter of the suckling pig and her treatment of Him. Porter addressed this particular element of the inner darkness in her essay "St. Augustine and the Bullfight." She recalls being at her first bullfight in reluctant and painful excitement with a man named Shelley, a descendant of the poet. The first bull out of the corral rushes at the picador and disembowels his horse, who then "trod in his own guts." She recalls sitting back and covering her eyes with her hands until Shelley pulls them away and says, "Don't you dare come here and then do this! You must face it!" She says that she "did look" and "did face it, though not for years and years." She goes on to say that she and Shelley "were not comfortable together after that day," for "there was bloodguilt between" them. "We shared an evil secret," she says, "a hateful revelation. He hated what he had revealed in me to himself, and I hated what he had revealed to me about myself, and each of us for entirely opposite reasons." That which stood revealed, which she calls "the falseness" she "had finally to uncover," was that she "loved the spectacle of the bullfights," "was drunk on it," and "was in a strange, wild dream" from which she did not want to be waked. She admits, "This had death in it, and it was the death in it that I loved." She wonders why she abhors Shelley "as if," she says, "he had done me a great injury, when in fact he had done me the terrible and dangerous favor of helping me to find myself out." She calls this bloodlust "evil" and says that it was not until she read St. Augustine that she was able to put the experience into perspective (CE, 99–101). Porter's account of her standing before the revelation of her own thirst for blood, for killing, to which "some deep corner" of her soul consents "not just willingly but with rapture," is what the child Miranda sees in the crowd of spectators at the circus—even in her own father, who when he directs Dicey to take her home has "not wiped the laughter from his face."

The thirst for blood, the capacity for violence, is treated extensively by Porter in "Noon Wine," a story which has been given much critical attention and whose genesis has been described by Porter herself.[38] It shares with "He" the backcountry setting and the focus on poor-white farmers, but it explores a more terrifying part of the darkness than does "He." "Noon Wine" is about three men—Royal Earle Thompson, Olaf Helton, and Homer T. Hatch—and a background of characters that include Mrs. Thompson, the two Thompson sons, the lawyer Burleigh, and various neighbors like the Allbrights and the Mc-Clellans. Specifically "Noon Wine" is about the relationship among these characters and the murder one of them commits. The crux of the story is Thompson's motive for killing Hatch. On the surface it may seem that Thompson simply sees Hatch for the evil person he is, and an evil person who moreover threatens Thompson's security by planning to take away Helton, whom Thompson needs to run the farm. Thompson's killing Hatch thus can be seen partly as a defense and partly as a gesture toward the destruction of evil. One of the more tempting interpretations of the story, however, is a psychological one which sees Helton, Thompson, and Hatch respectively as the Superego, the Ego, and the Id; thus the murder is the Ego's killing of the Id in order to preserve the Superego. Without such clinical terms, a part of that idea can be applied to the story in a way that is consistent with Porter's large design.[39]

In her analysis of "Noon Wine" Porter makes the specific point that "everyone in this story contributes, one way or another directly or indirectly, to murder, or death by violence." The three men, however, are more closely related than are the other characters and in ways that seem to be uncanny. Indeed, they have an understanding of one another that can be explained only as each one's representing some aspects of the other two. In the first paragraph, when Olaf Helton arrives at the Thompson farm seeking work, the narrator says that Helton "clumped down his big square dusty shoes one after the other steadily, like a man following a plow, as if he knew the place well and knew where he was going and what he would find there." Helton speaks "as if from the tomb" (an image that suggests his ghostly identity), and in spite of his being a "forriner" he swings "the churn as if he had been working on the place for years" (CS, 225). Helton is symbolically related to Thompson at a preconscious level, and that part of him which is "forrin" to the Thompson farm is his diligence and "good clean work." Mrs. Thompson at first misjudges him, when she sees him "sitting in the doorway of the hired man's shack, tilted back in a kitchen chair, blowing away at the harmonica with his eyes shut." She thinks he looks "lazy and worthless" and concludes in dismay, "It was just like Mr. Thompson to take on that kind," suggesting that Thompson, who does not take "trouble with his business," often hires people like himself (226). When she sees the order in the milk house, however, she knows that Helton is different.

There are other differences, in fact oppositions, between the two: Thompson is "noisy" and Helton is "silent." Thompson is full of bonhomie, takes a drink of liquor occasionally, and is hardly frugal. Helton is humorless, does not drink at all, and the money he earns is saved to send to his mother in North Dakota. Thompson divides work into categories of woman's work, man's work, hired help's work, whereas Helton makes no distinction. Thompson is concerned with appearance and what people will think; Helton is totally unconcerned with such superficialities.

In spite of all these oppositions, however, Thompson and Helton share some traits and experiences. Thompson once played an accordion, and Helton obsessively plays a harmonica (instruments which have a similar musical sound). In fact, the song Helton plays, "Noon Wine," which provides the title for the story, is, according to Hatch, about "starting out in the morning feeling so good you can't hardly stand it, so you drink up all your likker before noon. All the likker, y' understand, that you was saving for the noon lay-off" (246). In many respects, the song symbolizes the life of Thompson, who started out with grand hopes but through sheer self-indulgence and laziness has gone downhill to failure. He blames his wife's delicate health and his sons' "sitting around whittling or thinking about fishing trips" for the sad state of the farm: "The wagon shed was so full of broken-down machinery and ragged harness and old wagon wheels and battered milk pails and rotting lumber you could hardly drive in there any more. Not a soul on the place would raise a hand to it, and as for him, he had all he could do with his regular work. He would sometimes in slack season sit for hours worrying about it, squirting tobacco on the ragweeds growing in a thicket against the wood pile, wondering what a fellow could do, handicapped as he was" (234).[40]

The links between Thompson and Helton continue. Both Helton and Thompson have a potential for violence. Thompson thinks that slaughtering hogs is his job, and when the boys bother Helton's harmonicas, Thompson says knowingly, "It's a wonder he don't just kill 'em off and be done with it" (241). Thompson has come close to the truth, for Helton killed his own brother for bothering his harmonicas. Mrs. Thompson senses this capacity for violence when she happens upon Helton's "unnatural" shaking of the boys. Although he shakes them each with "the same methodical ferocity, the same face of hatred," something seems out of kilter. "If it had been a noisy spectacle, it would have been quite natural. It was the silence that struck her" (237). But Thompson seems to understand Helton, and from the outset protects him. For example, when Mrs. Thompson worries over Mr. Helton's soul and wants to invite him to church to "hear Dr. Martin," Mr. Thompson says, "Let him alone" (236).

Thompson protects Helton as the worker he might have been had sloth not led him to failure, and Helton seems still to be a mirror of some part of Thompson's personality. His ambiguous reality is much like that of Bartleby in Melville's story "Bartleby the Scrivener." Like Melville in his treatment of Bartleby, Porter suggests Helton's non-physical existence. Like Bartleby, Helton usually is silent, he seems not to hear, and he hardly eats. Once when he is forced to respond to the Thompsons's "Good night, Mr. Helton," his own "Good night" comes "wavering . . . grudgingly from the darkness." Mrs. Thompson says later, "It's like sitting down at the table with a disembodied spirit" (236).[41]

When Homer T. Hatch arrives at the Thompson farm, new sets of parallels and differences are established. Like Helton, Hatch is called "the stranger," a label which retains the irony if one is to assume that Helton, Thompson, and Hatch are not at all strangers to one another. In Hatch's case, however, it is the narrative voice that refers to him as "the stranger." The narrative voice, on the other hand, always refers to Helton as "the man," and it is rather the Thompsons who call him "the forriner" or "the stranger." To Hatch as "stranger" accrue connotations of devil or evil, as in Twain's story "The Mysterious Stranger."

Hints at relationship are numerous. From the outset, Thompson does not "take to" Hatch's looks, but "he couldn't say why." And just as Thompson guesses Helton to be "another of these Irishmen, by his long upper lip," Hatch, responding to Thompson's prideful statement that his "grampap immigrated in 1836," asks, "From Ireland, I reckon?" While they are talking, Thompson keeps glancing at Hatch's face because "he certainly did remind Mr. Thompson of somebody, or maybe he really had seen the man himself somewhere" (244). Both Thompson and Hatch laugh loudly. Early in the story, when Thompson is settling terms of work with Helton, he begins "to laugh and shout his way through the deal." He bawls and shouts in laughter through much of the story, usually at his own jokes. But Hatch's laughter sounds different, even though it is sometimes described in the same terms. He roars "with joy," shouts "with merriment," and once in response to Thompson's own "guffaw" (again uttered after his own "cleverness"), Hatch folds "his arms over his stomach" and goes "into a fit, roaring until he . . . [has] tears in his eyes." Thompson stops his own shouting and eyes the stranger "uneasily." Then he considers: "Now he liked a good laugh as well as any man, but there ought to be a little moderation. Now this feller laughed like a perfect lunatic, that was a fact. And he wasn't laughing because he really thought things were funny, either. He was laughing for reasons of his own" (245). The hint of madness links Hatch to Helton, who once was "in a lunatic asylum," and soon to Thompson, who asks, "You mean they had him

[Helton] in a strait jacket?" and then says, "They put my Aunt Ida in one of them things in the State asylum. . . . She got vi'lent, and they put her in one of these jackets with long sleeves and tied her to an iron ring in the wall, and Aunt Ida got so wild she broke a blood vessel and when they went to look after her she was dead" (247).

All three of them share lunacy or the seeds of it, and at least two of them are murderers. Helton killed his brother long ago, and Thompson kills Hatch. The imagery supports the violent relationship. Helton killed his brother with a pitchfork, Thompson slaughters hogs and eventually Hatch, and Hatch in Thompson's mind runs a knife in Helton's stomach and "slices up like you slice a hog," which symbolizes both what Hatch has done in essence, if not in fact, and Thompson's own role as hog-killer. Helton and Hatch are the two extremes, and Thompson stands between them and shares traits with them both. Hatch's name is Homer T. Hatch; his "middle name" is symbolically "Thompson," and his surname provides an image that suggests the "door" to the darkness of the hold below. Hatch in fact represents to Thompson his worst self. Hatch tells him, "I never had much use for a woman always complainin'. I'd get rid of her mighty quick, yes, sir, mighty quick. It's just as you say: a dead loss, keepin' one of 'em up" (248). But of course that is not what Thompson literally has said at all. What he said was that his wife was "a mighty delicate woman." But Hatch has summarized what was implicit in Thompson's saga of his wife's sickness and expensive operations, and he has voiced Thompson's repressed thoughts about his wife. It is as if Thompson has looked into his own inner blackness, with horror has viewed his own potential evil, and has destroyed it.

An important irony in the story is Mrs. Thompson's removal of herself from the violence and her righteous refusal to give her husband her personal absolution. Throughout the story she is described in rabbit images—she has "weak eyes" that often are "frightened," and when Mr. Thompson gives "her a good pinch on her thin little rump," he says, "No more meat on you than a rabbit" (232). She keeps her little sons "hopping" and once warns Herbert, "Cut those carrot tops closer" (238). A rabbit is gentle, skittish, and weak, but Hatch shows us another side, its viciousness. His "little rabbit teeth" that are "brown as shoeleather" are his distinguishing feature. Mrs. Thompson has not considered her own relationship to Hatch, her own inner darkness, because she is buoyed up by her pious adherence to social standards. She is doomed to an unenlightened life, symbolized by her weak eyes.

The rabbit image becomes a symbol for the oppositions of timidity and violence, which are irreconcilable to Thompson. They join together as his mind merges with them in the final scene: "Every time he shut his eyes, trying to sleep, Mr. Thompson's mind started up and began to run like a rabbit. It jumped from one thing to another, trying to pick up a trail here or there that would straighten out what had happened that day he killed Mr. Hatch" (265). Mr. Thompson's dilemma is inherent in the rabbit symbol that his subconsciousness has presented, but he is incapable of understanding his complex self. His imagination takes him through the maze of social disgrace and his wife's rejection, to what might have been, and finally back to Hatch and the murderous feeling again. He pleads for light, "Light the lamp, light the lamp, Ellie" (266). But she is incapable of shedding light, and he is too immersed in the blackness and so tied to what people think that he cannot "see" a larger truth, cannot place his experience in a meaningful perspective. He commits his last act of violence on himself.

Death is another element in the darkness. In "The Circus" Miranda glances at death in the clown's face but she does not fully understand it. Porter often has been concerned with death in her fiction; of the twenty-six stories and short novels, nine contain deaths, some of them violent, and others refer significantly to persons who have died before the stories' action begins. But the two stories that treat specifically Miranda's first encounters with death are the last two stories in "The Old Order": "The Fig Tree" and "The Grave." Miranda's adult acceptance of death as a part of life is presented in the last paragraph of "The Grave" and in "Pale Horse, Pale Rider."

In "The Circus" Miranda "sees" death but she has not fully made the leap to associate it with human beings and then with herself. In "The Fig Tree" she understands something more about it. She already knows that "Mama . . . [is] dead" and that "dead" means "going away forever." She knows the outward signs of death: the "long string of carriages going at a slow walk over the rocky ridge of the hill towards the river while the bell tolled and tolled" (354). And she knows other signs of death: "Lizards on rocks turned into shells, with no lizard inside at all. If caterpillars all curled up and furry didn't move when you poked them with a stick, that meant they were dead." When Miranda finds "any creature that . . . [doesn't] move or make a noise, or . . . [looks] somehow different from the live ones," she buries it "in a little grave with flowers on top and a smooth stone at the head" (354). Thus when Miranda finds a dead chicken, she wraps it in tissue paper, puts it in a shoe box, and buries it in a hole she has dug with her little spade. She then covers it up "with a nice mound, just like people's." She has hardly finished when she hears a sad little "weep, weep, weep," which she believes to be the buried chicken, but before she can exhume it to be certain, she is hurried away by her father to begin the journey with Grandmother to Cedar Grove, which he calls "Halifax," his word for Hell. "Hot as Halifax he would say when he wanted to describe something very hot." Although it is a common Southern expression, Miranda's suffering at the beginning of the trip makes the label for their destination especially appropriate. [42]

Through much of the trip Miranda agonizes over the fate of the buried chicken. Because she has understood the finality of death ("Death meant gone away forever"), she has understood something of the importance of life, suggested by the rituals she carries out for the dead animals. But because it is too horrible to face, she represses her worry about the buried baby chicken, suggested in her "forgetting" her usual interest at the farm, "kittens and other little animals on the place, pigs, chickens, rabbits, anything at all so it was a baby and would let her pet and feed it" (360).

She is distracted from her heavy worry by Great-Aunt Eliza, who has an almost sacred interest in science; she pores over "fragments" of "dried leaves or bits of bark . . . as if she were saying her prayers," an image that reminds us of Porter's seeing her own stories as "fragments" in a large plan. When Eliza is not on the roof "before her telescope, always just before daylight or just after dark," she is "walking about with a microscope and a burning glass, peering closely at something . . . on a tree trunk, something she [has] found in the grass" (360). Significantly it is Great-Aunt Eliza who directs Miranda to the comfort she needs. When they are out together in the fig grove and Miranda hears again the "weep, weep, weep, weep," the horrible memory leaps into her consciousness. But Eliza tells the suffering Miranda, "They're not in the ground at all. They are the first tree frogs, means it's going to rain . . . weep weep—hear them?" (361). Eliza gives a scientific explanation of the sound, and Miranda remembers "finally to say through her fog of bliss at hearing the tree frogs sing, 'Weep weep . . . ,'" " 'Thank you, ma'am' " (362).[43]

The fig tree—a variation of the tree of knowledge—is the story's controlling symbol, in which all the meanings merge, and it was apparently an important personal symbol to Porter herself. Among her notes and papers are many unfinished stories that begin "The figs are ripening . . . ," and in a letter to Caroline Gordon from Rome, she wrote, "I loved California too, but I love any place where you can grow figs and peaches and melons and camellias and roses and anemones in the open air the year round. I have thought seriously of trying to land something in the way of a house in Santa Barbara, because it is over the sea and I looked out at sailing ships, yet there was a great white camellia tree, twenty feet tall, at the door. And figs in the back yard."[44]

A symbol of the vast force of life, a fig tree is first seen in the story when the trip to Cedar Grove is announced and Miranda goes "hopping zigzag" down the crooked flat-stone walk, beyond which in a "very dark and shady" spot is the fig grove. She goes "to her favorite fig tree, where the deep branches bowed down level with her chin, and she could gather figs without having to climb and skin her knees" (354–55). The chickens roost there, too, "where the air . . . [is] sweet among the fig trees," and it is there that Miranda finds the dead chicken. She buries the chicken under the fig tree and mistakenly believes that a subsequent "weep weep" sound comes from the earth and therefore is a sound of suffering.

During the journey the distraught Miranda tries to repress the whole experience. Old Aunt Nannie tries to comfort Miranda by offering her some figs: "Look, honey, I toted you some nice black figs." Nannie herself is identified with the secret of the fig trees, for her face is "wrinkled and black and it . . . [looks] like a fig upside down with a white ruffled cap." Miranda rejects the offer vehemently, clinching her eyes tightly and shaking her head. Grandmother forces her to respond in a "pretty way" by saying "Thank you" to Aunt Nannie, "but she did not accept the figs" (358).

"The Fig Tree," not published until 1960, was written in the late twenties before the other Miranda stories were written, and it is thematically tied to them.[45] Beyond its being an obvious link in the Miranda saga, "The Fig Tree" is especially important to the group because in it the themes of death and the female principle, seen as separate elements in "The Circus," come together in an intertwined motif. The fig tree as the tree of knowledge has a sexual connotation because in the myth of Eden, Adam and Eve are said to have covered their nakedness with fig leaves. "The Fig Tree" does continue Miranda's sexual awakening begun in "The Circus." But more significantly, the fig archetypally is the symbol of the womb or the female principle, the final element in the darkness that contains the truth about self.

Old Aunt Nannie appears in "The Fig Tree" as the caretaker of the children, especially of Miranda, who is the youngest child, and it is she who offers love in the form of figs to Miranda and whose face itself looks like a fig. In rejecting the figs (and symbolically Aunt Nannie herself), Miranda is rejecting the female principle which she intuitively believes she has violated: instead of giving life she has taken it away, or so she fears; she imagines that she has buried the baby chicken alive.[46] Her rejection continues as she avoids the baby animals at the farm, which heretofore have been her interests.

Miranda intuitively tries to integrate herself with the female principle when she reaches up "by habit" and touches the fig tree "with her fingers for luck." Her distress is subsequently alleviated when she is assured by Great-Aunt Eliza that the sound she has heard is within the fig trees and is the sound of life and is not within the ground and the sound of death. All of Miranda's experience in the story occurs at the instinctual level, and she would not be able to explain what she has encountered and what she knows. The story is important as a base, however, for "The Grave," the events of which take place several years later.

In "The Circus" Miranda encounters, without understanding it, masculine interest in her femaleness. In "The Fig Tree" she intuits more of the truth of the female principle, and in "The Grave" still more. In the sequence of the three stories she also makes a similar journey toward an understanding of death. In "The Grave" the relationship between Porter's Miranda and her namesake in Shakespeare's *The Tempest* is more apparent than it is at any earlier point. Just as Shakespeare's Miranda confronts her own universe with rapturous cries of "Oh, wonder!" and "Oh, brave new world," Porter's Miranda in "The Grave" feels "thrills of wonder" and delights in "wonderful" little creatures. Both Mirandas illustrate the classical tenet notably expounded by Plato and Aristotle that wondering is the state preliminary to knowing, and Miranda of "The Grave" confirms her desire to have knowledge, or to find truth, when she says to her brother, "Oh, I want to *see*" (366).[47]

The first step toward Miranda's future awakening is made with the discovery of the treasures in the graves. Miranda finds the silver dove that is a screw head for a coffin, and Paul finds a wide gold ring carved with intricate flowers and leaves. Each child is drawn to the other's discovered bounty, and they make a trade. The reasons for Paul's attraction to the dove and Miranda's attraction to the ring are thematically important. The children have come out to hunt rabbits, surely, but also doves. The small silver dove represents a "killing" for Paul, and because he is able to get it from Miranda, who in the past has always claimed "as her own any game they got when they fired at the same moment," he sees the acquisition as a victory in a "tiresome and unfair" game with his sister. Moreover, Paul, in attempting to fulfill the archetypal role of the male as hunter, would regard possession of the dove as symbolic proof of his manhood. After he holds the silver dove in his hand, he discovers that it is a screw head for a coffin, but that fact holds little interest for him because he does not yet fear death. He is more impressed with its uniqueness, exulting, "I'll bet nobody else in the world has one like this!" (363).

The ring carries a set of symbolic meanings different from those of the dove. It first subtly suggests womanliness to Miranda, reminding her that she is wearing her summer roughing outfit that is socially offensive to the back-country law of female decorum. But the ring suggests to Miranda only superficial womanliness, womanliness as it is determined by outward appearances and not essential truths, for at the same time she has vague stirrings of desire for luxury and a grand way of living. The gold ring, clearly a wedding ring, is a link to the aristocratic past of leisure and wealth, in which women, presiding over the house and giving birth to children who would be cared for by slaves, embodied the ideals of beauty, grace, and gentility.

Thus, the gold ring alerts some of Miranda's female responses, but it does not yield an elemental truth. The real truth awaits discovery in the experience of killing the rabbit. She first discovers the meaning of mortality, and in doing so, paradoxically discovers her femaleness and her soul. At the beginning of the story Miranda and Paul have not understood death. When they come upon the empty graves, they try "to shape a special suitable emotion in their minds," but they feel "nothing except an agreeable thrill of wonder" (362). Miranda even leaps into the pit that has "held her grandfather's bones" and scratches around "aimlessly and pleasurably," the narrator says, "as any young animal" (363). At this stage, without the awareness of her own mortality and the attendant suffering and appreciation for life that the awareness will bring, she exists in only an animal, or physical, state. The silver dove, which Miranda finds and whose breast has "a deep round hollow in it," reflects at that early point in the story Miranda's own physical but "heart-less" or "spirit-less" existence.

The identification of children with animals has a firm place in both Porter's experience and her fiction. An early chatty letter from her sister Alice reports the birth of a son and her husband's proud response. "I said," she writes, "'All little animals like to cuddle up where its warm'—and Breck said, 'Animal—huh—that's *my* son.'"[48] In addition to "The Downward Path to Wisdom" there are several stories in which animal imagery is associated with children. In "Noon Wine," for example, the Thompson boys are seen "galloping through their chores" in "animals spirits." "They sprawled and fought, scrambled, clutched, rose and fell shouting, as aimlessly, noisily, monotonously as two puppies. They imitated various animals, not a human sound from them. . . . They were so idle and careless, as if they had no future in this world, and no immortal souls" (239). In "Holiday" the same imagery functions as the newest Müller baby bawls and suckles "like a young calf" and the grandchildren raven and gorge their food so that Hatsy, who is assigned to watch them, struggles "with them only a little less energetically than she did with the calves" (415). In play they "harness themselves to their carts and gallop away to a great shady chestnut tree on the opposite side of the house" (418).

Ironically, before children can be truly different from animals, and therefore truly human, they must discover their animal natures. Miranda herself follows these steps gradually. She and Paul think of the animals they kill as objects, or as "marks," with Miranda confessing that what she likes about shooting "is pulling the trigger and hearing the noise" (364). She makes no distinction between shooting at the rabbits and doves and shooting at the fixed, straw-stuffed targets on the range, saying that she would "just as soon" shoot at the latter. Despite their kneeling position and the hint at the ritualistic initiation that is soon to take place, it is with detachment and scientific objectivity that she and Paul examine the rabbit Paul has just shot. In fact, Miranda admires the way in which Paul skins the rabbit, "as if he were taking off a glove." The desecration of a once-living creature has no more meaning to her than does an act that suggests the superficial manners of social convention. Even when Paul discovers the embryonic sac and removes the dead rabbits, she is not frightened or repelled but feels a kind of "shocked delight in the wonderful little creatures for their own sakes" (366). It is only when she discovers the blood running over them that she begins to tremble, and like Hopkins's Margaret in "Spring and Fall: To a Young Child," she feels the emotion "without knowing why." And yet, "having seen, she felt at once as if she had known all along" (366). Porter says in " 'Noon Wine': The Sources," "We are born knowing death" (CE, 474).[49]

The next truth Miranda discovers has to do with herself. She identifies with the female rabbit who has carried the babies and thus she understands an important part of her own female nature that she had intuited in "The Fig Tree." She reaches the conclusions in steps, replying to Paul's comment that the babies "were just about ready to be born" with "I know . . . like kittens." Although kittens are also animals, they are domestic, not wild, and therefore provide a step to her final conclusion, "I know, like babies" (CS, 367). The awakening is emphasized throughout the paragraph with the repeated and varied use of *know*. The passage takes on added significance when we remember the earlier conversation between Miranda and Paul, who tells her that he wants the first dove or rabbit and that she may have the next. She idly asks in reply, "What about snakes? . . . Can I have the first snake?" (364). Like her archetypal mother, Eve, she indeed will have the "snake," the symbol of the way to knowledge of both sexuality and death.

A sudden sensitivity to her own part in a wanton destruction of life accounts for the terrible agitation she feels. She has discovered her own mortality and her own femaleness, with its frightening, awesome burden of procreation, and she has immediately violated it in participating in the destruction of life, as in "The Fig Tree" she only feared she had done. The experience, however, is too terrifying to fully grasp, and Miranda has not the maturity to mitigate the terror of her newfound knowledge. And so when Paul buries the young rabbits in their mother's body, Miranda begins to bury the terrifying experience itself deep within her mind. It remains there suppressed for nearly twenty years.

"Flowering Judas" has not been regarded as a story about inner darkness. It almost always is interpreted as a story about revolution and betrayal, and any critical confusion has revolved around the extent to which Laura is in fact the betrayer, the "Judas." Ray West's elaborate analysis of Laura as betrayer because she brings no love to the revolution has been the most widely accepted interpretation for many years. However, even West's theory does not answer all the important questions about the story, as Liberman, among others, has pointed out.[50] Porter has identified the model for Laura as her friend Mary Doherty, who like Laura taught Indian children in Xochimilco and participated in the revolution. Some critics, however, have correctly seen Laura as a combination of Mary Doherty and Porter herself and thus Laura as a somewhat autobiographical character, an embryonic version of Miranda, who first appears as a character in Porter's fiction five years after the publication of "Flowering Judas."[51] If Laura is examined as a version of the grown-up Miranda and her "betrayal" examined in the light of Miranda's experiences in "The Circus," "The Fig Tree," and "The

Grave," Laura herself emerges as a character better understood and the theme of betrayal in the story is more clearly defined. "Flowering Judas" is a link between Porter's concern with primitivism and her childhood experiences that created the Miranda cycle.

Laura's betrayal is indeed the crux of the story. However, Laura as the betrayer of the revolution because she brings no love to it, or Laura as the betrayer of herself because she does not allow herself love, or Laura as Eugenio's betrayer because she makes his suicide possible seems inconclusive. Moreover, the label that associates Laura with Judas Iscariot seems too strong, especially when her acts of "betrayal" are measured against those acts of "betrayal" by other characters in the story. The evidence that is cited as proof of Laura's self-betrayal centers on two elements in the story: Laura's "frigidity," symbolically grounded in her nunlike appearance and her "notorious virginity," and the dream at the story's conclusion, in which Eugenio's calling Laura "murderer" seems to hit its mark so directly that Laura is terrified of returning to sleep. Porter, however, does not intend to portray a frigid or even sexually repressed Laura. She shows a Laura who has simply withheld love, as "the incomprehensible fullness" of her breasts, "like a nursing mother's," indicates. In fact, the complete withholding of love has been Laura's protection against brutal violation from revolutionists like Braggioni, who swells "in ominous ripeness" but who will grudgingly honor the ideal of chastity.

Laura's withholding of love thus has a practical cause. But she has justified the withholding in two ways that defy rationality. She has displaced love on the one hand, and on the other she has idealized it. In her total commitment to the revolution, Laura has transferred libidinous passion into revolutionary fervor, as the conclusion of her scene with Braggioni clearly illustrates. Braggioni asks Laura to clean and oil his pistol, and the dialogue between them as Laura "peers down the pistol barrel" is heavy with sexual imagery and illustrates a subconscious collusion between them that Laura already has dreadfully intuited. Braggioni has told her, "We are more alike than you realize in some things," and after feeling "a slow chill, a purely physical sense of danger, a warning in her blood that violence, mutilation, a shocking death, wait for her," Laura thinks, "It may be true that I'm as corrupt, in another way, as Braggioni, . . . as callous, as incomplete" (93). In a parody of a consummating love scene, Braggioni speaks of the revolution as a process that engenders a new life: "No one shall be left alive except the elect spirits destined to procreate a new world cleansed of cruelty and injustice." He "strokes the pistol lying in . . . [Laura's] hands, and declares, "Pistols are good, I love them, cannon are even better, but in the end I pin my faith on good dynamite." Laura's response would be appropriate were she responding to a lover's sweet appeal. But the gentleness is in contrast to the content of her words. She holds up the prepared ammunition belt and says softly, "Put that on, and go kill somebody in Morelia, and you will be happier" (100).

Laura shows no aversion to the phallic suggestions in the scene. But if she has displaced her sexuality in the revolutionary moment, she also has idealized it, as is apparent in other important scenes. Her "tender" feelings about "the battered doll shape of some male saint whose white, lace-trimmed drawers hang limply around his ankles below the hieratic dignity of his velvet robe" point to an idealized phallic appreciation ("she loves fine lace") and show how her encasement of principles has removed her from the intimacy of human love in any form. The children she teaches "remain strangers to her." Indeed, she does not love *them*, but she does love "their tender round hands and their charming opportunistic savagery" (97).

Both Laura and Braggioni have substituted revolution for love, or death for life, as Laura's sleep-filling consciousness deduces immediately before she slips into the dream. Laura indeed betrays herself insofar as she denies herself the highest human fulfillment, which love makes possible. The dream, however, is cited as evidence that Laura is also the betrayer of Eugenio, who calls her "Murderer" and "Cannibal." In most interpretations the dream is seen as combining the two forms of Laura's betrayal. In betraying herself by refusing to give her love, she also has betrayed Eugenio by being unable to love him. Her providing the drugs which he uses for his suicide also supports the charge that Laura has betrayed Eugenio by making his death possible. The dream is of course crucial to the resolution of the story's theme, and it does merit careful consideration. It is important to remember, however, that the dream is created in Laura's subconscious with the symbols of her childhood religion and that it externalizes Laura's own fears rather than offering objective proof of Laura's responsibility for Eugenio's death.

In the dream Laura is called out of sleep by Eugenio and instructed in a parody of the words of Christ, "Follow me." When it is clear that he is taking her to the land of death, rather than life, Laura resists, saying she will not go unless Eugenio takes her hand. Eugenio is already dead, and instead of giving Laura his fleshless hand gives her flowers from the Judas tree, which she devours greedily. However, when Eugenio calls her "Cannibal!" and says, "This is my body and my blood," Laura cries "No!" and awakes trembling, "afraid to sleep again" (102).

The most important symbol in the story, the flowering Judas tree, reaches its culmination in the dream. Flower imagery in fact has permeated the story, although the only flower named and described in the story is that of the Judas tree. The children Laura teaches "make her desk a fresh garden of flowers everyday," and when they write "We lov ar ticher" on the chalkboard, they draw "wreathes of flowers around the words" (95). Flowers are traditionally a symbol of the female archetype, and there is sufficient reason to believe that Porter was using flowers in this sense in "Flowering Judas." Once when she was discussing symbolism, Porter remarked that the rose "begins as a female sexual symbol and ends as the rose of fire in Highest Heaven."[52] And in her sketch about Xochitl, whose name means "flower," she described the goddess of pulque as also the earth mother who "sends rain . . . and makes the crops grow—the maguey [from which pulque is made] and the maize and the sweet fruits and pumpkin." Thus Xochitl in Porter's sketch is the Great Mother who both gives life and provides pulque, a drug.[53] If flower symbolizes the female principle as it is embodied in Xochitl, then one can easily see how Laura has betrayed it, just as Miranda fears she has betrayed it in "The Fig Tree." If we recall Miranda's refusing the figs, another symbol of the female principle, and avoiding the baby animals at the farm because she thinks she has "given" death to the baby chicken, then Laura's detachment from the children she teaches is more easily understood. Her betrayal of her female self is represented by her throwing a flower to the youth who serenades her, not according to the custom of the culture to encourage his "love" for her, but in contradiction to make him "go away." The flower symbolically withers in his hat as he follows her through the city for several days.

Trees themselves, as the centers of vegetative symbolism, are another archetype of the female principle, and in this story flower and tree come together ironically in the Judas tree, the tree of betrayal, when the descriptive "Judas" is interpreted by Laura's discarded Christianity. The title and the dominant symbols in the story support the theory that Laura is betrayer of the female principle more than she is of anything else, and it is the recognition of this betrayal that terrifies her, much as it terrifies the young Miranda of "The Fig Tree" and "The Grave." The symbolism is completed in the dream when Laura devours greedily the "bleeding flowers" which satisfy "both hunger and thirst" in an attempt to integrate herself with the flower. Laura as the carrier of drugs has fulfilled only one role of the Great Mother and has denied the more significant role, that of giving nourishment, or life. Thus, Eugenio's telling her, "This is my body and my blood," horrifies her because what she had thought was an act of self-nourishment is actually an act of murder and cannibalism. Her awaking "trembling" is as understandable as Miranda's beginning "to tremble without knowing why" when she discovers the blood on the dead baby rabbits and understands at some place of "secret, formless" intuition that she has participated in death rather than life.

When Porter was writing "Flowering Judas" as well as some stories in the Miranda cycle, she would have been in her late thirties and early forties and, according to Joan Givner, unhappy over her childlessness. Letters Porter wrote to Eugene Pressly while they were separated in 1932 hint at a troubled relationship that may have been caused largely by Porter's unfulfilled maternalism. In one such letter, after saying that happiness for the two of them "seems possible, if not altogether reasonable," she immediately adds, as if by association, "I had the damndest dream last night." She then recounts a complicated dream in which she was a bystander who saw dead men, one with a heavy cross of flowers weighing him down," and dead women "clasping newly born babies." Her sister Alice was in the dream with another baby, which was Porter's, and regarded Porter with a "censorious look on her face." She tells Pressly that the dream was "very sinister, mysterious and portentous . . . and yet without meaning." The elements of guilt, flowers, and death—particularly in the form of dead mothers who could not nourish their babies—indicate that the dream may have related in a profound way to the stories Porter already had written and some she was planning.[54] She later recorded the details of a similar dream from the same period; it included both her and Pressly as well as a monkey that was starving to death in spite of her efforts to find milk and food for him. She says, "The dream ended I do not remember precisely how or when, except that my uneasiness was growing and the monkey was shrivelling up and lying in the palm of my hand almost perfectly still and silent. It was a very anxious and unhappy dream and very hopeless."[55]

The important flower symbolism in the story is supported by other symbolism, that of machinery and oil. In contrast to her concept of flowers, Porter consistently thought of machinery as life-negating, observing in "The Flower of Flowers" that "the world of evil is mechanistic," furnished with "the wheel, but not the rose." And she once told a former lover that she knew their love affair was dead when it became clear that he wanted them to "be machines . . . functioning with hair's breadth precision."[56] Laura senses this hovering negation, because she has a proper fear of machines ("I shall not be killed by an automobile if I can help it," she says) and a revulsion for them ("her private heresy" is that "she will not wear lace made on machines"). Braggioni's threat to Laura is suggested in imagery that links him to machines and particularly to the automobile. "His skin has been punctured in honorable warfare" ("puncture" is a word directly related to automobile tires), and when he asks Laura to oil and load his pistols, she "sits with the shells slipping through the cleaning cloth dipped in oil." When Braggioni sings, his cheeks grow "oily," and his smile is "suety." Thus his Sunday morning ride down the Reforma, the avenue that is dedicated to revolutionary vision and bravery, is highly ironic.

Machine and oil metaphors are particularly interesting here, as well as in "Hacienda," because they have specialized meaning to Porter that they could not have had to Faulkner, for example, who also used them as symbols of antilife and antinature, notably in *The Sound and the Fury* and *Sanctuary*. Porter's arrival in Mexico City coincided with the explosion of the so-called petroleum problem. Because Obregón stepped into the presidency during the depression that was the aftermath of World War I, he was immediately faced with many problems that grew out of the worldwide economic collapse. The Mexican federal treasury in 1921 was drained by the need to support the numerous unemployed in Mexico as well as to send help and railroad passage to the thousands of workers who had gone to the United States only to discover that depression and unemployment were there also. Thus, prices of raw materials dropped sharply, and Obregón had to suspend production taxes on silver, copper, and lead. However, the petroleum industry during these same years was remarkably healthy (1921 and 1922 were peak years in the production and exportation of Mexican crude oil). In order to replenish the treasury, depleted by loss of taxes on other raw materials, Obregón cited and upheld Article 27 of the Mexican Constitution as amended by Carranza in 1917; it was essentially a decree that the Mexican government had full title to all the lands in Mexico, both surface and subsoil, and had the power not only to break up and divide among the Indians certain unwieldy landholdings but also to tax subsoil products. The oil interests were enraged and suspended operations, throwing another four thousand persons out of work.[57] A compromise between the oil companies and the government was reached in which the payment of taxes was linked to the redemption of Mexico's defaulted foreign bonds, and although it was a compromise that would plague the Mexican government for more than a decade, it did lead to the United States's recognition of the Obregón government in 1924.[58]

Because Porter's reasons for going to Mexico in the first place were idealistic, she felt an immediate aversion to the capitalists and to oilmen, it seems, in particular. Shortly after her arrival there she described to her sister Gay her association with "rich men who are clever enough, but smell offensively of money, and who wish to hold your hand, and be a father to you—or rather, three fathers. And I tell one of them," she says, that "I am handsomely supplied with a perfectly spiffing father, and a brother beside, and a lover into the bargain, and I can only be a 'talking friend' to him. At which he sulks in his fat oil magnate way, and I order my favorite dessert."[59] Within seven months, she was able to write an incisive article she called "The Mexican Trinity," in which she analyzed the intricate relationships among "the great triumvirate, Land, Oil, and the Church" (CE, 402).

The crucial imagery in "Flowering Judas" is tied directly to Porter's experiences in Mexico, especially her research into primitive myths and her observation of the effects of machines and oil on Mexican society. The machine and flower imagery represent Laura's dilemma. The machine has been linked to the revolution because it was to free the peon from bondage, an illusion Porter elaborates upon in "Hacienda," but Laura's aversion to it is an instinctual female response to its antilife associations. The dilemma represents Laura's whole experience in the Mexican revolution, a subject Porter had put away by the time she started the Miranda saga in earnest. But she retained the most universal theme from "Flowering Judas," fidelity to the female principle, and integrated it into "The Old Order."

In many of her stories Porter examines the dark mysteries of our inner selves. The force of instinct contributes to the development of larger themes in "Virgin Violeta," "Rope," and "Pale Horse, Pale Rider." But in "María Concepción," "Hacienda," "The Circus," "The Fig Tree," "The Grave," "Flowering Judas," "He," "Holiday," "The Downward Path to Wisdom," and "Noon Wine," she particularly explores those corners of the darkness that must be penetrated in our perpetual groping toward truth. In isolation, the darkness is terrifying, but it is only a part of the whole. Nevertheless, those not able to transform the terror are doomed to the suffering and shortsightedness of a Mr. Thompson or to the fearful trembling of Laura in "Flowering Judas."

Chapter Two

Systems and Patterns

K atherine Anne Porter portrays persons who never look within and confront dark truths but look instead to external forms for affirmation of life's meaning. External forms, however, are made up of attractive deceptions, among which are codified aesthetic theories, philosophical and religious structures, political and revolutionary doctrines, social codes, and visible patterns. In pure form, art, religion, political and revolutionary ideas, and some philosophical tenets can point the way to truth by offering a sense of order that is a walkway to understanding. The problem lies in the systematizing of such sets of ideas, in their becoming ends unto themselves.

Porter believed that art and religion often were misused and became obstacles in the search for truth. She speaks of art's having the potential for making order out of this chaos that is the world, and she describes the artist's mission as that of the artificer of such order, but in her fiction she rarely depicts artists who have fulfilled the calling. She gives us "the martyr" Rubén, the shallow poets of "Flowering Judas," the would-be poet of "That Tree," "Hacienda"'s systematic Betancourt and ineffectual Carlos, and the struggling artists of "The Leaning Tower." In the same way, saintly religieuses are scarce in Porter's fiction. Instead she has created many characters who illustrate perverted religion or impotent religion that has become merely a hollow shell, providing, as she said, only "orthodox answers" to "the oldest, most terrifying questions."[1] She first develops the theme in "María Concepción," where all the rituals and outward acknowledgments of the alien faith fall away under the blind force of primitive instinct.

When Porter wrote "María Concepción" in the early 1920s, she was seeing the effects of many centuries-long forces in Mexico. When Hernando Cortés arrived in Mexico in 1519, he found a teeming Indian society with its own distinctive religions and with sophisticated scientific and artistic modes. But in spite of an admirable cultural level of the Aztecs and Mayans, the European conquerors were not content to let them exist unmolested; within a decade Pope Clement VII had sent twelve Franciscan friars to Mexico to convert the Indians to Christianity, and Augustinians and Dominicans soon followed. For the remainder of the sixteenth century the three orders built extensively, and the Roman Catholic Church imposed on the conquered Indians a new language and a new sociopolitical organization along with the new religion. In the three colonial centuries that followed, a rich and complex culture evolved that was characterized by racial blending and regional diversity. Over it all lay Hispanic customs, including worship practices, that were maintained by the aristocracy and its aspiring followers. [2]

It was not until the revolution of 1910 that the folk culture which had lain in the background for many years was brought forward and became a part of the larger movement that culminated in the reforms of 1917, when the authority of the church was reduced further. Tannenbaum explains the revolution of 1910 as simply "an attempt to liquidate finally the consequence of the Spanish Conquest."[3] This amalgam of cultures, one deeply rooted in the pre-Hispanic past and the other a transplanted one, is dramatically presented by Porter in "María Concepción." When the two cultures are in conflict, as they are in the characters of María Concepción and Juan, the older culture, with its ties to primordial antiquity, is victorious. The natural, mythic religion is stronger than the religion that has been imposed from without.

It was not Catholicism in itself to which Porter was objecting. Having been baptized into Catholicism when she was twenty, she remained sensitive throughout her life to the beauties of the faith. Although her own religious views are more difficult to categorize, there was much in the ritual that appealed to her aesthetic sense, and some of the church's history satisfied her appreciation for spiritual vigor.[4] In a letter to Caroline Gordon she said, in the stance of Henry Adams, that "a living practising born Catholic may be very healthy, is not nearly all art and literature of Western Europe Catholic, until the eighteenth century? And what health it has!"[5] Rather she was objecting to what she once referred to as the "moral blackmail" of dogma, the codification of religion or the perversion of it, abuses she had seen so dramatically in Mexico that she came to use Catholicism as the primary representative of hollow religion.[6]

In her essay "The Mexican Trinity" she lists among the church's abuses, in collusion with the other two powers in the triumvirate, Land and Oil, an attempt to subjugate the Indian to get his land and an exercise of unholy power "in an intricate game of international politics" (CE, 403), activities she labeled "sinister."[7] Years later, in notes for an unpublished review of James Magner's *Men of Mexico*, she castigates the author for defending the Catholic church in Mexico, saying that "act for act, nothing the Mexican revolutionaries ever did could match in cold blooded wickedness the methodical oppression of the Indian by the Church and the throne of Spain." She concludes that "in Mr. Magner's hands, truth becomes the most relative thing in the world. His impartial history is a piece of special pleading, an attempt to justify the unprincipled use of power by whatever means, and that Mr. Magner believes this power is divinely invested in the Catholic church is an added embarrassment to the reader."[8]

Porter, however, saw the spirit of stymie in religion outside of Mexican Catholicism. For example, in her unfinished biography of Cotton Mather she illustrates the negative elements of religion that inversely feeds on itself, and Puritanical self-righteousness is observed in the poet's wife Miriam in "That Tree," in the American Kennerly in "Hacienda," in Rosaleen O'Toole's neighbors in "The Cracked Looking-Glass," and in Mrs. Thompson in "Noon Wine."[9] In some stories it is simply the ineffectuality of dry religion that Porter treats, and whether the religion is Catholicism or Protestantism or a peculiar form of backwoods Fundamentalism is insignificant. In addition to its depiction in

"Flowering Judas" as Laura's discarded faith, dry Catholicism is examined also in Porter's Irish Catholics and in Granny Weatherall. In "A Day's Work" Mr. and Mrs. Halloran rely on the church for form in their lives, but neither they nor the others in their particular Irish Catholic society appear to have an inner light of true understanding and contentment. Rosaleen O'Toole, another of Porter's Irish Catholics, finds no solace in the religion of her upbringing but seeks escape from reality in her fantasies; trying to recall only the ecstasies of the feast days, she ignores the less romantic but more elemental truths in her childhood faith.

Porter's darkest discourse on ineffectual religion occurs in "The Jilting of Granny Weatherall." Granny's religion could be any other religion, but Catholicism served Porter's theme best because of its refined and elaborate structure. Structure is inherently important to Granny, who has spent her life looking for truth through systems and patterns, and it is the failure of systematic religion that is terrifyingly dramatized in her dying hour. In her muddled thoughts she confuses her jilting with her dying, remembering that she had to face the priest on that long ago day without her bridegroom. Now, at the hour of her death, she is facing the priest again, without a bridegroom. "For the second time there was no sign. Again no bridegroom and the priest in the house" (CS, 89). In the final instance, the bridegroom is unmistakably Christ—and she has not found the meaning focused through His life that her religion has promised and which she expected to have before she died. "This grief" wipes everything else away, and she dies in "endless darkness" that curls "around the light and . . . [swallows] it up," images that delineate her unenlightened state at her death.[10]

Although the theme of dry religion does not occupy a primary position in "Noon Wine," it nevertheless is important in understanding the character of Mrs. Thompson. She had been a "popular Sunday School Teacher in the Mountain City First Baptist Church" before she married Mr. Thompson.[11] She continues all the rules of propriety within her religion, offering a "Christian invitation" to Mr. Helton to attend church with the family on Sunday, and worrying over Helton's soul when he refuses. But after her husband's killing of Hatch, the uselessness of her religion is seen in her inability to find in it solace for her suffering and courage to face social ostracization. Her religion fails to lead her to a higher truth, as the light's hurting her eyes symbolizes. She, in fact, wears shaded glasses to guard against it. Porter uses light here as she does in "The Jilting of Granny Weatherall" to symbolize understanding, for Granny's blowing out the light symbolizes her relinquishment of the search for truth as much as it does her relinquishment of life.[12]

Porter viewed black magic, or spiritualism, as a form of religious perversion, dangerous rather than merely stifling or useless. When her sister Gay's child Mary Alice died, Porter's letters to her sister are full of sympathy and expressions of her own grief over this favorite little girl; occasionally she offered advice to Gay, who was struggling to accept the tragedy, and once she warns Gay about "keeping on with spiritualism." She says, "I have gone about a bit here, and have seen one or two of the best—and spiritualism is a superstition for darkened minds. It is the same as a belief in witchcraft, and a personal devil. . . . It is not for enlightened people, or thinkers. And I tell you, emotion without intelligence is not worth anything."[13] She elaborates on this idea of witchcraft in her essay "The Flower of Flowers," in which she writes, "Evil is dull, that is the worst of it, and black magic is the dullest of all evils" (CE, 153).

"Magic" is a little story about witchcraft, written about the same time as "The Jilting of Granny Weatherall."[14] It is a Jamesian dialogue that subtly tells the reader something, however slight, about Madame Blanchard and her Creole maid, who tells her employer the story of the maid Ninette to entertain her while she dresses her hair.[15] Ninette, according to the story, once worked in a New Orleans brothel where she saw many things Madame Blanchard "wouldn't believe" and the maid "wouldn't think of telling," but she justifies the story she presents by saying, "Maybe it will rest you while I brush your hair" (CS, 39).

It is a story of extraordinary seaminess and cruelty, and it is told as a diversion for Madame, whose name coincidentally suggests her purity or her whiteness and thus her opposition to her dark-skinned maid and the characters in the narrative.[16] The story turns upon a witchcraft charm in which the maid and apparently all the characters in her story put stock, even the cruel madam of the brothel. After the madam beat

Ninette and threw her out for insubordination, men who had favored Ninette kept asking for her, and the madam saw that she had made a bad economic decision. Because Ninette had gone altogether out of Basin Street and thus out of the jurisdiction of the corrupt policemen who protected the brothel, the madam turned to the cook, who "lived among people who worked spells" and whom the madam trusted "above everything." The charm which the cook used and which was said to work in New Orleans required their taking "the chamber pot of this girl from under her bed, and in it . . . [mixing] with water and milk all the relics of her they found there: the hair from her brush, and the face powder from the puff, and even little bits of her nails they found about the edges of the carpet where she sat by habit to cut her finger- and toe-nails; and they dipped the sheets with her blood into the water, and all the time the cook said something over it in a low voice" (41). The girl Ninette came back in seven nights and "after that she lived there quietly." The irony in the story is provided in the sordidness and cruelty of the setting. The "magic" of the charm, like the "magic" of systematic religion, is shown to be an illusion. Ninette returns only because the loveless world that created her made it impossible for her to go anywhere else.

If the black magic underscores the loveless, mechanistic world of the brothel and the evil of the seamy world that surrounds it, its opposite is not seen in the character of Madame Blanchard, who interrupts the narrative to say only, "You are pulling a little here" or to close her perfume bottle "with a thin click" (40–41). She shows her interest in the story by saying, "And then what?" or "Yes, and then?" There are obvious contrasts between the two pairs, Madame Blanchard and her Creole maid and the brothel's madam and Ninette. But the ironic parallels are even more significant. Madame Blanchard by her lack of compassion nourishes the social evil, and none of the characters in the story reveals an understanding of life.

"Theft" is a story that has received considerable critical attention because of its complexity and puzzling conclusion. Although it is a study of the modern wasteland and of empty human relationships, it is also an ironic study in a systematic way of living. The system here is not atheism, an active disbelief in God, but rather is a code based on the absence of dynamic belief in anything. The protagonist of "Theft" has not replaced the missing or lost religion with anything so elaborately structured as Laura's revolutionary ideal, or even a philosophical stoicism, but she has replaced it with a stasis and what she boasts of as a "faith" in the honesty of others. A careful look at the passages which illuminate her static existence and her "faith," however, reveals that the stasis is not the stability of reconciled opposing forces but is the paralysis of emotional apathy. And her faith that leads her to leave her doors unlocked is borne not out of a belief in the essential goodness of fellow human beings but is an indifference that grows out of her discomfort in "the ownership of things." In short, she leaves her doors unlocked because she has no possessions she cares about protecting, and her faith is "a certain fixed, otherwise baseless and general faith which ordered the movements of her life without regard to her will in the matter" (64).

That Porter intended the reader to see the protagonist's set of actions as a replacement for a religion is supported in the numerous biblical allusions and in the religious structure of the story. Like the Christian imagery in "Flowering Judas," the allusions and the structure of "Theft" act as an ironic standard to show the disparity between the active life of religious fervor and the static existence of irreligious dispassion.[17] The three men in the protagonist's immediate past represent different versions of the same stasis or irreligion. Camilo, with whom she has just left a party at Thora's house, lives by a "set of smaller courtesies" that ignores "the larger and more troublesome ones" (59). His code of behavior is grounded on chivalric principles derived from his Latin heritage (like those principles that motivate the male characters in "Flowering Judas"); he walks the lady to the subway in the rain, risking her health and his own hat. She indulges his sentimentality as far as the foot of the platform and makes his remaining at the foot of the stairs a favor to herself, which he must honor. Only out of sight, or so he thinks, can he take off his new hat and hide it under his raincoat for protection.

She next meets Roger, who lives by no such romantic code. He already has his hat carefully buttoned inside his raincoat, his face consequently streaming with water. In the taxi she and Roger witness two scenes, one with three boys and one with two girls. In the first instance, two of the boys are razzing the other about his declaration that he will marry for love. They represent the opposition of sacred and profane love, and Roger's comment on the scene is "Nuts . . . pure nuts." Neither extreme has any appeal to him because each represents a position or a belief. In the other scene the monologue of one of the girls apparently is a rejoinder to something the other has said, and it is filled with self-concern. "Yes, I know all about *that*. But what about me? You're always so sorry for *him*" (61). The full significance of the scene emerges later in the story. As the ride continues, Roger reveals that Stella, whoever she is, will be home, that "she's made up her mind and it's all settled." The protagonist's comment that she thinks "it is time for you and Stella to do something definite" is ironic because Roger is not doing anything definite, only Stella is. Roger is like the protagonist. They are the passive recipients of other people's actions, exercising no will of their own. The narrator's rhetorical observation about Roger's show ("It's a matter of holding out, isn't it?") represents both their habits of insulating themselves against involvement and protecting themselves against the exercising of will. It is significant that she and Roger have had "long amiable associations."

The least admirable of the protagonist's male friends is Bill, who lives in her apartment building and exhibits the worst traits of all the characters in the story. He has no sense of chivalry, like Camilo, or even mild concern for the protagonist, as does Roger, who has told her to take aspirin and a hot bath to keep from getting a cold. Bill observes, "You're perfectly sopping," when on his invitation she goes into his apartment for a drink, but he shows no concern for her health. He becomes the mirror of the adolescent girl's self-pity and self-indulgence as he complains about his wife's "ruinous" insistence on child support payments in the face of his own expenses (for costly luxuries). His distance from the Christian standard of charity is underscored ironically first when he calls to the protagonist, "For Christ's sake, come in and have a drink with me. I've had some bad news," and later in his response to the protagonist's request that he pay her the fifty dollars he promised for some writing she had done for him. He says, "Weeping Jesus . . . you, too?" (62). Jesus wept out of pity but not self-pity. Bill's words are reminiscent of Juan Villegas's "Oh, Jesus! What bad luck overtakes a man" and look ahead to Braggioni's self-pitying sobbing while his wife washes his feet.

Alcohol is the catalyst for Bill's "feeling"—inverted as it is, and alcohol is the sacrament of all the main characters in the story. The protagonist and Camilo have left Thora's house "nicely set up on Thora's cocktails," and Roger laments in the careening taxi, "I could do with a cocktail this minute." The protagonist already has said, "I really must be drunk," but she nevertheless has two more drinks with Bill before she goes to her apartment on the floor above. In the bohemian world in which the protagonist and her friends move, alcohol provides both the ecstasy and the insulation against feeling and commitment, making their apathy possible in the same way that pulque numbs the will of the Indians in "Hacienda."

The rain motif in the story supports the biblical irony and points again to the wasteland theme of impiety. As the protagonist begins the reminiscence that is the major part of the story, she recalls that it was raining when she and Camilo left Thora's house. It was rain that triggered their actions: Camilo walks her to the elevated in order to share the inconvenience of the rain, but he will protect his new biscuit-colored hat from it when he can do so without losing face; Roger hastens the protagonist to a taxi in order to avoid the rain from which he already has protected his hat; the protagonist and Roger view the scenes with the boys and girls through the rain that distorts their sense of reality and causes the taxi to slide dangerously through the streets. Once in her apartment building, she goes toward her apartment after Roger has urged her to take a hot shower and aspirin to ward off the effects of the rain; and Bill, who wants company for his misery, looks at her soppiness with disgust. The point is that rain, the fructifying symbol, is avoided by these dry, impotent, unfeeling inhabitants of the twentieth-century wasteland. The religious meaning of water as cleansing or redemptive agent is lost on them. They want only to avoid it, and thus they avoid life itself. [18]

The structure of "Theft" is that of a religious myth, but ironically it does not lead to the high place of fulfillment. In the subway the protagonist is led away from "the elevated" by Roger, who says, "Come on let's take a taxi" (60). In her apartment the next morning, having realized that the janitress has taken her gold purse, she descends to the basement furnace room to confront the thief. The scene is filled with images of hell. The janitress, whose face is "streaked with coal dust," is "shaking up the furnace," the red light from which is reflected in her "hot flickering eyes" (63–64). The pattern is not completed, for following the symbolic descent into hell, the protagonist never ascends to true understanding. She does have a small insight, however, which in Porter's fiction is a significant accomplishment. She understands her losses, both "material and intangible," that are brought together in the symbol of the purse. The losses have occurred because of her own failure of will and not because of active agents of adversity. There is no suggestion that the protagonist has had the kind of epiphany that will change her life, but by a trick of reversal she has been made to see a small truth about herself. The janitress who stole the purse from the protagonist tells her that in asking for its return she is stealing it from the niece who was intended to receive it. In momentarily seeing herself as thief, however, she is continuing her refusal to claim her possessions, whether the love of the absent Eddie, the love of either Camilo or Roger, the money Bill owes her, or the stolen purse. Despite the irrationality of the janitress's charge, through it the protagonist is able to see herself as thief in addition to victim and is able then to recognize the truth that through failure of will she is responsible for the things she has lost.

The religious structure of "Theft" is like that of other Porter stories, "María Concepción," "Virgin Violeta," "The Martyr," "Magic," "The Jilting of Granny Weatherall," "Flowering Judas," "Noon Wine," "Pale Horse, Pale Rider," and "Holiday." To some degree, in each of these there is a descent to the underworld. In most instances there is no real ascension. This pattern can be directly linked to writers like St. Augustine, Dante, and Spenser, whose works were continuing inspiration for Porter.[19] The so-called Pauline pattern, central to *The Faerie Queen* and *The Divine Comedy*, is described by St. Augustine: "The fact is that every individual springs from a condemned stock and, because of Adam, must be first cankered and carnal, only later to become sound and spiritual by the process of rebirth in Christ."[20] When Porter was describing her early plans for "Old Mortality," she identified the working title of the middle part, "Midway of this Mortal Life," as a translation of the first line from Dante's Inferno. She went on to explain that it referred to "the season in hell which any being who can think or feel must pass through at least once," presumably before the pattern could be complete.[21]

That which makes the pattern incomplete is the missing self-sacrifice, the Adam or the Christ. The persons depicted in the world of the protagonist of "Theft" are either vain and shallow, like Camilo, kindly apathetic like Roger, self-indulgent like Bill, or unwilling to suffer like the missing Eddie, who writes that whatever they once had is no longer "worth all this abominable . . . ." For the moment, she is simply looking on the emptiness of her rootless, fragmented existence and acknowledging, in however small a way, her responsibility for it.

Apathy particularly terrified Porter because she had seen the same kind of motiveless existence not only in her generation but in her own father. Near what would have been her father's one-hundredth birthday, had he lived, she wrote her nephew Paul that she had "never seen a more terrible example of apathy" or "an almost unconscious refusal to live" than in her father's life. "Let me tell you," she says, "I have turned in hope to other strains in my ancestry, for I have sometimes felt myself under a curse with such a father; I had to find in other sources the courage to outlive and outgrow him."[22] She was even more explicit about the dangers of apathy when she discussed with friends Malcolm Lowry's *Under the Volcano*, which Albert Erskine apparently had sent her. Referring to the hero of the novel, Geoffrey Firmin, she declared that it was his inability to believe in anything—his moral, psychic, and spiritual impotence—that led him to assist evil.[23] It is the theme that she develops fully in *Ship of Fools*.

According to Porter, mere sets of ideas fail to lead to truth. It was a failure she once summarized in a reference to "the mean sick little souls on a high falutin search for God via Kirkegaardism."[24] In "Flowering Judas" she shows one failure of philosophy in Laura's "system" that is an alternative to the dying idealism. It is necessarily a philosophical one rather than religious because it is consciously adopted and mindfelt rather than heartfelt. Laura "persuades herself that her negation of all external events as they occur is a sign that she is gradually perfecting herself in the stoicism she strives to cultivate" (97).

"Holiday" also reveals the inability of philosophical systems to provide either balm for suffering or answers to crucial questions. The Müller family governs itself by a system of positivism, atheism, and Marxism, and they dredge up their Lutheran heritage for a ceremony at Mother Müller's death. All their systems fail, however, and the bewildered family cannot understand or articulate their grief. They scream and call and implore in "a tumult utterly beyond control" (431). None of Father Müller's philosophies brings him understanding or acceptance of his wife's death, and he is further unable to draw any conclusions about the meaninglessness of his own. Although he handles *Das Kapital* as if it were a Bible, the truth is that he no more adheres to *Das Kapital* than he does to the Christian Bible; it is only a superficial symbol of doctrinal obedience because he in fact uses his wealth to exploit poorer neighbors who disapprove of his atheism but are so dependent on him economically that they do his bidding. In the one instance he cites, despite their fear and dislike of him, they elect his son-in-law sheriff. More than any others among Porter's fictional characters, with the exception of Granny Weatherall, the Müllers symbolize the uselessness of patterned thoughts and philosophical systems in the face of life's mysteries.

Philosophical and religious systems often are tied to political and social systems in such a way that it is difficult to separate one from the other. Porter has warned of the dangers the artist faces if he or she links the aesthetic vision to a political end, and she likewise has warned of the dangers and evils of political religions and religious politics. All are perversions of the two primary possibilities for finding order in life's chaos. However, political systems, whether tied to religion or not, in time become corrupt shadows of their original intents, as Porter discovered firsthand in the Mexican cultural revolution.

When she first arrived in Mexico City in 1920, she was full of enthusiasm for the revolution that was going on there; no doubt her enthusiasm had been set into motion in Greenwich Village by Best-Maugard and other Mexican artists and idealists she had met there. Her letters to her family and friends during the early months after her arrival are heady with the excitement of the cultural and political climate and reveal the level of her idealism. In an early letter to her family, she says, "There are a thousand delicious things to tell you—of amazing contrasts and amusing situations." And she continues by describing her exciting social schedule:

> How one goes to a party at Chapultepec Castle one afternoon and drinks tea and champagne with the President—a former marauding General— and in no time at all attends the Lottery ticket sellers ball in company with the greatest Labor leader in Mexico—and many others—and dances until two o'clock with one eyed men, and marvelous carbon colored Indians in scarlet blankets, who dance divinely—and one staggers home in the gray of the morning with vine leaves and confetti in one's hair. And goes that afternoon to a bull fight, and the next day to have tea.

In the same long letter she reiterates her excitement. "Life here is a continual marvel to the eye, and to the emotions," she says. "Politically, Mexico is amazingly primitive. I meet all the holders of the government reins, and the process of governing is naively literal. . . . Later, I expect to be connected by a small thread to the affair, and now I dabble a bit at times, for it is very amusing."[25] She later would describe her thread-connection to the amusing affair as a part of "that wild escapade to Mexico, where I attended, you might say, and assisted at, in my own modest way, a revolution."[26]

Her Leftist sympathies are apparent during these times in the activities and scenes she describes and in her references to her new acquaintances. She tells her family of her plans to teach dancing in the new Institute of Social Sciences, headed by "a socialist connected with the National University." And she says that she is "to write a revolutionary text book of English for use in our Institute." "Nobody," she says, "seems to realize elsewhere that a full fledged revolutionary government is in full swing here, with everybody from the President down a seething radical."[27]

Her disdain for capitalists is as apparent as her admiration for some of the revolutionaries. She recreates for Gay a conversation she had with a representative of the Hearst papers before she left for Mexico. "I wouldn't work for Hearst, not for any price," she declares, but says she returned the Hearst editor's call "to hear what was up." She then says, "Here is the conversation exactly as I remember it—I mean the important parts:

> Editor—"We want you to interview Pancho Villa for us. What is he really doing now that he has a ranch of his own under government protection? Has he reformed?"

> I—"He didn't need to reform. He always was a perfectly good revolutionist working for the peons. But he is making inter[es]ting experiments on his ranch, I think—I mean such experiments as paying his workers a living wage, and establishing schools for their children."

> Ed—"Yes, I know that is what they are trying to tell us. I find it hard to swallow. Well, you can get help from the Mexican government in this, can't you?"

> I—"What makes you think so?"

> Ed—"I was told that you could. Why don't you manage it, and get us a corking story with pictures—you know what we want. Villa in all his glory, whiskers and guns if any, running his new show."

> I—"What else do you want?"

> Ed—"How do you mean?"

> I—"Do you mean to tell me you will pay all my expenses to get just a simple color story for your Sunday magazine?"

> Ed—"O, we'll syndicate it, and make a lot of money out of it. But naturally, the more sensational your story is, the better we would like it—Listen to me! If you get us a good story with pictures, we will pay you twenty five hundred dollars and expenses. If you get kidnapped, we'll raise it to three thousand . . . and of course, any price if you make an international affair of it!!!!"

Ah, ha! Well, I declined with thanks, and got out, and am going to write a book on bandits, but not for Hearst. And I am going to put that story in the very beginning of the book. Wait and see. [28]

By the same token, she speaks admiringly of the Habermans, Lincoln Steffens ("a charming teller of stories, a cynic, a follower of revolutions"), and others in the movement designed to correct long-standing social injustices in Mexico.[29]

Before long, however, she was beginning to understand the complexity of events in Mexico, and although she had not lost her sympathy for the aims of the movement, she appears to have begun to lose some of her idealism. Among her notes and papers is the recording of some random thoughts about the "impossibility of writing a story at short notice on Mexico." She says, "It ma[y] b[e] five years before I can really write about Mexico. I am not one of those amazing folk who can learn people or countries in a fortnight. They come dashing in here, stay two weeks, gather endless notes and dash out again. In two more weeks their stories are in the weekly reviews. While here am I, not yet able to say for sure that the things I see are the true state of affairs. Or that my present impressions of Mexico are rightly proportioned. Or that if I write profoundly of events here at the moment I shall not be making a profound idiot of myself." She summarizes the difficulty as the thing's "being too complex and scattered and tremendous. I want first of all to discover for myself what this country is. Everybody I meet tells me a different story. Nothing is for me but to wait, and gather my own account."[30] She says more or less the same in "The Mexican Trinity," published in July 1921: "I have been here for seven months, and for quite six of these I have not been sure of what the excitement is all about. Indeed, I am not yet able to say whether my accumulated impression of Mexico is justly proportioned; or that if I write with profound conviction of what is going on I shall not be making a profoundly comical mistake. The true story of a people is not to be had exclusively from official documents, or from guarded talks with diplomats. Nor is it to be gathered entirely from the people themselves." And perhaps her most telling statement in the essay concludes the second paragraph: "The life of a great nation is too widely scattered and complex and vast; too many opposing forces are at work, each with its own intensity of self-seeking" (CE, 399–400).

The essay continues to explore the forces within Mexico that are at cross-purposes, primarily the big three: Land, Oil, and the Church. Her loss of idealistic expectations and her disillusion with the government were apparent in a letter she had written to Paul Hanna some two months earlier: "Things happen so quickly here, I have not been able to record them. From one day to the next, events were monstrously out of proportion. I gave false values to everything. Now that they are finished, or nearly so, they are all dwindled to the true measures of their triviality. I can write of them now." She describes to Hanna the troubles there: "We are having deportations, riots, arrests; an elaborately prepared comedy of respectability is being staged by the Mexican government with the American high politicians as directors."[31]

When Porter was planning "María Concepción," she wrote that "the revolution has not yet entered into the souls of the Mexican people," and she contrasted the Mexican revolution to the Russian revolution, the difference being that the Russian revolution had been "made" by the Russian writers. Mexican writers, Porter declared, were concerned with nothing more important than "the pain of unrequited love" (CE, 401–402). The problem, however, went beyond the absence of serious writers, for as she observed, the Indian could not read. "What good would a literature of revolt do them?" she asks.

But if the Indian could not read, he nevertheless could see, and Porter credits the muralists for providing the revolutionary spark that the writers had failed to offer. The painters made it possible for the Indians to "read" their history on the walls. Porter in fact said that the Mexican renaissance began with Diego Rivera's entry into Mexico in 1922 and "kept up nicely for about four years. Riots, manifestos, and manifestations, syndicates, shows, a fine warm hullabaloo, all mixed up with politics on the one hand and personal animosities on the other. . . . And some damned fine work came out of it."[32]

When, in her interview with Barbara Thompson, Porter was remembering early experiences in Mexico, she said of the Revolution that "it was a terribly exciting time. It was alive, but death was in it."[33] That hindsight is not reflected in her early letters from Mexico, even after she had begun to see some of the problems within the movement. But by the end of the twenties, when she was writing "Flowering Judas" and "Hacienda," she was able to trace astutely the failure of the revolution through fictional characterization. In 1941 she wrote that "there exist documents of political and social theory which belong, if not to poetry, certainly to the department of humane letters. They are reassuring statements of the great hopes and dearest faiths of mankind and they are acts of high imagination. But all working, practical political systems, even those professing to originate in moral grandeur, are based upon and operate by contempt of human life and the individual fate."[34]

In "Flowering Judas" Porter shows the vestiges of great hopes and dearest faiths that have nearly run out. When she described to Thompson the genesis of the story, she told, as she does elsewhere, of walking past a window and seeing her friend Mary sitting with a big fat man. She says that Mary was not able "to face her own nature" then but that she herself was "more skeptical."[35] Laura represents the alien who came to Mexico "uninvited" to participate in the revolution. In so doing she ostensibly had to abandon her own Catholicism and take on the "religion" of revolution because the church was an enemy of the revolution in Mexico. One supposes that Laura has joined the revolution with the kind of fervor that shows in Porter's own early remarks about it. But now Laura has become disillusioned with the hypocrisy of the movement, even with her own participation. She goes to union meetings, takes food, cigarettes, messages, and a little money to prisoners, "smuggles letters from headquarters to men hiding from firing squads in the back streets in mildewed houses," borrows money from one agitator to give to another, and teaches English to Indian children. But Laura feels betrayed. Her idealistic view of the revolution has not been borne out. "Sometimes she wishes to run away, but she stays" because "she has promised herself to this place; she can no longer imagine herself as living in another country, and there is no pleasure in remembering her life before she came here." She cannot define "the nature of this devotion, its true motives, . . . its obligations" (CS, 93). Like many other outsiders who came to aid in the revolution, she feels obligated to stay through to some conclusion, even in the face of disillusionment.

Braggioni is the symbol of Laura's disillusions, for she had thought of a revolutionist as "lean, animated by heroic faith, a vessel of abstract virtues," essentially a Christ figure. Braggioni's distance from this standard is implied in all the descriptions of him. The irony is established early in the story when "the Indian maid meets Laura at the door and

says with a flicker of a glance towards the upper room, 'He waits' " (90).
He who is waiting has already been described as "sitting there with a
surly, waiting expression, pulling at his kinky yellow hair, . . . snarling
a tune under his breath," surely not the description of a "vessel of
abstract virtues." The reference to the upper room is an allusion to the
place of the Last Supper, and the maid's warning, "He waits," is an
allusion to Christ.[36] The story thus is framed by symbolic, if ironic,
allusions to the sacred supper at which Christ and his disciples celebrate the Passover, significantly a celebration of one people's escape
from bondage. It is at the Last Supper that Jesus instructs his disciples
in the meaning of feet washing, that the Sacrament of Holy Communion is observed, and that Jesus predicts Judas's betrayal. Later in the
story Mrs. Braggioni washes her husband's feet, Laura symbolically
betrays herself, and in her dream she participates in a parody of Holy
Communion.

Braggioni once had been closer to Laura's revolutionary ideal; he
once at least had been "lean," if not animated by heroic faith. Indeed,
"once he was called Delgadito by all the girls and married women who
ran after him; he was so scrawny all his bones showed under his thin
cotton clothing, and he could squeeze his emptiness to the very backbone with his two hands. He was a poet and the revolution was only a
dream then" (98). He has forgotten his hunger, however, and in spite
of his incompetent singing is a symbolic figurehead of the poets who
write "about romance and the stars, and roses and the shadowy eyes of
ladies, touching no sorrow of the human heart other than the pain of
unrequited love." In fact, it was unrequited love that animated Braggioni. "When he was fifteen, he tried to drown himself because he
loved a girl, his first love, and she laughed at him. 'A thousand women
have paid for that.' " And so he indulges himself with food and women
and nourishes his self-love. "Too many women loved him and sapped
away his youth, and he could never find enough to eat anywhere,
anywhere!" He has good food and abundant drink . . . and enjoys
plenty of sleep in a soft bed beside a wife who dares not disturb him;
and he sits pampering his bones in easy billows of fat. He tells Laura,
"One woman is really as good as another for me, in the dark. I prefer
them all" (99). He perfumes his hair with imported Jockey Club.

The same ideal motivates others in the story who mirror Braggioni's misplaced fervor. For example, the "shock-haired youth" who serenades Laura is "one of the organizers of the Typographers Union," and yet he spends hours on consecutive nights singing to Laura "like a lost soul" and following her by day "at a certain fixed distance around the Merced market, through the Zócolo, up Francisco I. Madero Avenue, and so along the Paseo de la Reforma to Chapultepec Park, and into the Philosopher's Footpath."[37] His movement is a superficial pattern only, however, because he has not the zeal or vision of the leaders whose names adorn the streets and parks of the city, monuments to the true revolutionary spirit. He begins also to write poems to Laura which he prints on a wooden press (why else but for wider distribution?), and Laura knows that his "unhurried" and watchful black eyes "will in time turn easily towards another subject" (96). Another version of the same chivalric lover is seen in the attentions of the young captain who once had been a soldier in Zapata's army and who now channels his fervor into "amusing" ardor for Laura. He writes to Laura: "I am a very foolish, wasteful, impulsive man. I should have first said I love you, and then you would not have run away. But you shall see me again" (96). The ideal they are expressing is neither tragic nor graceful but is the "most trivial" version of romantic love which Porter described as "the pretty trifling of shepherd and shepherdess" (CE, 185).

Braggioni is the professional revolutionist. He wages war for gain and not for idealistic commitment. But he acts the part of the idealist well. When "crafty men" whisper in his ear, "hungry men . . . wait for hours outside his office for a word with him," or "emaciated men with wild faces waylay . . . him at the street gate with a timid, 'Comrade, let me tell you . . . ,'" he is always sympathetic (CS, 98). He gives them handfuls of small coins from his own pocket, he promises them work, he tells them "there will be demonstrations, they must join the unions and attend the meetings, above all they must be on the watch for spies. They are closer to him than his own brothers, without them he can do nothing—until tomorrow, comrade!" Tomorrow of course will never come, for Braggioni is in fact cruel and unsympathetic and says to Laura, "They are stupid, they are lazy, they are treacherous, they would cut my throat for nothing." He says of Eugenio who has taken all the drugs that Laura brought him because he was bored, "He is a fool, and his death is his own business. . . . We are well rid of him" (100–101). He also tells her that he himself is rich, "not in money . . . but in power, and this power brings with it the blameless ownership of things and the right to indulge his love of small luxuries" (93). Braggioni is so far removed from the original revolutionary zeal that he cannot understand why Laura is involved in the revolution at all, "unless she loves some man who is in it" (100).

This, then, is the death that was in the revolution. The heroic faith is not present in the "revolutionaries" who are left to carry on the fight. In this sense Braggioni and the shock-haired youth and Eugenio and Laura and the Zapatista captain have betrayed the revolution. They simply go through the motions of being revolutionaries but without idealistic commitment. The failure of the revolution, however, is centered in the Braggionis, who consistently have been interpreted in a particular light. Bad as Braggioni is, he has been regarded by most critics to be salvageable in that he after all is moved to contrition and tears by his sad-eyed wife's washing his feet. Mrs. Braggioni, by the same token, has been regarded as a foil to Laura and as one whose capacity for love and forgiveness enables her husband to transcend his human weakness. Laura's view of Mrs. Braggioni as one "whose sense of reality is beyond criticism" has been interpreted to mean that Mrs. Braggioni is an ideal in the story. However, a more careful look at Mrs. Braggioni and at the feet-washing scene reveals that both she and her husband have misplaced values. Feminism was an important part of the revolution, and Mrs. Braggioni is active in the feminist movement. She "organizes unions among the girls in the cigarette factories, and walks in picket lines, and even speaks at meetings in the evening." The narrative voice adds, "But she cannot be brought to acknowledge the benefits of true liberty" (99). The irony lies in the two meanings of "liberty," neither of which she accepts. She does not free herself from male domination and yet will not concede to Braggioni's freedom from fidelity. "I tell her I must have my freedom, net. She does not understand my point of view," Braggioni says. Mrs. Braggioni may be a feminist leader, but she is not a true feminist. It is significant that we never know her given name; she is known only as an extension, or a possession, of her husband. She is not dedicated to an idea but to a man.

As tempting as it is to see Braggioni's tears as a sign of his redemption, the tears clearly are tears of only self-love and self-pity. Braggioni's vanity is his most obvious trait from the outset; Laura listens to him "with pitiless courtesy, because she dares not smile at his miserable performance." Nobody dares to smile at him. "Braggioni is cruel to everyone, with a kind of specialized insolence, but he is so vain of his talents, and so sensitive to slights, it would require a cruelty and vanity greater than his own to lay a finger on the vast cureless wound of his self-esteem" (90–91). "The excess of self-love" has flowed out, "inconveniently for her, over Laura." And it is evident again when Braggioni enters his own house and sees his wife weeping, as she has done every night since he left. He is filled with tenderness at seeing her love for him. That love he can understand. She asks him whether he is tired, and it is then that he bursts into tears. "Ah, yes, I am hungry, I am tired . . ." (101). Tired? Braggioni can be tired only from "the labor of song." And hungry? Braggioni has not been hungry for years. Mrs. Braggioni, cast in the image of Mary Magdalen, has placed a poor substitute in a god's role.

In addition to her betrayal of the female principle, Laura also has betrayed the revolutionary ideal because she has refused to admit to the absence of proper zeal among the leaders like Braggioni. She has protected herself against the reality of the revolution by protecting herself against feeling. Eugenio's total negation of feeling is the extreme of Laura's repression of feeling. It is that to which she is destined, if she continues her course. And therein lies an additional horror.

Among Porter's papers is a sketch hand-dated 1921, preliminary to the story that undoubtedly became "Flowering Judas." It is not inconsistent with her description of the genesis of the story in her interview with Thompson and in Whit Burnett's *This Is My Best*, and it does help illuminate the character of Laura.[38] It is worth examining carefully:

Yudico cam[e] tonight bringing his guitar, and spent the eve[ning] singing for Mary.

    Mary sat in a deep chair at the end of the table, under the light, a little preoccupied, infallible and kindly attentive. She is a modern secular nun. Her mind is chaste and wise, she knows a great deal about life at twenty three, and is a virgin but faintly interested in love. She wears a rigid little uniform of dark blue cloth, with immaculate collars and cuffs of narrow lace made by hand. There is something dishonest, she thinks in lace contrived by machinery. She is very poor, but she pays a handsome price for her good, honest lace, her one extravagance.

Being born Catholic and Irish, her romantic sense of adventure has guided her very surely to the lower strata of revolution. Backed by a course of economics at the Rand School, she keeps her head cool in the midst of opera bouffe plots, the submerged international intrigue of her melodramatic associates.

She had meant to organise the working women of Mexico into labour unions. It would all have worked beautifully if there had been any one else in the whole country as clear and straight minded as Mary. But there wasn't, and she has got a little new pucker of trouble between her wide set grey eyes, within four weeks of her arrival. She doesn't in the least comprehend that revolution is also a career to the half dozen or so initiates who are managing it, and finding herself subtly blocked and hindered at every turn, she set it down to her own lack of understanding of the special problems of labour in Mexico. . . . She has been bludgeoned into a certain watchful acquiescence by that phrase. So that now she has the look of one who expects shortly to find a simple and honest solution to a very complicated problem. She is never to find it. [39]

When the notes were made Porter would have been in Mexico probably less than a year, but according to published essays and her letters to Paul Hanna, she already had lost many of her illusions. The story "Flowering Judas," completed some years later, relies upon the essential elements of the sketch, but Mary has become Laura, Yúdico has become Braggioni, and it is Mrs. Braggioni who organizes the working women. In the note Mary has been jolted into the realization that no one else in the revolution is "as clear and straight minded" as she is. And so she "has got a little new pucker of trouble between her wide set grey eyes." But she nevertheless "has the look of one who expects shortly to find a simple and honest solution to a very complicated problem." The Laura of the published story, however, is a step beyond the Mary of the sketch. She no longer expects to find a simple solution. She has glimpsed the reality and the dangers and has avoided both by withdrawing to a state of deadened feeling while simply carrying out the ritual of the revolution. "Like a good child," she "understands the rules of behavior" (92).

Revolution that aims at correcting authoritarian abuses originates in the left of the political spectrum, and the left in theory was attractive to Porter in the twenties and thirties as it was to many intellectuals and artists of the times. Porter flirted with Communism for a while because she saw it as offering the best hope for solving the world's social injustices, and like many of her contemporaries, she was particularly sympathetic to the Russian revolution. She told an interviewer that "there was a time, almost, when if I hadn't been in Mexico I might really have gone left." She says, "But I was inoculated against communism down there. I saw the way they worked, the way they behaved to each other, to say nothing of the way they behaved to me!"[40] Nevertheless, in 1933 in a letter to Peggy Cowley, she says flatly, "I was a Communist twelve years ago."[41] That would have placed her "membership"—we can only speculate whether it was formal—in the party in 1921, when she wrote to Paul Hanna about Morones, whom she described as "a Bolshevik, a perfectly good one"—and added, "It is not a defamation of character to call a man that in this country."[42]

Whatever idealistic faith she might have had in the idea of Communism must have evaporated before she passed much time in Mexico. Long before she finished "Flowering Judas" or made her statement about "all working practical political systems," she had come to see Communism as a once good idea that had become codified. As early as 1926 she was voicing criticism of systematic Communism. Commenting on the second issue of the Marxist organ *New Masses*, she says it is "better than the first maybe, but yet none so good." She asks, "What makes them all so glassy-sharp, and ill-humored, and why do they write so very badly about everything?" And then laments, "I still hope for something sound, simple, intelligent and warm from some of them. But they are radical in the manner of the petty bourgeoisie convicted of . . . the commonplace. That's only one way of being progressive, and I believe the least effective."[43]

Thereafter, sprinkled through her letters and essays are statements about the dangers of political systems. In a letter to the editor of the *Nation*, 11 May 1947, Porter discusses the relative dangers of Communists and Fascists and advocates a moderate position unpopular with liberals at the time.[44] But her position moved again left in the same year when she attended a "Town Meeting of the Air" debate and was appalled at the tactics of the Anti-American Activities Committee. She was offended by the committee's supporter, California State Senator Jack Tenney, who relied, according to Porter, on "intuition and rumor" and "seized every opportunity to shout 'Red, Communists' into the microphone, whether in turn or out of it." She said it seemed to her "that there were a great number of people in that house who don't like Communism, and who will fight it, but not in the Senator's company." She concluded, "I still don't know how many Communists there are in Hollywood, nor where they are; but I will trust Mr. Dekker and Mr. Lavery and that audience to fight them more effectively than any number of Anti-American Activities Committees, whose activities have seemed to me from the beginning the most un-American thing I know."[45]

A few years later, in a review of E. M. Forster's *Two Cheers for Democracy,* she had occasion to comment about her and Forster's participation in the International Congress of Writers in 1935 in Paris. She says that she "distrusted the whole thing for good reasons and attended only on the one evening when Mr. Forster was to speak. At that time, the Communists were busy dividing the whole world into two kinds of people: Fascist and Communist. They said you could tell Fascists by their abhorrence of culture, their racial prejudices, and their general inhumanity. This was true. But they said also that Communists were animated solely by a love of culture and the general good of their fellow man. Alas, this was not true."[46]

If Porter's hand-dating of the sketch that became "Flowering Judas" is accurate, then she must have planned and thought about the story long before she actually wrote it or published it. That would help explain the difference in theme between it and "Hacienda," which appeared only two years after "Flowering Judas." If "María Concepción" pointed out some of the great difficulties facing the revolution, and if "Flowering Judas" depicted the played-out revolution with only shallow leaders left, then "Hacienda" shows the aftermath of the failure. Harry Mooney, Jr., in *The Fiction and Criticism of Katherine Anne Porter,* complains that the narrator of "Hacienda" "makes no effort to go beyond the surface of any given situation" and "has no integral function in the story itself."[47] The disappointment many reviewers expressed in "Hacienda" had to do in part with the story's viewpoint and the seeming lack of plot. However, if "Hacienda" is considered an extension of "Flowering Judas," the narrator and the story become more logical. The narrator of "Hacienda" is present at the postmortem of the revolution, but she has succeeded in detaching herself from the pain ot it—precisely what Laura in "Flowering Judas" was in the process of doing.

In a letter to Ernestine Evans, notes to which survive among Porter's papers, Porter recorded a number of impressions that are relevant to an understanding of "Hacienda." She begins by saying, "I always travel on walloping little tubs and sleep in a berth, and the pen refuses to stick between my fingers," a scene which anticipates the train ride in the story. She describes her disillusionment with the revolution and with her part in it. "Mexico is a curious place," she says, "a very strange place, but not surprising, for it is rather the place a great many persons—myself a little included—have helped to make in the past ten years. God knows I was not working towards this end consciously, but my short-sightedness is to blame." Some of the evidence of the revolution's failure lies in the poverty of the Indians, she implies, as she says, "The Indian is poorer than ever, his heels are cracked as deeply, his face as despairing." And then she names the hypocrisies that are further indicators of the failure of the aims of the revolution. She speaks of the primitives who come to paint the poor Indian and see him as "a more paintable object," but they are "make-believe primitives." Like others, she believes that Diego Rivera has become corrupt; she says with high irony, "But the Mexican Renascence is in full swing, with Diego getting . . . twenty-two thousand dollar[s] . . . from Morrow— the Good Will Ambassador—to spoil Cortes palace with his dummies—and is paying his assistant, a talented Russian painter, with three children, five pesos a day." The Avenida Madero, named for the 1910 revolutionist, has been taken over with "lousy . . . Arty Shoppes where you pay a peso for a blue goblet that used to cost ten centavos." She continues the catalog of corruption:

> Bill Spratling sleeps with his mozo, and encourages the laquerware industry, and the Sonora News is stacked up with raw, crude and frightful objects

in this craft. An American woman went to Tonala—which was a town famous for its fine pottery when the Spaniard came to show the Tonala potters how to "refine" their product and make it more acceptable to the market. I've forgotten the animal's name, but I have seen enough of the bastard stuff she turns out. The much advertised Fresh Air Schools mostly take it out in publicity, there are no funds for their support. One of the Esculeas de Bellas Artes gets its main revenue by making and painting fancy beds—with American canned paints—and carving imitation Aztec statues for the house and garden of one of our more homosexual politicians. The major opus is a squat female figure with a hose attachment running under the seat, through the vagina, and arranged to spout water from one of the breasts. The country is stuffy with Hubert Herrings holding seminars, and dessicated females looking for romance and attaching themselves to such nice, such charming inverts, and good old Frank Tannenbaum still busily "writing up" in his faithful wooden way, everything he sees, with statistics to back him up, and a thesis to begin with. He can't move a leg without a thesis as a crutch.[48]

She also writes about the Crane Foundation ("the fancy plumbing fixtures company") which "has a representative here taking surveys of this and that, acting on the official, but secret, dream of gaining moral power by boring into the country, like a worm, and establishing himself as the Mexican member of a little group of the Elect, such as Pythagoras and Plato dreamed of. They're going to achieve this by helping establish Big Business Firms in the different countries, preaching the gospel of higher standards of living—which will of course include fancy plumbing, and aiding the government they live under so effectively that they will become men to be reckoned with."

One can imagine Porter's sitting down with the notes to this letter to Evans as she is reconstructing "Hacienda" for the second version and finding in them the inspiration for the long train ride that begins the story and the train and automobile rides that conclude it. The letter in fact contains a great many important clues to the story's meaning. In addition to the evidence of decay and perversion she cites, throughout much of the letter Porter's own bitterness, resignation, and self-blame are apparent and are a believable sequence to Laura's sense of being betrayed and her attempt to escape the force of the horror by withdrawing from feeling, appropriate reactions that are a prelude to the complete moral objectivity of the narrator of "Hacienda," who simply looks on and records the events and the scene without participating in them. The hypocrisies and perversions Porter treats somewhat obliquely in "Flowering Judas" are described in lurid detail in the letter and presented artistically in the second version of "Hacienda."

The train and the automobile are more than a framing device for the story; they become important symbols in the narrative, extensions of Braggioni's Sunday morning automobile ride down the Reforma and his own identification with machine imagery. Whereas in "Flowering Judas" machines symbolize antilife forces, in "Hacienda" they serve as reminders of the revolution's failure. Machines were to free the peons from servitude to the land and were to raise their standard of living. After a decade, however, the lives of the peons have been transformed in only one way by the machine. Now a train's engine, "mysteriously and powerfully animated, draws them lightly over the miles they have so often counted step by step" (136). But it is a mere illusion of movement, a journey to nowhere, because the plight of the Indian remains unchanged.

Both the illusion of change and the inevitability of change are especially important elements in the revised version of "Hacienda."[49] Shortly before the first version was published, when Porter already may have started thinking about the revised version that would appear two years later, she discussed at length her philosophy of change in a letter to William Hale, whose recent study of nineteenth-century romanticism she had read. She calls his work "a bill of particulars against our present times," but she cautions him against advocating change without specifying what the change should be, implying that change for change's sake is dangerous. She goes on to explain her theory of immutability. She says that trying to recover something of the past (Goethe's philosophy is the example she cites) is "fatal, because, since all life is a change and a becoming, all definite rules are inevitably outdated certainly within two generations and sometimes earlier, unless they are modified by the minds that accept them, and gradually become something else."[50]

The theme of change versus immutability is advanced in the very first paragraph of "Hacienda" II when a mildly bitter narrative voice says, "Now that the true revolution of blessed memory has come and gone in Mexico, the names of many things are changed, nearly always with a view to an appearance of heightened well-being for all creatures" (135). Growing out of that thematic germ, several truths become apparent in the developing story: change sometimes is an illusion; mere motion is sometimes confused with change; immutability is impossible; and change itself does not ensure melioration. The appearance of change is mistaken for true change, as in the case of the young Indian who boards the train to tell Andreyev of the shooting at the hacienda. Because he is playing the leading role in the film, he is followed by "several of his hero-worshipers, underfed, shabby youths, living happily in reflected glory" (146–47). He has double fame because he also is a pugilist, and with "a brilliant air of self-confidence" he approaches Andreyev's group "with the easy self-possession of a man of the world accustomed to boarding trains and meeting his friends" (147). But the change is an acquired one, and "the pose would not hold. His face, from high cheekbones to square chin, from the full wide-lipped mouth to the low forehead, which had ordinarily the expression of professional-boxer histrionic ferocity, now broke up into a charming open look of simple, smiling excitement." Assigning new names to people and things does not change their essential natures or basic truths; and sometimes a change in a truth makes a name no longer accurate. Velarde, for example, may once have been a true revolutionist. But now, although he is called "the most powerful and successful revolutionist in Mexico," the truth is that he is the opposite, an entrepreneur and an oppressor.

Those who mistake motion, the medium of change, for change itself, consider speed to be still better. Like the Indians, don Genaro prefers speed, but he favors high-powered automobiles rather than trains and is "thinking of an airplane to cut the distance between the hacienda and the capital." The narrative voice says flatly that "speed and lightness at great expense was his ideal" (151). The illusoriness of his ideal is revealed in the fact that he is always late. As Betancourt observes, "Always going at top speed, . . . 70 kilometers an hour at least, and never on time anywhere" (154).

For others it is the seemingly unchanged nature of the hacienda that has an appeal. Andreyev explains to the narrator why the hacienda was chosen for the filming:

> "It was really an old-fashioned feudal estate with the right kind of architecture, no modern improvements to speak of, and with the purest type of peons. Naturally a pulque hacienda would be just such a place. Pulque-making had not changed from the beginning, since the time the first Indian set up a rawhide vat to ferment the liquor and pierced and hollowed the first gourd to draw with his mouth the juice from the heart of the maguey. Nothing had happened since, nothing could happen. Apparently there was no better way to make pulque. The whole thing," he said, "was almost too good to be true. An old Spanish gentleman had revisited the hacienda after an absence of fifty years, and had gone about looking at everything with delight. 'Nothing has changed,' he said, 'nothing at all!'" (CS, 142).

Andreyev and the old Spanish gentleman are wrong, of course, for even if the architecture and the method of making the pulque have remained the same, other things have changed. Moreover, stasis itself is death, which paradoxically is also change; the pervasive smell of decaying maguey underscores the "change" at the hacienda, which is a microcosm of postrevolutionary Mexican society.[51]

The story of don Genaro and doña Julia illustrates particularly well the social death that the revolution has caused. Don Genaro has claimed his right to philandering, as was customary within the aristocratic conventions of the past. But doña Julia is not a part of the old tradition, and she does not behave in a traditional way. She is "modern . . . very modern," she says, with "no old-fashioned ideas at all" (143). It is this modernity that offends don Genaro's grandfather, "a gentleman of the very oldest school," who thinks of this woman his grandson marries as only fit for a "gentleman's education" but totally inappropriate to marry. When doña Julia becomes the lesbian lover of her husband's mistress, don Genaro does not know what to do. "He had borne with his wife's scenes because he really respected her rights and privileges as a wife. A wife's first right is to be jealous and threaten to kill her husband's mistress" (144). The Julia-Lolita affair is one more example of the breakdown of the patriarchal system of the past, but it has been replaced with unnaturalness, perversions, and hypocrisies. Integrity, pride, and strength have decayed, showing what happens when aristocrats lose place, as in Chekhov's plays and Faulkner's fiction. Little doña Julia, who represents decay and unnaturalness, is more in control of events than is her husband, "who had no precedent whatever for a husband's conduct in such a situation." He "made a terrible scene, and pretended he was jealous of Betancourt" (145).

Decay and pretense are pervasive. The actress Lolita dresses for the film in costumes circa 1898, and yet in reality she is as far removed from being an aristocratic lady as possible. Doña Julia, likewise, loves "Chinese dress made by a Hollywood costumer" and walks "softly on her tiny feet in embroidered shoes like a Chinese woman's." Her eyes are painted "in the waxed semblance of her face," and she appears "to be an exotic speaking doll" (152). The baby image, a perversion of womanhood that found its greatest expression in the American songs and female attire of the twenties, is carried still further. Doña Julia, in her husband's frequent absences—it is his wont to roar away in one of his powerful automobiles when troubles start—sits at the head of the table, "a figure from a Hollywood comedy, in black *satin* pajamas adorned with rainbow-colored bands of silk, loose sleeves falling over her babyish hands" (154). Like a child, she does not want to go to bed at night. "Let's go on with the music," she says to the narrator. "I love sitting up all night. I never go to bed if I can possibly sit up" (161). Her room, which is "puffy with silk and down, glossy with bright new polished wood and wide mirrors," is made "restless with small ornaments, boxes of sweets, French dolls in ruffled skirts and white wigs." The narrator observes that the air in doña Julia's room is "thick with perfume which fought with another heavier smell" (161). The heavier smell is literally the smell of fermenting pulque, but it is figuratively the smell of death: the death of the old feminine ideals of gentility, procreation, and patience, and the old male ideals of strength and honor.

The soldiers also illustrate the decline. Sent to protect the hacienda against the agrarians, they only sprawl "in idleness eating their beans at don Genaro's expense." The extent of the degradation is seen when "one of the polite, expensive dogs" chases "with snarls of real annoyance, a little fat-bottomed soldier back to his proper place, the barracks by the wall opposite the Indian huts." The indignity is emphasized in the way "the soldier scrambled and stumbled silently away, without resistance, his dim lantern agitated violently" (162).

Kennerly, who is the most despicable character in "Hacienda," exists as further evidence of the corruption of the revolutionary ideal. He is the foreigner who comes to the revolution with a mission that is hostile to the natural way of the people. Although he is in Mexico officially to represent the moving picture men who are being financed by his brother-in-law and other Americans who are sympathetic to the socialist aims, Kennerly is narrow-minded and provincial, speaks no Spanish, and is both disdainful and fearful of the Mexicans. He is especially sensitive to laws, worrying that the filmmakers might be sued for Rosalita's death, but not to human life (he is annoyed that Rosalita's death and Justino's imprisonment may delay the filming). "It just means more time wasted," he says, and regrets only that they couldn't have filmed the actual murder. He finds comfort and excitement in the thought that when Justino returns (he does not consider that he will not), "he'll have to go through the same scene he has gone through twice before, once in play and once in reality. *Reality!* He licked his chops" (164). Kennerly is from "God's own Hollywood," accustomed "to . . . clean, four-square business methods," and trembles to think what he might be getting into. He is like Hatch of "Noon Wine" in his adherence to the letter of the law and in his failure to grasp larger human meanings.

Kennerly shares literal-mindedness with Betancourt, who is concerned with details. Partially modeled on Adolpho Best-Maugard, Betancourt is "Mexican by birth, French-Spanish by blood, French by education," and "completely at the mercy of an ideal of elegance and detachment perpetually at war with a kind of Mexican nationalism which afflicted him like an inherited weakness of the nervous system." He is reed-thin, with "burning fanatic eyes and a small tremulous mouth." When Carlos sings his little song about "poor Rosalita with two bullets in her heart," Betancourt wags a finger and corrects him, "One bullet. . . . One bullet!" Carlos laughingly stands corrected, "Very well, one bullet! Such a precisionist!" (160).

Betancourt and Carlos are a study in contrasts that provide further insights into the revolution. After explaining to Andreyev a proposed background tune for the film, Carlos says with "unhappy certainty" that Betancourt will not like it because "either it will not be modern enough, or not enough in the old style, or just not Mexican enough" (158). Betancourt, who "had spent his youth unlocking the stubborn secrets of Universal Harmony by means of numerology, astronomy, astrology, a formula of thought transference and deep breathing, the practice of will-to-power combined with the latest American theories of personality development; certain complicated magical ceremonies; and a careful choice of doctrines from the several schools of Oriental philosophies which are, from time to time, so successfully introduced into California," has "constructed a Way of Life which could be taught to anyone, and once learned led the initiate quietly, and surely, toward Success: success without pain, almost without effort except of a pleasurable kind, success accompanied by moral and esthetic beauty, as well as the most desirable material reward" (158–59).[52]

It is easy to see how by Betancourt's standard Carlos is a failure. Carlos once had been director of the Jewel Theatre, and ten years before "had composed half the popular songs in Mexico." Now he is "a large lumpish person in faded blue overalls and a flannel shirt" and "a fine set of whiskers." Although Betancourt assures the narrator that "it's not only the whiskers and the fat" that have determined the failure of Carlos, Betancourt's determinants are just as superficial: Carlos has no evident success.[53]

But Carlos is the only character in the story who has artistic vision. He gets to the heart of the Justino-Rosalita story, as his *corrido* indicates. As the only true artist in the story (the filmmakers are linked to political motives and thus by Porter's standards have abdicated the artist's responsibility), he is a departure from his former self when he was composing half the popular songs of Mexico, presumably those songs about unrequited love. The irony is that now that he offers a more profound view of life, he is not taken seriously and is moreover considered a failure.[54]

Other characters in "Hacienda" reinforce the theme. Andreyev and Stepanov are the other Russian filmmakers; Andreyev is introduced first because he travels with the narrator on the train. He shows her pictures from the film, and the narrator observes that the camera had captured something of the doom in its mechanical accuracy that the propagandists did not know it caught. "The camera had seen this unchanged world as a landscape with figures, but figures under a doom imposed by the landscape" (142). Andreyev knows that the natural fact will yield to the truth; he knows that the propaganda is not working. The filmmakers have made an agreement with the Mexican government that certain statements will be implied in the film; for example, in the hacienda a large chromo portrait of Porfirio Díaz looms "from a gaudy frame on the walls" in order to show, as Andreyev says, "that all this really happened in the time of Díaz, and that all this [the plight of the Indians] . . . has been swept away by the revolution." He tells the narrator this "without cracking a smile or meeting . . . [her] eye" (145).

Stepanov is more enigmatic than Andreyev. He is a champion at tennis, polo, and billiards, an expert pilot, and, one presumes, an expert photographer; in fact, "he excelled in every activity that don Genaro respected." He captures reality with the camera in ways that don Genaro, doña Julia, Kennerly, and others cannot understand. When Kennerly accusingly asks why he missed the opportunity to film the murder as it really happened, Stepanov responds, "Light no good, probably." Then "his eyes flickered open, clicked shut in Kennerly's direction, as if they had taken a snapshot of something and that episode was finished" (163). Kennerly continues to complain, and Stepanov says to the narrator, "The light, . . . it is always our enemy" (163). As she does in other stories, Porter is pointing out that truth is the enemy of some people, in this instance Kennerly.

One other character is worth noting. The last night at the hacienda the narrator is "learning a new card game with a thin dark youth who was some sort of assistant to Betancourt. He was very sleek and slim-waisted and devoted, he said, to fresco painting, 'only modern, . . . like Rivera's, the method, but not old-fashioned style like his'" (168–69). He goes on to tell the narrator that he is decorating a house in Cuernavaca and invites her to come look at it. He may be partially modeled on Juan O'Gorman and partially on David Siqueiros, and he represents change within change. In 1922 Rivera had been the radical destroyer of the old aesthetic standards, and now a decade later there is a need to revolutionize Rivera himself. This is change that is inevitable, growing out of the staleness of any movement. Rivera in time has become old-fashioned.[55]

The revolutionary background to "Hacienda" is always evident. Although the picture of Porfirio Díaz in the background is intended by the filmmakers to date the events depicted in the film, it assumes an ironic meaning in Porter's story. When Díaz became president in 1866, succeeding the Juárez regime, he instituted some reforms and programs that led to greater prosperity for Mexico. He was a dictator, however, and as the years passed he became more and more autocratic and more and more entrenched in his ways. By 1910 there was strong sentiment against him, even much hostility, and the country was ripe for his overthrow by Madero. He symbolized the change that in the beginning was fresh and good but in time became ossified, even corrupt, and antagonistic to human needs. He represented what the revolution had become for Porter, for Laura in "Flowering Judas," and for the narrator of "Hacienda."[56]

"Hacienda" is a story woven of many threads. It is on one hand an account of some of the conflicting interests involved in the filming of *Que Viva Mexico,* and it is about the Mexican revolution that Porter "ran smack into" and which failed to fulfill the aims she and other revolutionary sympathizers of the twenties idealistically hoped it would fulfill. On a universal level, it is about a changing of orders and how change itself is not necessarily better than that which is yielding place, and about revolutions that become systems, which seem to hold the answers to life's questions but yield only disillusion.[57]

Throughout Porter's fiction are not only characters who embrace religious, philosophical, or political systems but also characters who are literal-minded in their belief that visible, outward, or concrete order provides a satisfying pattern for life. Social decorum is a set of implicit laws by which people live in order to ensure their own virtue and to find truth.[58] They believe that being "proper" is the same as being virtuous; the appearance of virtue in turn is proof to themselves and others that they have found life's meaning.

It is a belief with which Porter would have been intimately familiar. She grew up in a region of the country that was more stringently structured socially than others and that placed much value on the appearance of things. Although it was reinforced by the nationally pervasive colonial Puritanism, the background of Southern stratification was also aristocratic, even European, and it was self-fulfilling. Poor whites and blacks were kept in their places for so long in a belief in white supremacy, in God-ordained class stratification that included noblesse oblige, that they had little opportunity to change the appearance of the things that gauged a person's worth: where he lived, the way he dressed or spoke, his deportment, and his material possessions. [59] Regardless of the immorality of the system, it has been deeply ingrained in Southern life, and one doubts that Porter ever emotionally escaped the notions of how a lady behaved and how "trash" behaved. She complained about the play *Dylan*, which dramatized on stage a meeting between the poet and Porter. "The worst thing," she said, "was that they had me sitting alone at a bar, which is something I've never done and never would. That made me most annoyed."[60] One of Porter's landladies confirmed this trait. Señora Soledad Guzmán recalls that Porter was always very charming, always wore hats, worked long hours at her typewriter, and never attempted to entertain men in her room. [61] There has been a tendency to see Porter as a free spirit, roaming from one marriage to another, and perhaps living a bohemian life that was antagonistic to her upbringing. There is truth in both views, but throughout her life Porter gave the appearance of genteel upbringing and ladylike deportment.

In "Noon Wine: The Sources" Porter comments directly about the social structure of south Texas towns. She provides what she calls "a rather generalized view of the society of that time and place [the setting of "Noon Wine"] as I remember it, and as talks with my elders since confirm it" (CE, 471). She says that her elders "all talked and behaved as if the final word had gone out long ago on manners, morality, religion, even politics," and the rulers of the daily life were the grandparents and their generation. "They showed plainly in acts, words, and even looks . . . the presence of good society, very well based on traditional Christian beliefs."

After the Civil War, which she calls the "fatal dividing change in the country," it was the upward-bound lower class or the middle class that was most class-conscious and struggled so hard to maintain a sense of propriety and to follow rules of decorum that would give them the appearance of "place" and link them to the upper class and thus by implication to "divine rights." It is these people about whom Porter writes in "He" and "Noon Wine." She describes them as "the petty middle class of fundamentalists who saw no difference between wine-drinking, dancing, card-playing, and adultery." She once chided Malcolm Cowley for speaking of "the middle-class virtues." "Middle class virtue," she wrote him, "is a kind of code of behavior based on fear of consequences, an artificial line set up, but to [be] sneaked over if one can manage it with secrecy."[62]

Class consciousness and a sense of social decorum cause Mrs. Whipple to present a false face to her neighbors. Because "she couldn't stand to be pitied," she tells her husband, "Don't ever let a soul hear us complain." She says, "Nobody's going to get a chance to look down on us" (CS, 49). It is this pride, this desire to be thought grateful for the Lord's blessings, that causes Mrs. Whipple to declare that she loves her retarded son more than she loves her other children. And although she worries constantly about "people coming around saying things all the time," she is not aware of the comments that are indeed made behind their backs. She does not really fool the neighbors in spite of her vociferous declarations of piety and conscientious mothering of Him. It is class consciousness also that forces Mrs. Whipple to kill the suckling pig when her brother, "his plump healthy wife, and two great roaring hungry boys" come to dinner; she wants to give the appearance of prosperity lest her relatives think she is lower class than they.[63] Although she wants to appear better off than her brother, the opposite is implied in their rosy plumpness and hearty good humor.

Class consciousness is even more of a force in "Noon Wine," for it is Mr. and Mrs. Thompson's fear of what their neighbors think that finally forces the concluding tragedy of the story. "All his carefully limited fields of activity were related somehow to Mr. Thompson's feeling for the appearance of things, his own appearance in the sight of God and man. 'It don't *look* right,' was his final reason for not doing anything he did not wish to do" (233). Because it is "his dignity and his reputation" that he cares about, Mr. Thompson, in spite of the fact that he has been "going steadily down hill," finds solace in the fact that he is "a prompt payer of taxes, yearly subscriber to the preacher's salary, land owner and father of a family, employer, a hearty good fellow among men" (234).

Because of Thompson's desire to give a good appearance, the events that follow his killing Hatch are predictable. Although Thompson was exonerated at the trial and neighbors keep saying, "yes they know it was a clear case and fair trial," they look "like they don't really take sides with him" (258). Obsessed with having society's approval, his "eyes hollowed out and dead-looking" and "his thick hands gray white and seamed from washing them clean every day before he started out," Thompson goes from place to place and family to family, telling his story of self-defense over and over again. He becomes more and more desperate, and his decline is mirrored in the class of the people he stoops to convince. The last memorable visit is at the McClellans'. When McClellan comes "out in his sock feet, with one gallus up, the other broken and dangling" and Mrs. McClellan joins him "barefooted, in a calico wrapper," Mr. Thompson begins his liturgy: "Well, as I reckon you happen to know, I've had some strange troubles lately, and, as the feller says, it's not the kind of trouble that happens to a man every day in the year, and there's some things I don't want no misunderstanding about in the neighbors' minds, so—." When he pauses and stumbles forward, "the two listening faces took on a mean look, a greedy, despising look, a look that said plain as day, 'My, you must be a purty sorry feller to come round worrying about what *we* think, *we* know you wouldn't be here if you had anybody else to turn to—my, I wouldn't lower myself that much, myself'" (263). Thompson is ashamed of his lowering himself, and enraged, he suddenly knows that "he'd like to knock their dirty skunk heads together, the low-down white trash—but he held himself down and went on to the end." In their own way, even the McClellans refuse Thompson. Mr. McClellan says, "I kaint see no good reason for us to git mixed up in these murder matters, I shore kaint," and his wife adds, "Now we don't hold with killin'; the Bible says—" (264). It is subsequent to this final social degradation, compounded by his wife's refusal to offer her own form of forgiveness, that Thompson, who already is symbolically a dead man, shoots himself with his double-barreled shotgun.

The Thompsons and the Whipples, in their efforts to ascend the social ladder, are so caught up in what people think and so fearful of breaking, or of having broken, the social code that they are blinded to truths that lie all around and within. In other stories are people who also are daunted by rules of social decorum, for they too understand that in their society they are going to be evaluated by the degree to which they adhere to the rules or flout them. Rosaleen O'Toole in "The Cracked Looking-Glass" is the victim of the social code because she keeps young boys in her house, goes on trips away from her husband, and dyes her hair. Rosaleen is able to escape into her fantasy world and avoid the agony of ostracization, but when the native boy's mother castigates her ("A pretty specimen you are, Misses O'Toole, with your old husband and the young boys in your house and the traveling salesmen and the drunkards lolling on your doorstep all hours"), Rosaleen, after stopping in her tracks and listening, levels a barrage of Irish curses at the stringy-haired woman and wishes, just for a moment, that she had the strength to strangle "all at once" the people who have been telling lies about her. One of the ironies in the story is that while Rosaleen is judged by her mean-spirited neighbors according to the appearance of things, she, too, does the same. She puts great emphasis on labels, often judging a person by the part of Ireland from which he comes. Dennis recalls that the night he met Rosaleen she had told him that the only thing against him was that he came from Bristol, "and the outland Irish had the name of people you couldn't trust. She couldn't say why—it was just a name they had, worse than Dublin people itself. No decent Sligo girl would marry a Dublin man if he was the last man on earth" (106). Rosaleen in turn is identified by the slant-eyed youth in Boston as a County Sligo woman, apparently by her brogue, and he uses that knowledge to gain Rosaleen's confidence, which leads to the free meal. "I'm County Sligo, myself," he says. After the misunderstanding and altercation, however, he taunts Rosaleen with "Farewell to ye, County Sligo woman. . . . I'm from County Cork myself!" (129).

A similar kind of stringent adherence to social decorum is seen in Lacey Halloran in "A Day's Work."[64] She is so concerned with giving the appearance of propriety that she distorts the truth to others and to herself. When Halloran crows out the window, "What's a father these days and who would heed his advice?" Lacey comments, "You needn't tell the neighbors, there's disgrace enough already" (390). Later in the story, when Halloran in a drunken delirium tries to kill "the ghost of Lacey Mahaffy," she is too proud and too conscious of social condemnation to admit to Officer Maginnis that her husband hit her with an iron. She says, "I fell and hit my head on the ironing board. . . . It comes of overwork and worry, day and night. A dead faint, Officer Maginnis" (405). She is merely doing her "duty," for according to the rules of her social class, a good wife must be patient and "do right first." She admires most the persons who have fulfilled the rules of decorum, which, as Porter pointed out, included rules of religion and morality. The Connollys are her standard of achievement and success because they are "good practical Catholics" who go to mass every day. She is judging by outward appearances, as she always has been inclined to do. When Mr. Halloran learns that Connolly is being pursued by the G-men for being mixed up in the numbers racket, his response is ambivalent. Unoffended by the immorality or of the breaking of the law, he at first is sympathetic to Connolly, who is "a great fellow," but his sympathy turns to joy as he thinks, "Wait till I give Lacey Mahaffy the news about Connolly, I'll like seeing her face the first time in twenty years." Connolly's predicament is proof that appearance belies reality and that social respectability is no guarantee of virtue; the message will be lost on Mrs. Halloran.

Other kinds of visible ordering set up even more explicit illusions of truth. Granny Weatherall has thought she found answers to life's mysteries in the rules of her religion. But she goes beyond religion to structure her life and relies also on visible patterns. As she lies and drowses and loses her sense of time, she thinks, "Tomorrow was far away and there was nothing to trouble about. Things were finished somehow when the time came; thank God there was always a little margin over for peace; then a person could spread out the plan of life and tuck in the edges orderly. It was good to have everything clean and folded away, with the hair brushes and tonic bottles sitting straight on the white embroidered linen: the day started without fuss and the pantry shelves laid out with rows of jelly glasses and brown jugs and white stone-china jars with blue whirligigs and words painted on them: coffee, tea, sugar, ginger, cinnamon, all-spice" (81).

Everything labeled and arranged neatly in rows. The irony is that Granny's mind at her dying hour is not orderly at all. The past is getting confused with the present, and her tired mind is rambling freely from one memory to another, through the years that are metaphored as "the bright field where everything was planted so carefully in orderly rows" (84). Moreover, "she had her secret comfortable understanding with a few favorite saints who cleared a straight road to God for her" (86).

Reinforcing the image of orderliness is the image of light. Order should have brought with it its own light, its own truth. But the order that has characterized Granny's life has been a deceptive order, no meaning at all. Light first appears in her memories as an association with the fog that is creeping in at the edges of her dying consciousness. She translates it symbolically as a memory: "A fog rose over the valley, she saw it marching across the creek swallowing the trees and moving up the hill like an army of ghosts. Soon it would be at the near edge of the orchard, and then it was time to go in and light the lamps. Come in, children, don't stay out in the night air" (83–84).

Throughout the rest of the story, light, as symbol of truth or of understanding, dominates the story. Its opposite, fog or smoke, represents the breakdown of order or meaning. The important symbols in the story, the jilting sixty years ago, the orderly rows, light, and fog, come together in a crucial passage near the end of the story. On that long-ago wedding day everything had seemed right: "Such a fresh breeze blowing and such a green day with no threats in it." But the groom fails to show up. "What does a woman do when she has put on the white veil and set out the white cake for a man and he doesn't come?" (84). That was the day that chaos, doubt, confusion, and disillusion entered her soul, when "a whirl of dark smoke rose and covered it, crept up and over into the bright field where everything was planted so carefully in orderly rows." That was hell itself, and for sixty years Granny Weatherall has repressed the thought of the missing bridegroom (the thought of him was "a smoky cloak from hell"), but now at her dying the smoke is threatening to surface. The light seems to hurt her eyes, just as the old grief wounds her anew. But she allows the memory of the first bridegroom to surface: "Yes, she had changed her mind after sixty years and she would like to see George. I want you to find George. Find him and be sure to tell him I forgot him. I want him to know I had my husband just the same and my children and my house like any other woman. A good house too and a good husband that I loved and fine children out of him. Better than I hoped for even. Tell him I was given back everything he took away and more. Oh, no, oh, God, no, there was something else besides the house and the man and the children. Oh, surely they were not all? What was it? Something not given back" (86). That which was not given back was her faith, but instead of living out her days in bitter resignation she suppresses the trauma and searches for meaning in orderly rows, one of which is a path to God, or truth.

Among Granny's dying memories is that of hunting for matches to get light when one of the children screamed in nightmare; throughout her life she continued to hunt for a truth that would alleviate her fears of the darkness. She recalls that lighting the lamps had been beautiful: "The children huddled up to her and breathed like little calves waiting at the bars in the twilight. Their eyes followed the match and watched the flame rise and settle in a blue curve, then they moved away from her. The lamp was lit, they didn't have to be scared" (84).

As Granny's death approaches, the room is "like a picture she had seen somewhere" in "dark colors with the shadows rising towards the ceiling in long angles." Black is beginning to dominate. "The tall black dresser gleamed," and in the picture on the dresser her husband's eyes were "very black" when "they should have been blue." The light beside the bed is blue, however, because the bulb is covered by Cornelia's blue lampshade, and the blue light becomes first the replacement for the blue eyes and then it becomes Granny herself. "The blue light from Cornelia's lampshade drew into a tiny point in the center of her brain, it flickered and winked like an eye, quietly it fluttered and dwindled. Granny lay curled down within herself, amazed and watchful, staring at the point of light that was herself" (89).

Granny is not able to find the meaning that should have been approachable through her life with the "good husband" whom she loved. All three—truth, John, and she herself—are brought together in the blue light and submerged in the renewed agony of there not being a "visible" sign from God. When Granny blows out the light, she is acknowledging a wasted life led by the promise of meaning through her religion or intuitively sought in the ordering of her life and her rows of preserves and crops. She has identified the absent George with Christ and feels abandoned by both. "There's nothing more cruel than this—I'll never forgive it" is her final thought (89). It is the ultimate agony that is created when one pins one's faith on formal systems or on an external order that is not natural to one's spirit. It is a theme of betrayal like that of "Flowering Judas," and it is underscored by the Hapsy story that is only hinted at within the larger story of Granny's dying. She waits for Hapsy, too, who does not return, and we can only speculate about the details. In the dream vision Granny sees Hapsy with a baby that is Hapsy's child, Hapsy herself, and Granny all at once; in another dream memory, the birth of this child is suggested in Granny's recalling having announced to John that Hapsy's "time has come." Hapsy is the love child, the only one Granny truly wanted, and she, like George sixty years ago and Christ now, fails to appear. Perhaps she is dead, or perhaps away, perhaps sent away. The details are unimportant. It is only significant that this story within the story underscores the theme of betrayed faith that permeates "The Jilting of Granny Weatherall." Cornelia is the faithful and weeping child who is there throughout, and her name suggests the Cordelia-Lear tragedy, without Lear's uplifting vision at the tragedy's end. The story ends at Lear's "Never, never, never, never, never" speech.

"Holiday" is also set in central Texas, and like Granny, the Müllers are orderly. As German immigrants who have retained and transplanted the customs and family structure of the old country, they live in an order that is exotic to the Southwestern American soil. The tenacity of the Müllers, who have held on to their heritage, is pointed out by the narrator when she explains that their low German dialect has been corrupted by three generations in a foreign country; they therefore are not recent immigrants. This fact is given further meaning in the ensuing digression as she remarks that "a dozen miles away, where Texas and Louisiana melted together in a rotting swamp whose sluggish under-tow of decay nourished the roots of pine and cedar, a colony of French emigrants had lived out two hundred years of exile, not wholly incorruptible, but mystically faithful to the marrow of their bones, obstinately speaking their old French by then as strange to the French as it was to the English" (413). It is important to note that the old "order" of the French exiles was acted upon by the new land and was rendered meaningless to both the old and the new. Not only the impossibility of retaining past systems is illustrated here, but also the foolishness of trying to do so. The reader obviously is expected to draw a parallel between the French immigrants and the Müller family.

The Müllers believe that outward orderliness ensures an understanding of life. It is not they who learn otherwise, but rather the narrator who learns by observing them and by some trials and errors of her own. For a while she, too, believes that an ordered life allows for a meaningful life, and from the moment of her arrival at their farm she thrills to their efficiency. Like persons cut from a pattern, they can be identified by their physical similarities, notably their pale, tilted eyes and taffy-colored hair. Within the patriarchal society of their farm, every family member knows what is expected of him or her and carries it out dutifully; indeed, they work together like parts of a precisioned machine. On the basis of their likenesses the narrator makes a hasty assumption that is to be the catalyst in her awakening at the journey's end; she illogically concludes that the servant girl, tangential to the family in function and different in outward appearance, is not a part of the family proper. She says, "I got a powerful impression that they were all, even the sons-in-law, one human being divided into several separate appearances. The crippled servant girl brought in more food and gathered up plates and went away in her limping run, and she seemed to me the only individual in the house" (417).

Ottilie, the servant girl, is further described in images that contrast to the vision of the vigorous Müllers: "The blurred, dark face was neither young nor old, but crumpled into criss cross wrinkles, irrelevant either to age or suffering; simply wrinkles, patternless blackened seams as if the perishable flesh had been wrung in a hard cruel fist" (420). Ottilie symbolizes disorder and confusion. The cause of her affliction is never known to the narrator, and thus it cannot be explained by logic; the wrinkles exist for mysterious reasons, without a pattern, in a face that is ageless. Human suffering, brought about by absurd, irrational forces, is illogical, too, and as the victim of such forces, Ottilie symbolizes the dark, unfathomable side of life.

As long as the narrator can view Ottilie as a universal accident, beyond the pale of the Müller family, she is able to bask in naiveté, content within the Müllers' fresh-scrubbed pleasantness and complete order, in which even the play of the Müller grandchildren is "disciplined," and even the Müllers' recreation is regulated—always on Sunday, always at the Turnverein. Gradually the narrator moves toward understanding that external order is irrelevant. Equally important to the story's theme is the narrator's simultaneous perception of the subversion of human love by external order. This undermining is most apparent at the primary events of human life: marriage, birth, and death. For example, love is merely hinted at during the wedding of Hatsy and her gentle-tempered bridegroom. The strongest statement the narrator is willing to make is that Hatsy's husband "looked at Hatsy as if he liked what he saw." The glimmering of love is obscured in the rituals that take over after the marriage—the chasing of the bride, the feasting, the dancing, the drinking. After the chase Hatsy returns to the dining room with the other women, "still wearing her square of white cotton net bound on her hair with peach blossoms shattered in the bride's race." Throughout the story the peach trees and their blossoms reflect nature's cycle of life, death, and rebirth and underscore the superficial order of the Müllers. Hatsy's shattered blossoms symbolize her retrieval from natural, or spiritual, vitality; herewith she will live in the ritual of serving her husband and bearing children. In the Müllers' world, there is little difference between the marriage of two persons and the mating of two animals. Love, that which gives meaning to life and raises humans above animals, is noticeably obscured by the overwhelming pattern.

During the celebration of the birth of Gretchen's child, the lack of the human difference is again apparent. The hardworking wives and mothers are not awed by the miracle of birth, but rather see the birth as a low joke, an occasion for obscene improprieties. In their view the baby, who bawls and suckles like a young calf, is no different from any newborn animal. And conversely, animals are described in human terms. The calves, for example, "bawled like rebellious babies." In addition, the Müller grandchildren, who mimic their elders, go through their games of pretend mechanically and dispassionately, changing effortlessly from horses to humans whenever the game requires. Moreover, as they come at call "to be fed and put to sleep with the docility of their own toys or animal playmates," their mothers, who handle them with "instinctive, constant gentleness," are "as devoted and caretaking as a cat with her kittens" (419). Obviously, as nothing more. Again, Porter has used animals and animal imagery to show the absence of the humanizing element.

The Müllers' very lives symbolize order. That which does not fit into their patterned lives must reside beyond them, for they can "understand" only that which seems to have a visible logic. Nature's cycles surround them, and yet they learn no lessons from them; they continue to cling to surface patterns as a way of life. The narrator thinks that in spite of the great tumult of their grief when Mother Müller dies, life for them will eventually "arrange itself again in another order" and yet it will be the same (432–33).

The narrator of "Holiday" makes the obvious mistake of trying to understand Ottilie Müller in terms of her own experiences and by what she wrongly perceives to be the laws of human nature. At the same time that the story illustrates the insufficiency of patterns and systems to lead to truth and life's meaning, it also shows the separateness of humans and the inability of one person to completely understand another. As Porter said, "There are only a few bits of absolute knowledge in the world, people can learn only one or two fundamental facts about each other, the rest is decoration and prejudice" (CE, 254).

The Müllers' visible order is like that of Granny Weatherall. The order of the Thompsons and the Whipples is the order of social decorum, and yet it is visible order as well. Porter reveals that none of these people learns that clinging to a superficial order is useless and that a natural order is to be found within the spirit and cannot be measured by grids or charts. Neither can it be found in methodized religion, art, or politics. She summarized her philosophy when she told Thompson, "The thing is not to follow a pattern. . . . The thing is, to accept your own life and not try to live someone else's life."[65]

Chapter Three

Ideals

Systems become illusions of truth as people place all their faith in them. Other illusions are created in the human tendency to idealize persons or places, making them seem the embodiment of truth and perfection. Such ideals are important elements in some of Katherine Anne Porter's stories. In one sense, the placing of a human being in a divine position is just a form of perverted religion, as it is with Mrs. Braggioni in "Flowering Judas," which also includes the related theme of self-love in the person of Braggioni. But in other stories the religious significance is eliminated, and Porter shows such misplaced devotion as simply a deluding idealism that fails to yield to the large understanding.

In addition to "Flowering Judas" the idealizing of human beings appears as an important element in "The Jilting of Granny Weatherall" and "The Martyr." Porter has spoken outside of fiction about this tendency in human beings, including herself, and scoffs at it. She offers counsel to her nephew Paul about the Stroke of Lightning school of love (to which she says she "long adhered"), in which an "Object" becomes a "Subject . . . instantly transfigured with a light of such blinding brilliance all natural attributes disappear and are replaced by those usually associated with archangels at least." She says that "it is probably the silliest kind of love there is."[1] The archangel image is important in this comment, for it may be the signal for the theme of deification in her fiction. Mrs. Braggioni, for example, asks her prodigal husband, "Are you tired, my angel?"[2]

"The Martyr" was one of the first of Porter's stories to treat the theme, and it goes far beyond the deification of human beings in its analysis of false ideals. The story was written and published at a time when Porter was seeing all around her the development and the decline of the Mexican revolution at the same time she was taking notes for stories that would depict the process and the aftermath of the revolution's failure. She credited the Mexican muralists for much of the revolutionary spirit in Mexico in the twenties, and she believed that Rivera, as the leader of the muralists, made significant contributions to art and to the revolution. As she said to Robert McAlmon, "Some damned fine work came out of . . . [the cultural renaissance led by Rivera]."[3] But like others she also had early fears about Rivera's potential for self-aggrandizement and the difficulty of keeping him on track. Through reviews, essays, and letters her changing attitude toward Rivera can be traced and in fact can help explain the character of Rubén in "The Martyr."

Porter's relationship with Rivera probably began soon after he returned to Mexico in 1922 to take up the Mexican Renaissance. Porter already had published "The Mexican Trinity," in which she discussed with keen perception what she saw as Mexico's internal enemies. After Rivera's arrival she published "María Concepción," which depicts the difficulty of "educating" the Indian. During these first two years of her stay in Mexico she was becoming wary, and she saw problems and potential problems, but she still had some hope, as her praise of José Vasconcelos, the minister of education, and her sketch "The Children of Xochitl" would indicate.[4] In the midst of the development of her complex feelings, Diego Rivera arrived. To Porter he must have seemed Mexico's answer to the literary artists she thought missing from the Mexican revolution.

Porter apparently knew Rivera well, even spent time grinding his paints during the execution of the murals, as she told Lopez.[5] Whether she was among the women who actually had affairs with him, as his colleague David Siqueiros told Lopez she was, one can only speculate.[6] But other details of the association are confirmed. Among her papers is the note, "I went to the Escuela Preparatoria and saw the finished fresco," and Carleton Beals comments in *Glass Houses* that he and

Porter went together to see the Rivera fresco at the Preparatory School.[7] In 1924 she knew Rivera sufficiently well to publish an interview with him, and in 1925 she translated an excerpt from his notebooks which was published as an essay called "From a Mexican Painter's Notebook"; it is an explanation of the artistic revolution in Mexico and its relation to European movements. In 1929 she reviewed *The Frescoes of Diego Rivera*, and while she questions his political views, she calls him "the most important living painter."[8]

Moving as she did within artistic circles, Porter was certain to become acquainted with Rivera. If there ever was an intimate relationship, it did not last long. She wrote to Ernestine Evans in October 1930 that she recently had seen Rivera:

> He did not recognize me, I have so changed. Changed so. But he was gallant and said, "You are more *Guapa* than ever," and we drank together, and ended by embracing and slapping each other on the back, which was a very uneven exchange, considering the weights of his slapper and mine, and I thought, in spite of everything he has done, I have done as ill no doubt, and we cannot but be friends after a fashion. He asked me to come to Cuernavaca for a day to watch him work, "and we will eat together and talk as in the old times," he said, but I have not got there. His wife [Frida Kahlo] is a most unusually beautiful and charming creature, a face altogether out of the ordinary. Lupe comes now and then and stamps with her big mule hoofs in the middle of their lives, but she doesn't do as much damage as she would like.[9]

Somewhat pleased with that meeting, Porter was critical of him seven years later when she reviewed *Portrait of Mexico*, the result of his collaboration with Bertram Wolfe, who wrote the text for this collection of photographs of Rivera's work. She says that Rivera is "half hero, half mountebank, as artists sometimes are," but if she stops short of saying he was "the most important living painter," she does attest to his importance. She says, "For myself, and I believe I speak for great numbers, Mexico does not appear to me as it did before I saw Rivera's paintings of it. The mountains, the Indians, the horses, the flowers and children, have all subtly changed in outlines and colors. They are Rivera's Indians and flowers and all now, but I like looking at them."[10]

Much later, when she reflected on Rivera and what he meant to

Mexico, she cast him in a still different light. She wrote to Mary Doherty in 1963 about David Siqueiros, who had been imprisoned for subversive activities and whose friends were signing petitions hoping to get him released. "Siqueiros," she said, "is basically stupid, or he need not be in this fix. He is not really a communist, and never was: no more than Diego Rivera. They just hopped on the bandwagon and made the most of the publicity; and there we are again. Diego, who was as great a crook as Siqueiros, was smart, and knew how to call the shots."[11]

Whatever Porter's relationship with Rivera and whatever she finally thought of him, there is no doubt that he fascinated her as a subject for her fiction. Among notes she took in the twenties for future stories are the heading "Stories of Diego" and a sketch identified as "Lupe." The sketch shows Porter's habit of beginning with factual details and then selecting and shaping them into art. The sketch follows:

> Lupe: her history of poverty, pride and bitterness as one of a family of fast beautiful girls in Guadalajara, not really fast, but poor, unconventional, and therefore prey to men . . . her affair with Diego. Her demand for marriage. The confession episode . . . Diego marries her by proxy, no church wedding, not legal. The fights, the uproar afterward. Her character, her . . . feroceness [sic]. Tito's remark about her. Diego goes to Russia, has a half dozen mix-ups. When he returns she shows him a written list of her lovers with their occupations. Boot black, truck driver, saloon sweeper, policemen—I wanted to keep you in with the lowest I could find. The beatings, the separation. The women who came to worship Diego, Paca, Tina, Ione, keeping friendly with Lupe while sleeping with her husband. His marriage—legal—with Frida. L's marriage. Death in childbirth, hawklike, ferocious, unappeased, untame, to the last . . .
> Her clothes and eating habits. Her hatred of everything.[12]

There is little doubt that "The Martyr" is based on Rivera and his relationship with Lupe (Guadalupe) Marin, his first wife. On the surface, the story is an expansion of the theme of deifying human beings and the tragedies that result. Rubén, the central character in the story, is in love with his model, Isabel. He adores her and calls her "my poor little angel." When Isabel leaves him for his rival, Rubén becomes "altogether a changed man." He can talk about nothing except Isabel, "her angelic face, her pretty little tricks and ways." Although his friends privately think Isabel's going is a good thing—calling her "the lean she-devil"—Rubén will not be distracted and declares, "There is no other woman like that woman" (34). He is unable to paint, refusing "to touch the nineteenth figure of her, much less to begin the twentieth, and the mural was getting nowhere." All that Rubén can do is eat—"sweets and fruits and almond cakes," and "when his friends took him out for dinner, he would sit quietly and eat huge platefuls of every sort of food, and wash it down with sweet wine." And so Rubén sits immobile, and weeps and eats and grows fatter and fatter.

His friends are concerned, offering advice to him and finally deciding among themselves that since none of them can tell him the true cause of his pain, a physician must be the one to do so. Thus, the doctor from the university is enlisted in the cause. The doctor finds Rubén seated before his easel, facing the half-finished nineteenth figure of Isabel, weeping and eating "spoonfuls of soft Toluca cheese, with spiced mangos." He hangs "in all directions over his painting-stool, like a mound of kneaded dough." But the doctor succumbs to Rubén's "malady," saying, "I have only crass and vulgar remedies" and tiptoeing out "respectfully" (36).

The friends give up in boredom and exasperation, and Rubén sees no one except the proprietor of a small café called The Little Monkeys, where he often had gone to dine with Isabel and where he now went alone for food. And here one night Rubén, clasping his heart with violence and rising from his chair, hurriedly whispers something to the proprietor and dies.

Rubén is an early version of Braggioni, who as a lean and hungry youth and a poet had been rejected by a girl and for the rest of his life had not allowed himself to be hungry. He, too, is "a gluttonous bulk," his "gasping middle" hanging over "his ammunition belt of tooled leather worked in silver" (91–92). And he, too, sings songs of self-pity, of loneliness, and of unrequited love.[13] Both Braggioni and Rubén exemplify the artistic perversion that Porter complains of in "The Mexican Trinity," idealizing unrequited love instead of using their art to present a truthful picture of life. Rubén idealizes love in the person of Isabel, and although he declares throughout his grief that he is dying for love of her, it is clear in the narrative voice that he eats himself to death.

Perhaps the greatest irony is that others are willing to propagate the lie. They, too, place great stock in the chivalric convention of unrequited love. Even the caricaturist Ramón, who has told Rubén that he should finish his "great mural for the world, for the future," forgets his own advice. At Rubén's death Ramón begins to gather materials for Rubén's biography, which is to be dedicated to his "Friend and Master, Inspired and Incomparable Genius of Art on the American Continent." Ramón hastens to the proprietor of The Little Monkeys to learn Rubén's last words, and primes the proprietor by telling him that "the last words of a great artist, they should be very eloquent. Repeat them precisely, my dear fellow! It will add splendor to the biography, nay, to the very history of art itself, if they are eloquent" (CS, 37).

There is every reason to believe that the proprietor makes up Rubén's last words, because he nods his head "with the air of a man who understands everything" and says, "Well, maybe you will not believe me when I tell you that his very last words were a truly sublime message to you, his good and faithful friends, and to the world." The message the proprietor quotes, however, is nothing so grand, in fact is merely another testament to the romantic love ideal. "He said, gentlemen," says the proprietor, " 'Tell them I am a martyr to love. I perish in a cause worthy the sacrifice. I die of a broken heart!' and then he said, 'Isabelita, my executioner!' That was all, gentlemen." And then they all bow their heads. Ramón, who should have known better, says, "I thank you. It is a superb epitaph. I am most gratified." Ramón's thanking the proprietor indicates that the proprietor has given him something, and when the proprietor adds modestly, "He was also supremely fond of my tamales and pepper gravy. . . . They were his final indulgence," the "pay-off" is implied in Ramón's response: "That shall be mentioned in its place, never fear, my good friend." It is more likely that Rubén's final words had something to do with the tamales and pepper gravy, as "supremely" and "final" hint at in the proprietor's afterthought.

Rubén was the greatest artist in Mexico ("earnest minded people made pilgrimages down the narrow cobbled street, picking their way carefully over puddles in the patio, and clattered up uncertain stairs for a glimpse of the great and yet so simple personage"), but he no longer deserves the label.[14] Earnest-minded people have idealized him just as they idealized Rivera, and just as Rubén has idealized Isabel, who does not deserve the pedestal either. She is far from the pure lady of the romantic tradition. She is greedy, cruel, bored, and reckless, and stays with Rubén only until her lover, Rubén's rival, sells a painting and can afford to keep her as she wishes to be kept: she will never have to cook again but will have instead "red slippers and a gay life." Rubén symbolizes the perversion of art to an unholy end. Instead of worshiping at the sacred fount, he is worshiping at the shrine of a human being, a particularly unworthy one, according to the story.

If the greatest artist in Mexico has lost both his artistic purpose and his revolutionary aim, so, too, have all the others. The doctor, who represents the professional class and the academics (he is on the faculty at the university) and combines "a sufficiently refined sentiment with the highest degree of technical knowledge," is himself awed and "profoundly touched" at Rubén's grief. He can offer only consolation to this "man of such delicately adjusted susceptibilities" (36). The friends, who have no respect for Isabel, have abdicated their responsibilities to the great artist, shunted them instead to the ineffectual academic technician, the doctor. And Ramón, the fellow artist, not only fails to uphold the truth but actually propagates the perversion and the lies. Instead of writing the biography of Rubén the artist, he will write the biography of Rubén the martyr to love.

The final irony in the story occurs at the end when Ramón tells the proprietor of The Little Monkeys that his café "will be a shrine for artists" when the story becomes known. The ideal has passed from Isabel the person to Isabel the embodiment of unrequited love to Rubén the martyr to love to the absurd café appropriately called The Little Monkeys.

It is not difficult to see that there were real-life experiences, mood, and acquaintances behind "The Martyr." Rubén has much in common with Rivera, including his great bulk and his obsession with food. Isabel shares many of the traits of Guadalupe Marin, whom Rivera's biographer, Bertram Wolfe, describes as "the wildest and most tempestuous beauty in Jalesco," "long limbed and tall," "wayward of thought and speech and action," "primitive, cunning," and "absorbed in herself."[15] Ramón is modeled partly on Miguel Covarrubias, the caricaturist who remained Rivera's only friend to the end. Covarrubias was also a friend of Porter, in fact had worked with her on the OMPAC exhibit.

Although revolution is not mentioned in "The Martyr," the story must have been inspired by the events of the Mexican revolution. Because it is about misguided idealism and its inevitable failure to lead to truth, it represents Porter's own fears about the obstacles to the revolution's success, obstacles she examines at their later stages in "Flowering Judas" and "Hacienda." Like the earlier "María Concepción," which exhibits the difficulty of "civilizing" the Indians, "The Martyr" exhibits the abdication of the artists. The story was written and published during the years of the cultural renaissance's peak as it was led by Rivera. There are important clues in the story that link it not only to Rivera and his circle but also to the cultural revolution. The name of the café is similar to a real café called *Monotes* ("Big Monkeys"), which was frequented by artists and intellectuals as well as revolutionaries.[16] The café's name has another significance in the cultural context. There was much controversy about Rivera's murals during the early days of his rise to success. More traditional art critics and Mexican patrons of the arts were offended by the bold human visages—less than "pretty" people—in his paintings. There were numerous public threats to cover "Diego's monkeys" with whitewash, until progressive foreign art critics' praise of Rivera's style quieted the native traditionalists.[17] Rivera's "Monkeys" came to symbolize his commitment to art in the face of bourgeoise taste, a theme that is not omitted in "The Martyr." Rubén's rival sells a painting to a rich man "whose decorator told him he must have a panel of green and orange on a certain wall of his new house. By a felicitous chance, this painting was prodigiously green and orange. The rich man paid him a huge price, but was happy to do it, he explained, because it would cost six times as much to cover the space with tapestry" (34). Rivera himself had talked to Porter about the bourgeoise taste, or at least had provided her with some written thoughts about it. In "From a Mexican Painter's Notebooks" she quotes Rivera as having written or said the following:

> Here in Mexico, I find that very simple intuitive persons, in common with a highly sophisticated and prepared type, accept my way of painting. But the bourgeoise mind (here as elsewhere called "cultured," I believe) does not. This bourgeoise mind of Mexico is of a special virulence, for being mixed in race for only a few generations, it is also lamentably mixed in its "culture." It is, in a word, saturated with European bad taste, the finer European influences having been almost wholly rejected by the Creole of Mexico.[18]

Porter would have sympathized with Rivera's sentiment. Many times she spoke about the tendency to be "fashionable," by which she meant bourgeoise, which Rivera certainly was not. She wrote to John Hermann in 1931, "I think we've all been a little timid. That is, sat upon by a notion of literature. . . . I'm all for just beginning and being our little selves, and the devil take the hindmost. There will come a time when we will be in fashion, and another when we are out of it: but in the meantime we will have had the magnificent, the irreplaceable pleasure of having said our say—as for me, I'd willingly lose my skin in such a cause."[19] Perhaps even more to the point, in a review of Ezra Pound's letters she makes the comment that "greatness in art is like any other greatness: in religious experience, in love, it is great because it is beyond the reach of the ordinary, and cannot be judged by the ordinary, nor be accountable to it."[20] For a period in the twenties Rivera would have qualified for greatness, according to Porter. An additional irony in the story is that the café debases the ideal to which its name alludes.

If there were any doubt about the real-life models for Rubén and Isabel, an important detail in the story dispels it at the same time that it illuminates the theme and explains Porter's later attitude toward this story. Rubén has planned drawings of Isabel, eighteen of which are finished. After she leaves, he sits immobile before the unfinished nineteenth and has not even begun to think of the twentieth. So much is made of the unfinished nineteenth figure of Isabel and of the unstarted twentieth that the reader cannot ignore the suggestion of symbolic weight. One would immediately think of possible biblical significance, but the allusion does not yield any connection. However, one of Rivera's murals provides the key, and while she must have seen many of them, it is the one that Porter is documented as having seen at the Preparatoria School. The mural is called "Creation" and is made up of one male figure and twenty female figures in a context of symbolic forms. In addition to Woman, who is the counterpart to Man, there are Knowledge, Fable, Erotic Poetry, Tradition, Tragedy, Prudence, Justice, Strength, Continence, Science, Dance, Music, Song, Comedy, Charity, Hope, Faith, and Wisdom. The nineteenth female figure is Wisdom and it is the most important, according to Rivera's notes of explanation for the mural, for it is a uniting figure that "shows through her two hands the gesture which signifies Microcosm and Macrocosm and Infinity."[21] The twentieth figure is the Tree, from which arises the Pantocrat. If the nineteenth figure is to be a uniting figure, the allusion explains why Rubén cannot complete it. He has lost sight of his artistic commitment to bring order out of chaos and no longer has an integrating vision. He only pines away in the seductive charade of unrequited love.

Porter did not include "The Martyr" in her early collections of stories.[22] Although she offered various reasons for the omission, one suspects that in this instance she recognized a flaw in it. The number symbolism makes the story personal to the artist and damages its universal statement. But the story remains a depiction of the dangers the artist faces when his art becomes tied to a hollow ideal: it could be revolution or religion or courtly love, and this is its most universal theme. The story also is about the Mexican revolution and one of its weak links; it is about the cultural renaissance led by Diego Rivera and about Rivera's fall from the pedestal where he was placed by adorers. In both cases it is about false gods as obstacles in the progress toward knowing.

Porter's second published story, "Virgin Violeta," was probably also inspired by events associated with the revolution in Mexico; nevertheless, it too can stand on its own, apart from the topical events that fed it. "Virgin Violeta" is on one hand a story about feminism and on the other about the disservice of idealism that is not grounded in reality. In this story the two themes are inextricably related, for Porter blamed paternalism and the church for fostering sexism.[23] She had her own sense of what constituted femininity long before she arrived in Mexico at the age of thirty. An early letter from her brother, Paul, responds to a letter Porter had written him about the injustices heaped upon women. In her letter she apparently had presented her case for women's suffrage, and he in turn was trying to refute her argument.[24] Obviously he never changed her mind, because she left him and the rest of her family, including a husband, not many years afterward and set out on her own.[25] In the year following the publication of "Virgin Violeta" Porter was still sufficiently engulfed in the feminist issue to bitterly attack W. L. George, a well-known leader in women's rights. In her review of his *The Story of Women* (1925) she takes him to task for being patronizing and insincere, and traces her own feminist outrage to her adolescent years.[26] She later would be critical of the subservient attitude of the young woman in *My Chinese Marriage*, a work she had ghostwritten.[27]

She would have been made even more acutely aware of feminism as a political issue soon after she arrived in Mexico, because it was an important part of the revolution.[28] She herself participated in the feminist movement to some extent. She writes of attending union meetings to organize female workers, and among her papers is the first issue of *Redencion*, the organ of the Mexican Feminist Council (La Liga Feminista Obrera). It calls for strong action to overcome the effects of ages-long oppression. ¡EMANCIPARA LA MUYER! permeates the booklet. Also included are a "Program of Action of the Mexican Feminist Council" (in English) and two pages of notes, partly typed and partly handwritten, that Porter may have intended to use for an article or treatise on the subject. Obviously she had not written these notes; the style is not hers, and the comments describe the establishment of the council by "We" in August 1919, a year before Porter's arrival.[29] It is likely that the notes were provided by Mary Doherty, who is described in the sketch that became "Flowering Judas" as wanting to organize women into unions. On the back of the Program of Action there are notes in Porter's handwriting that refer to Avelina, who went to Vera Cruz, to Miss Torres, and to "Mary." The typed notes identify Miss Torres and

Mrs. Avelina Royas as among the "principal and most enthusiastic members" of the council when it was reorganized in September 1919. In the program of Action of the Mexican Feminist Council, under "II. Social Emancipation," is the stated objective: "to urge the same moral criticism for men as for women." It is on this point that Mrs. Braggioni fails the feminist movement, in addition to committing the more serious offense of idealizing a man. While Mrs. Braggioni's perversion of one of the revolutionary ideals will be stated as fact in "Flowering Judas," Porter explores one of the causes of the perversion in "Virgin Violeta."

Lopez says that the central idea of "Virgin Violeta" was inspired by Porter's relationship with Salomon de la Selva, a Nicaraguan poet who was probably her lover for a time and whom she described to Lopez as "totally without scruple" and "beyond redemption."[30] She once characterized Salomon's preying nature, like that of Carlos in the story, in the humorous suggestion that if "he ever met the Virgin Mary he would introduce himself as the Holy Ghost."[31]

While the character of Carlos may have been inspired by Selva, the theme of the story encompasses much more. The idea of the church patriarchy's relationship to sexism, pervasive in the Mexican society she observed in the twenties, must have interested Porter long after she wrote "Virgin Violeta"; notes she made on the back of a theater program dated August 1930 contain a conversation, real or imagined, that had they been earlier could have formed the kernel of "Virgin Violeta":

"At the age of six, he enticed his 3 year old cousin Antonia into the closet under the servants stairway, and there God knows what damage had not occurred except for the giggles of the servant Xictemp, who mistook it for pure cousinly attention. At the age of 11, he was caught in the very act of examining the blameless organs of his 2 years old cousin Maria de los Angeles through his grandmother's reading glass—such were his pastimes before his twelfth year! And do you expect me to believe they have changed except for the horse, since he has an allowance and is 21 years old? And is given free run of the theatres."

"Such, with vanalimas, were my own pastimes before twelve, said Don Miguel.

"I am not surprised to hear it," said Dona Heraclia—no, after thirty years of marriage, I am not surprised to hear anything you may wish to tell me."

"Can you say I have not been an excellent husband for all that?"

"We are not discussing your qualities as a husband," said Dona Heraclia, "we are talking about that Son of yours, who by some unacceptable fatality is precisely like you—Yes, My Jesus, just like you!"[32]

Implicit in the conversation is the suggestion that sexist tradition is handed down from father to son. Porter later will place the blame for such sexism on any paternalistic system, not only Roman Catholic society.

Delineation of sexual roles is present in "Virgin Violeta" from the outset. Violeta, her sister Blanca, and her mother, Doña Paz, are aligned against Papacito and the cousin, Carlos. All their ideas about male and female rights and about love have been formed by the church and the church-dominated aristocratic society that is their background. Mamacita and Blanca accept their world and their place in it; "Mamacita's eyes were always perfectly clear when she looked at Papacito," and Blanca plays very well the dual role summarized in the parents' comments: "Blanquita blooms like a lily!" Mamacita says, and Papacito replies, "It is better if she conducts herself like one!" (23).

The conflict lies in Violeta, who has been away to a convent school for a year and has returned home for the summer. Fifteen-year-old Violeta is becoming aware of sexuality, her own and that of others. What she sees in her cousin Carlos's face is lust, like that which Miranda encounters at the circus. But she also sees herself, projecting her own sexual thoughts onto Carlos "as if his face were a mirror" (29). Violeta thus is horrified at her own blossoming sexuality as well as that of Carlos. However, she has romantic ideas about love. She has focused this idealized love on Carlos, who writes poems about the agonies of forbidden or unrequited love. For a year Violeta has clipped Carlos's poems from magazines and has concealed them in the pages of her books, to read during study time. Her favorite is about the ghosts of nuns who, returning to the square in front of their ruined convent, dance in the moonlight "with the shades of lovers forbidden them in life, treading with bared feet on broken glass as a penance for their loves" (24).

Violeta's ideal self is a virgin self whom others will admire from a distance. She thinks that the painting that hangs in their parlor, identified as "Pious Interview between the Most Holy Virgin Queen of Heaven and Her Faithful Servant St. Ignatius Loyola," is "perfectly proper" in spite of its being "very ugly and old-fashioned." She thinks of herself as being bridelike, "wearing a long veil" and being trailed by flower girls and pages as she begins her real, adult life, which will "unroll itself like a long, gay carpet for her to walk upon." She thinks of life as a festival, of which she will be the virgin queen, "miraculously lovely," admired by "fascinating young men" and particularly by Carlos (24–25).

This idealized self is inconsistent with the sensuality that is struggling within Violeta for recognition. At the convent in Tacubaya she is taught "modesty, chastity, silence, obedience" and does as she is told, but she is confused because she cannot understand "why the things that happen outside of people . . . [are] so different from what she . . . [feels] inside of her" (23). "Something inside her" feels as if it is "enclosed in a cage too small for it . . . like those poor parrots in the markets, stuffed into tiny wicker cages so that they bulged through the withes, gasping and panting, waiting for someone to come and rescue them" (26). In the next paragraph Violeta identifies the cage as "church," and it seems clear that she is experiencing the ancient conflict between cupidity and romantic love.

Violeta cannot reconcile lust with her idealized version of love. She feels enormous guilt for thinking "I love Carlos," and she prays frantically for forgiveness. As Blanca and Carlos sit together reading poetry, Violeta is annoyed when "a tiny spot of light" reveals moisture on Carlos's underlip, but she does not know why. She is likewise annoyed when she sees Blanca posing and making herself pretty and feels acutely wounded when she sees Blanca and Carlos murmuring intimately.

The climax in the story occurs when Violeta offers to find Carlos's missing book of poems and he follows on the pretext of helping to look. In the warm moonlight in the small room above the patio, Carlos kisses the frightened Violeta. No doubt the scene is the realization of one of Violeta's adolescent dreams, for she expects "to sink into a look warm and gentle." Instead she sees his "bright and shallow" eyes, "almost like the eyes of Pepe, the macaw" (29). Like the bold and unfriendly stare of the little boy under the plank seats at Miranda's circus, Carlos's kiss communicates pure lust without the mitigating presence of spiritual love. Violeta, whose idealistic illusion has been shattered, wants to cry. Instead, running back to the parlor she falls asleep with her head in Mamacita's lap until the departing Carlos begins his farewell kisses. Carlos's macaw eyes come "closer and closer" to Violeta, and his "tight, smiling mouth" seems "ready to swoop"; she begins to tremble, and when he touches her she slides "up and back against the wall" and hears herself "screaming uncontrollably" (31). Thus, Violeta, who has been trained well in the convent, is not able to reconcile the two kinds of love and so rejects them both. She makes ugly caricatures of Carlos, and feeling betrayed by the church, she weeps and complains to her mother that there is "nothing to be learned" at the convent. A "painful unhappiness" possesses Violeta, because she cannot "settle the questions brooding in her mind" (32). Like Young Goodman Brown, she is unable to accept the opposition within and will doubtless spend her days in bitter resignation.

Violeta has placed her young faith in a romantic view of love that leaves no room for sexuality, lust, prurience. It is an obscuring view of life and an attitude that inevitably leads to dismay. Porter not only delves into this polarized view of love in her fiction; she also defines and discusses it in several essays. Violeta's idea of romantic love has come from the church's distinction between sacred and profane love. In "The Fower of Flowers" Porter writes that "sacred and profane love in the Western World had by . . . [the twelfth century] taken their places at the opposite poles, where they have remained to this day" (CE, 147). She elaborated in a letter to her nephew Paul: "Of course, Times do change and vocabularies change, too, but in *my* time there was among certain advanced spirits a determined effort to identify—or at least confuse—Sex with love; that is, to disprove the old theological doctrine that sex took place entirely below the belt, and love entirely above it."[33] That love is romantic love, which Porter describes as "changeless, faithful, passionate," and she says that it "has no obstacles save those provided by the hazards of fate (that is to say, society), and such sufferings as the lovers may cause each other are only another word for delight: exciting jealousies, thrilling uncertainties, the ritual dance of courtship within the charmed closed circle of their secret alliance; all *real* troubles come from without, they face them unitedly in perfect confidence." She concludes, "Marriage is not the end but only the beginning of true happiness, cloudless, changeless to the end. That the candidates for this blissful condition have never seen an example of it, nor ever knew anyone who had, makes no difference. That is the ideal and they will achieve it."[34]

Porter traces the reasons that the two kinds of love became confused. She asks, "How did Romantic Love manage to get into marriage at last, where it was most certainly never intended to be? At its highest it was tragic: the love of Héloïse and Abélard. At its most graceful, it was the homage of the trouvère for his lady" (images that are similar to Violeta's daydreams). Porter continues, "But Romantic Love crept into the marriage bed, very stealthily, by centuries, bringing its absurd notions about love as eternal springtime and marriage as a personal adventure meant to provide personal happiness. To a Western romantic such as I, though my views have been much modified by painful experience, it still seems to me a charming work of the human imagination, and it is a pity its central notion has been taken too literally and has hardened into a convention as cramping and enslaving as the older One."[35]

Porter believed that spiritual love and sexual love had to coexist harmoniously and that neither should be confused with the other. She describes the opposite kind of distortion as that which is a "pious attempt to purify and canonize obscenity, to castrate the Roaring Boy, to take the low comedy out of sex. We cannot and should not try to hallow these words because they are not hallowed and were never meant to be."[36] She makes it clear that she is not objecting to either sexuality or obscenity. Having accused Lawrence of trying to hallow sex, she writes, "I do not object, then, to D. H. Lawrence's obscenity if it were really that. I object to his misuse and perversions of obscenity, his wrongheaded denial of its true nature and meaning."[37]

In "Holiday" Porter displays an equally limited view of love in people who live such mechanically ordered lives that they exercise no imagination at all in their notion of what constitutes love. The women who come to Hatsy's wedding whisper things in her ear that cause her to turn red and all the other women to burst out laughing. The same women are "ribald and jocose at births." When Gretchen's baby is born, the "honest hard-working wives and mothers" allow the talk to grow broad, and with "hearty gutterals . . . swallowed in the belly of laughter" see life "for a few hours as a hearty low joke" (CS, 428). While such a view of life fails to lead to high, encompassing truth, as Porter illustrates throughout the story, it nevertheless is a lesser crime than Lawrence's or that of those who try to ignore the obscenity in life.

What Porter approved of was the interrelatedness of profane and spiritual love, their dependence on one another, neither of which was to be ignored or denied. She says it best in her essay "The Flower of Flowers": "With very few exceptions among wild roses, they thrive best, any good gardener will tell you, in deep trenches bedded in cow manure. One famous grower of Old Roses . . . advises one to bury a big beef bone, cooked or raw, deep under the new plant, so that its growing roots may in time descend, embrace, and feed slowly upon this decayed animal stuff in the private darkness" (CE, 148). She later concludes, "Like all truly mystical things, love is rooted deeply and rightly in this world and this flesh."[38]

In several other stories Porter expounds on the deceptiveness of an idealized view of love that ignores another reality of it. "The Cracked Looking-Glass" presents Rosaleen O'Toole, who worships her ideals about love because of an inability to face harsh truths. According to Joan Givner, the story was inspired during Porter's lonely stay in a Connecticut farmhouse in 1928, when she heard an account of a former occupant, a rich Irish widow, who had created a scandal by "adopting young boys."[39] When Porter later said that she thought of calling her version of the story "St. Martin's Summer," for the false season of warmth that comes in November after the first chill, she was confirming the theme of illusion in the story.[40] Although Rosaleen's husband, Dennis, is thirty years older than she and now frail and feeble, she refuses to face the truth. Instead she asks, "Somewhere inside of him there must be Dennis, but where?" (CS, 116).

Rosaleen's trip to Boston allows her to find the idealized Dennis again, the Dennis she remembers as "a fine man, oh, a fine man . . . in his black suit and white gloves, a knowledgeable man who could tell the richest people the right things to order for a good dinner, such a gentleman in his stiff white shirt front, managing the waiters on the one hand and customers on the other, and making good money at it" (108). The journey itself is a symbol of Rosaleen's escape from the realities of her hard life. She thinks "how she had always been a great traveler" and "how a train was like home to her." Not seeing a sad face anywhere at the station, she considers it a lucky sign. In New York she goes to a movie theater where she sees *The Prince of Love*, "about two beautiful young things, a boy with black wavy hair and a girl with curly golden hair, who loved each other and had great troubles, but it all came well in the end, and all the time it was just one fine ballroom or garden after another." She sees another moving picture, called *The Lover King*, and it is "about a king in a disguise, a lovely young man with black wavy hair and eyes would melt in his head, who married a poor country girl who was more beautiful than all the princesses and ladies in the land" (124).[41] Rosaleen cries because the films realize her idealized, romantic view of love. The prince of love and the lover king are the Dennis she seeks inside the old and infirm husband. The movies, like her dreams, provide the illusions by which she escapes.

Rosaleen's escape journey continues as she takes a taxi to Christopher Street (St. Christopher is the patron saint of travelers) to catch the boat that will take her to Providence and a step closer to her destination, Boston. When she reaches Boston she cannot "remember any good times there" and goes to a church, once again as an escape from reality. She seeks the ecstasy of the church ("How long had it been since she had seen the church as it should be, dressed for a feast with candles and flowers, smelling of incense and wax?"), but finds no truth. The despair of the city, her failure to find Honora, and her unpleasant encounter with Hugh Sullivan make her want to escape Boston. Thus home and Dennis become the refuge from the larger and more alien reality.

Home again, she experiences another unpleasantness when she takes the slow-witted native boy home and is accused by the boy's mother of being a loose woman. Life all around her is filled with ugliness, and Rosaleen has difficulty clinging to her illusions. Her final desperate solution is to conclude that life itself is the dream and that dreams themselves do not always reveal the truth, as she once had convinced herself. Finally the reality becomes all she has: "Here in the lamplight sat Dennis and the cats, beyond in the darkness and snow lay Winston and New York and Boston." Her last illusion is her unrealistic desire to preserve Dennis, who must be approaching his death. She tells him, "If anything happened to you, whatever would become of me in this world?" (134).

Rosaleen's idealized world is created by dreams, self-delusions, superstitions, and distorted vision that does not allow for a glimpse of reality for very long. The cracked looking glass is a symbol of that distortion, and Rosaleen conveniently forgets to get a new one in New York, in spite of having told Dennis before she left, "One thing I must remember, Dennis, . . . is, to bring back a looking-glass that won't make my face look like a monster's" (122). Rosaleen is contrasted to Dennis, who is "a sober, practical, thinking man, a lover of truth" (105). He admits to himself that "it's just a born liar she is," but at once feels as if "he had leaped head-first into a very dark pit" (122). Nevertheless, even though he knows he will never hear a straight account of Rosaleen's trip to Boston, he wants to hear her "story" about it. She is his connection with the romantic, just as he is her connection with reality.

"Old Morality" also revolves around romantic ideals, romantic love and the past. The ideal of romantic love is embodied in the love story of Amy and Gabriel, told in part 1: 1885–1902. The story centers on the beautiful Amy, who died young, and the somber, tenacious Gabriel, who had everything, "youth, health, good looks, the prospect of riches, . . . a devoted family circle," and after five years, Amy herself (181). The Amy legend was based on a Porter family legend, the unhappy story of Annie and Thomas Gay. It probably also incorporated Porter's idealistic view of her own mother, a view created by her father's sentimental and guilt-ridden recollections of his wife.[42]

The viewpoint of the first part is that of the little girls Miranda and Maria, and their perception of romantic love is analyzed in an irony that contrasts an implied truth with what the little girls believe to be truth. The romantic ideal is fostered by their elders, and they accept their elders' assertions even in the face of conflicting evidence. Miranda and Maria are disturbed by the "evidence"—"the visible remains"—but trust the "truth" that exists in the memory of the elders. Even though Amy of the photograph has a "reckless indifferent smile" and her clothes are "terribly out of fashion," they believe their father, who says of the photograph, "It's not very good. Her hair and her smile were her chief beauties, and they are not shown at all." And they believe their Uncle Bill, who answers their "Was she really beautiful?" with "As an angel, my child" (176).

Amy has been idealized as the beautiful, unapproachable woman of chivalric tradition—idolized by the dashing and patient suitor in the person of Gabriel. The legend does not pretend that Amy herself had romantic notions about love and marriage; it admits indeed to Amy's having not loved Gabriel at all. But the Gabriel of memory is fully developed in the ideal of romantic love. Even his tendency toward profligacy, apparent early on, is explained as the result of Amy's coldness to him. Ostensibly he suffers Amy's rejection for five years, plies her with extravagant gifts from caged lovebirds to enameled flowers, endures jealousies, challenges a rival to a duel, and goes forth to exile until Amy changes her mind and agrees to marry him. She dies six weeks after the marriage, and in their minds' eyes the little girls see Gabriel suffering from a broken heart through the long years after. Once he wrote a poem about Amy, had it printed in gold on a mourning card, and sent it to a great many members of the family.

Thus Miranda and Maria's romantic ideal is centered in Uncle Gabriel, whose name identifies him as a celestial being; the ideal is amplified by their adolescent reading of sentimental and Gothic romances in which virtuous and beautiful heroines are immured in convents by villainous religiouses. The girls, who attend the school of the Convent of the Child Jesus, identify with the "unlucky" immured maidens of their forbidden reading matter.[43] Their awakening and the concurrent disillusionment occur when Miranda and Maria are "freed" from the convent for a Saturday outing with their father, who comes to take them to the horse races, where their Uncle Gabriel, whom they never have seen, is running a horse. The release from the

convent will be more than a day of freedom from the school's re-
strictive rules; the girls also will be released from their false notions
about Uncle Gabriel and about love itself.

Uncle Gabriel proves to be "a shabby fat man with bloodshot blue
eyes, sad beaten eyes, and a big melancholy laugh, like a groan." He
towers over them and shouts to their father, "Well, for God's sake,
Harry, it's been a coon's age. You ought to come out and look 'em over.
You look just like yourself, Harry, how are you?" Miranda and Maria
are horrified, staring first at him and then at each other. "Can it be our
Uncle Gabriel?" their eyes ask. "Is that Aunt Amy's handsome romantic beau? Is that the man who wrote the poem about our Aunt Amy?"
(197). Their disillusion is completed in Gabriel's coarseness, his
drunken poverty, and the embittered wife who is the successor to Amy.
The disillusionment and the understanding they absorb are tied to
their greater disillusionment and understanding of the past, of which
Gabriel and Amy are an important part.

The ideal of romantic love is a part of the general romantic idealiza-
tion of the past, which is really the subject of "Old Mortality." The past
figures in Miranda's disillusionment, which is a step toward her growing awareness within the saga. Part 1 of "Old Mortality" is largely
Grandmother's Rhea's exploration of the past, which she represents
throughout the Miranda stories. The past is made up of the family
legend and the family "feeling," which often belies the truth. Harry,
Miranda and Maria's father, for example, declares that "there were
never any fat women in the family, thank God," and the little girls
wonder how he can account for Great-Aunt Eliza, "who quite
squeezed herself through doors, and who, when seated, was one solid
pyramidal monument from floor to neck"—or Great-Aunt Keziah,
whose husband, Great-Uncle John Jacob, "had refused to allow her to
ride his good horses after she had achieved two hundred and twenty
pounds" (174). And yet the little girls understand that there is truth and
then truth. "This loyalty of their father's in the face of evidence con-
trary to his ideal had its springs in family feeling, and a love of legend
that he shared with the others. They loved to tell stories, romantic and
poetic, or comic with a romantic humor; they did not gild outward
circumstance, it was the feeling that mattered. Their hearts and imag-

inations were captivated by their past, a past in which worldly considerations had played a very minor role. Their stories were almost always love stories against a bright blank heavenly blue sky" (175).

Miranda and Maria associate the past with poetry, with art. To them, the story of Amy and Gabriel was such a story as one would find in books, "unworldly books, but true, such as the Vita Nuova, the Sonnets of Shakespeare and the Wedding Song of Spenser; and poems by Edgar Allan Poe." Moreover, to the little girls, "Aunt Amy was real as the pictures in the old Holbein and Dürer books were real."[44] They "lay flat on their stomachs and peered into a world of wonder, turning the shabby leaves that fell apart easily, not surprised at the sight of the Mother of God sitting on a hollow log nursing her Child; not doubting either Death or the Devil riding at the stirrups of the grim knight; not questioning the propriety of the stiffly dressed ladies of Sir Thomas More's household, seated in dignity on the floor, or seeming to be" (178).

Miranda and Maria's innate appreciation of art partly explains their love of the theater, and their father, who ignores "entertainment," takes them to see Hamlet, The Taming of the Shrew, Richard the Third, "and a long sad play with Mary, Queen of Scots, in it. Miranda thought the magnificent lady in black velvet was truly the Queen of Scots, and was pained to learn that the real Queen had died long ago, and not at all on the night she, Miranda, had been present" (179). A few years later, however, by the time part 2 begins and Miranda and Maria are in school in New Orleans, they have refined their distinctions between life and art. Avid readers, "they had long since learned to draw the line between life, which was real and earnest, and the grave was not its goal; poetry, which was true but not real; and stories, or forbidden reading matter, in which things happen as nowhere else, with the most sublime irrelevance and unlikelihood, and one need not turn a hair, because there was not a word of truth in them" (194).

The essential truths of the past and of art are revered by the family and by Miranda and Maria. The disillusion occurs when the truths claimed for the idealized past are discovered to be lies. The entire past is held up for examination when Miranda and Maria discover the truth of the Amy-Gabriel legend. It is here that the title should be considered, for it provides some clues to the work's meaning. George Hendrick's interpretation of the title as a reference to Sir Walter Scott's *Old Mortality* (1816) was refuted by Porter, who said she had never read a word of Scott.[45] A more likely source of the title is Sir Thomas Browne's "Urne-Burial" (*Hydriotaphia*), which contains the phrase "old mortality" and is a treatise on the various modes of disposal of the dead.[46] Thus, it provides an illuminating background against which to measure the disposal of "the dead" in Porter's "Old Mortality." In the latter case, the dead, whether Amy or the whole past, are only disposed of selectively and idealized.

Miranda's lessons about the past include her understanding the truth about victory and racing, just as she understands the truth about luxury in "The Grave." It is a building upon another truth about the aristocratic past that she has absorbed from Uncle Jimbilly's stories of "the horrors of slave times," the economic base that made the luxuries possible. Gabriel's horse, "Miss Lucy," wins the race that Miranda and Maria attend, and although they thrill to the race they view from the stands, they see afterwards, up close, that Miss Lucy is far from the racing steed of romantic illusion. "She was bleeding at the nose, two thick red rivulets were stiffening her tender mouth and chin, the round velvet chin that Miranda thought the nicest kind of chin in the world. Her eyes were wild and her knees were trembling, and she snored when she drew her breath" (199). An important reality, associated with the past, is reluctantly accepted by Miranda; she had idealized horse racing as a genteel pastime, just as she had idealized Uncle Gabriel. Now she must look at the other side of "winning," just as she must look at the real Gabriel. More significantly, she must share in the guilt, for she had wanted to be a jockey. As she looks at the exhausted horse, she thinks, "That was winning, for Miss Lucy." And then, "instantly and completely," her heart "rejects" the "victory." She "hated it, and was ashamed that she had screamed and shed tears for joy when Miss Lucy, with her bloodied nose and bursting heart had gone past the judges' stand a neck ahead. She felt empty and sick and held to her father's hand so hard that he shook her off a little impatiently and said, 'What is the matter with you?'" (199). Miranda's shame is compounded by the fact that she won money on Miss Lucy's victory.

Miranda has discovered the full truth of the ideal of victory and some important truths about the idealized past. Miranda in "The Grave" makes a similar discovery when she fully understands that the silly and frivolous fur coats Uncle Jimbilly made for her dolls were made from the skins of rabbits that once had been alive. Her experience with Uncle Gabriel and the races has been the catalyst for these small illuminations, and Gabriel himself symbolizes the disparity between the ideal and the reality. Certainly far from the picture of him in the family legend, he does not even write decent verse. In fact, Harry, who is reluctant to criticize the poem Gabriel writes about Amy, says that "it should have been better." Presumably, the standard was "our greatest poet," Poe, whose favorite subject, like Gabriel's, was the death of a beautiful woman. Poe's lines which are read to the little girls, "Her tantalized spirit now blandly reposes, Forgetting or never regretting its roses" (a slight misquotation from "For Annie"), represent the ideal that Gabriel shames.

Gabriel is the link to "old mortality," a selective burial of the dead. Amy's family, who generally attempt the same selectivity with the past, a Southern preoccupation it seems, share Gabriel's interest in keeping alive the honor of the past, even at the expense of truth. Miranda is the truth-seeker, however, and she readily abandons the romantic version of things when she discovers their falsity.

In the last of the three subdivisions of "Old Mortality," Miranda, who is disillusioned with the family and with the past as well as with romantic love, is moving toward a renunciation of all three. However, she meets Cousin Eva, who already has renounced everything romantic. Confronted with Eva's disdain for the legend and with her cruel destruction of the beautiful, if false, legends, Miranda suddenly shifts toward a rejection also of practical reality. Her rejection of Eva and what she represents is symbolized in her refusing to ride in the backseat of the car with her. "No, thank you," says Miranda, in a firm cold voice. "I'm quite comfortable. Don't disturb yourself" (220). Miranda at the end of "Old Mortality" is not able to reconcile what she sees as two false views of life: the romantic view of her family and the unromantic one of Eva. She rejects them both, thinking, "It is I who have no place." She in fact resents all these people telling her what is true and what is not. "She resented, slowly and deeply and in profound silence, the presence of these aliens who lectured and admonished her, who loved her with bitterness and denied her the right to look at the world with her own eyes, who demanded that she accept their version of life and yet could not tell her the truth, not in the smallest thing. 'I hate them both,' her most inner and secret mind said plainly, '*I will be free of them, I shall not even remember them*'" (219).

Miranda, not able yet to bring the past into the present, puts all her faith in the future. "Her mind closed stubbornly against remembering, not the past but the legend of the past, other people's memory of the past, at which she had spent her life peering in wonder like a child at a magic-lantern show. Ah, but there is my own life to come yet, she thought, my own life now and beyond. I don't want any promises, I won't have false hopes, I won't be romantic about myself. I can't live in their world any longer, she told herself, listening to the voices back of her. Let them tell their stories to each other. Let them go on explaining how things happened. I don't care. At least I can know the truth about what happens to me, she assured herself silently, making a promise to herself in her hopefulness, her ignorance" (221).

The necessity for integrating the past and present was a longtime obsession with Porter, at least dating to her early days in Mexico. She saw in the cultural renaissance an admirable attempt to bring to the surface the already existing integration. In the *Outline* she wrote, "In this country the past is interwoven visibly with the present, living and potent."[47] She also planned a novel based on her Mexican materials that she tentatively called "The Historical Present." Her use of the historical present tense in the first version of "Hacienda" and in "Flowering Judas" seems to be an implicit attempt to bring temporal elements together by a stylistic device, one which she later claimed to be unaware of using.[48]

In "Old Mortality," however, Miranda wishes to reconcile more than the past and the present. When she admits to herself that she does not know what life is or what good and evil are, her "disturbed and seething mind" receives "a shock of comfort from this sudden collapse of an old painful structure of distorted images and misconceptions" (220–21).

Porter has revealed a Miranda who in spite of her new awareness that rested on the disillusion of ideals remains confused not only about the romantic and the real but also about good and evil and life and death. Not yet able to integrate them in a total perspective, she must wait for greater maturity. Porter at one time thought of the work that became "Old Mortality" as a longer novel, which she referred to as "that book of Amy." Giving working titles to the three parts that finally were identified only by dates, she listed the parts as "(1) Introduction to Death: the Beginning. (2) Midway of this Mortal Life. (3) Beginning Again: The End."[49] Whether Porter intended her central character to have a total rebirth at the end of the novel is not clear. But she surely intended all along to show a degree of progress toward truth.

"That Tree," published in 1923, shares with "Old Mortality" the theme of the delusion of ideals and of powerful ideals in conflict with one another. The characters act according to ideals they cherish as ways to truth and success. The unnamed journalist in the story, by his own admission a writer of poems that are "no good," nevertheless has idealized the "idle free romantic life of a poet." Even after he has become "an important journalist, an authority on Latin-American revolutions and a best seller," he still talks about "the thing he believed he loved best" (66). His ideal broadens to include other romantic notions, for example, machismo: he admires the way the Mexican girls in the café once seized their men as shields when trouble started and remembers the humiliation he felt by his wife's diving under a table for protection (she explains the disgrace by saying that she refuses to pander to male vanity); he also has "a sackful of romantic notions about artists and their destiny"—trying to explain the poverty, gluttony, and raggedness of his artist friends in idealistic terms: Carlos never changes his shirt because he does not have any other; Jaime is a glutton because he is famished; they do not work because they hold to Franciscan notions of holy poverty as being the natural companion for the artist. He has idealized these Mexican artists, trying to define "his mystical faith in these men who went ragged and hungry because they had chosen once for all between what he called in all seriousness their souls, and this world" (76). In fact, he has idealized Mexico itself, its primitive beauty and its easy way of life. "He had thought it rather a picnic to wash a lot of gayly colored Indian crockery outdoors in the sunshine, with the bougainvillea climbing up the wall and the heaven tree in full bloom" (75). He believes that here in Mexico he will find the muse and fulfill his ideal, which in his mind's eye is a picture of himself as "a cheerful bum lying under a tree in a good climate, writing poetry." He tries to live and think in a way that he hopes will "end by making a poet of him" (77).

His ideals are almost totally destroyed, however, for, as he says, "It hadn't worked." Moreover, his wife Miriam shatters his illusions about his artist friends. She insists that these friends are not "being poor on purpose," that they are "looking for the main chance." And she proves to be, according to the journalist, "abominably, obscenely right" (76). Jaime takes up with a rich old woman; Ricardo turns film actor; and Carlos gets an easy government job that only requires him to paint revolutionary frescoes "to order."[50]

Miriam has her own set of recognizable ideals. She values work, duty, reason, cleanliness, and possessions; she distrusts artists, and she calls her husband "Parasite" and "Ne'er-do-well." She prefers the poetry of Milton to that of her husband, and she finds little in Mexico that she truly likes. She holds her nose when she goes to the market, refuses to eat Mexican food, will not have an Indian servant near her, and despises her husband for thinking that washing "gayly colored Indian crockery outdoors in the sunshine" a picnic. She does not approve his even using the word "temperament," thinking it "a kind of occupational disease among artists, or a trick they practiced to make themselves interesting" (68).[51]

The conflict in the story is between the two sets of ideals—the romantic, carefree one and the serious, insulated, puritanical one. But the primary conflict lies not between the journalist and his wife Miriam. Rather, the conflict lies within each of them, and it is this conflict that reflects the theme of the story and raises it to universal significance. The truth is that both the journalist and Miriam are drawn to the other's ideal. The journalist thinks there is "a special kind of beauty in Miriam," and he recalls that "in certain lights and moods he simply got a clutch in the pit of his stomach when he looked at her" (67). When she leaves him, he is shocked into accepting her standards.

He becomes a successful journalist whose "sympathies happened to fall in exactly right with the high-priced magazines of a liberal human-itarian slant which paid him well for telling the world about the op-pressed peoples." Consequently, he makes "the kind of success you can clip out of newspapers and paste in a book, you can count it and put it in the bank, you can eat and drink and wear it, and you can see it in other people's eyes at tea and dinner parties" (78). The extent to which she represents an ideal to him is seen in the fact that his second wife's cattiness about Miriam leads to divorce. "He could not bear hearing Miriam called a mousy little nit-wit—at least not by *that* woman," even though he already has admitted that Miriam's mind would fit "in a peanut shell" (68). Five years after she leaves, Miriam writes to him, asking him to take her back. "She had read everything she could find of his in print, and she loved all of it." Affluent now, and twice di-vorced, he is able to send her money for the trip.

In spite of Miriam's disdain for the filth and sloth of Mexico, the country nevertheless is an ideal—as is her husband—to which she is drawn. Before their marriage she "spent three mortal years writing him how dull and dreadful and commonplace her life was, how sick and tired she was of petty little conventions and amusements, how narrow-minded everybody around her was, how she longed to live in a beau-tiful dangerous place among interesting people who painted and wrote poetry, and how his letters came into her stuffy little world like a breath of free mountain air, and all that" (73–74). Even after she undergoes the dreadful four-year experience of "trying to cook wholesome civi-lized American food over a charcoal brasier, and doing the washing in the patio over a stone tub with a cold water tap," she is able to write him five years later that she hopes it is not "too late for them to make a happy life together *once more*" (italics mine). She has succumbed to the illusion of a romantic ideal that requires forgetting the reality from which she fled, "shabby and thin and wild-looking" with only a few belongings.

This story has a firm foundation in the social reality of the 1920s in Mexico, especially in the expatriate community there, of which Porter was a visible part. And although the real-life counterparts to the jour-nalist and Miriam were surely Carleton Beals and his first wife,

Lillian, the inspiration for the story was probably the pervasive conflict Porter recognized within the Anglo-American community. She was very much aware of the appeal Mexico had for Anglo-Americans. It offered a primitivism that was on the one hand an escape from economic and social turmoil in other parts of the world and on the other an opportunity to return to an idyllic plane of existence, a desire that seems to be more indigenously American than anything else. Mexico attracted political idealists like Lincoln Steffens and John Reed; journalists and historians like Anita Brenner, Ernest Gruening, Frank Tannenbaum, and Lesley Byrd Simpson; and writers and artists like John Dos Passos, D. H. Lawrence, Dylan Thomas, Edward Weston, and Tina Modotti.[52]

Porter knew Beals well and probably knew Lillian, who was with Beals in Mexico in the early twenties when Porter was there. Beals mentions Porter twice in *Glass Houses*, and his personal papers include a letter from her dated 1926 and written from the United States.[53] Among her notes and papers are references to "Carleton" at various parties she attended in Mexico.

There are many significant parallels between the journalist and Miriam in Porter's story and Carleton and Lillian Beals. Lillian, like Miriam, had been a schoolteacher, and in Beals's estimation she had had a priggishness that he told his mother he was glad to have "escaped from."[54] In the story Miriam is described as having "a professional habit of primness." The fictional journalist has dismayed Miriam by his association with "bums" and by his unwillingness or inability to hold a job; he had lost his politically acquired teaching job when the Minister of Education was suddenly put out of office. Miriam calls him "a failure," "worthless and shiftless and trifling and faithless." There is evidence to suggest that Beals was part of a rowdy group of writers and artists, and when the government was overthrown in 1920 he lost the job he had had as English instructor to President Carranza's general staff; during the next three years he was not regularly employed, although unlike the journalist and Miriam, he and Lillian lived most of that time in Spain and Italy rather than in Mexico. They were in Mexico again, however, in 1924, when Lillian left. At the time of her departure, Beals was two and a half months behind in his rent, as he told his mother, and had no certain prospects for income.[55] And like the journalist after Miriam left, Beals fell into a depression when Lillian left. He described his state to his mother as one in which he was "just marking time" and in which "everything seems to run in a blind circle."[56]

There are other similarities. The description of the journalist by a hostile newspaper reporter as a "banjo-eyed chinless wonder" also could have applied to Beals, who had a weak chin and large eyes. Moreover, the journalist's best-selling success "as an authority on revolutions in twenty-odd Latin American countries" was close to an accurate description of Beals's own success.

The similarities and differences between the characters of "That Tree" and Carleton and Lillian Beals define some real-life models for Porter's fiction and show also where Porter deviated from fact when it was necessary to make an artistic point. The Bealses' marriage and personalities within the context of the Mexican social scene provided a convenient medium in which she could distill her theme, which rests upon the dilemma posed by two ideals in conflict with one another. The viewpoint of the story, significant tree symbolism, and certain key phrases and words show what Porter finally thought about an ageless paradox that was deeply embedded in the American experience. The viewpoint is objective and restricted, limited to the journalist, and filtered through a narrative voice that describes indirectly the content of the journalist's self-revelation that is a bittersweet reminiscence of his life with and without Miriam. Mixed with this description are dialogue and action taking place in the café where the monologue is being delivered to an unnamed auditor. The immediate dialogue and action are presented against the decaying revolutionary climate. When an automobile backfires in the street, the patrons jump nervously and a "smart cracker" newspaperman says, "Another revolution," which the journalist labels "the oldest joke since the Mexican Independence" (68). The fight that follows points up the chaos at all levels of the tottering government and its revolutionary hangers-on.

The viewpoint variously has been described as a "dramatic monologue" involving "the journalist telling his story and his companion, perhaps a woman, through whose eyes we see and hear the events of the story" and as "a superficial conversation between the protagonist and a friend."[57] The first description of the viewpoint is partly right in that the story is primarily a dramatic monologue. But the notion that the companion to the journalist provides the narrative voice is based on the first version of the story rather than the revised version. In the first version, the narrative voice says that after the backfiring of an automobile, "We both jumped." In the revision, the narrative voice says, "They both jumped," and thereafter the companion is referred to in the third person. In the first version the companion is never referred to again.

The narrative voice of the revised version—one assumes it represents Porter's intention in the story—is nonparticipating and acknowledges the presence of both the journalist and an auditor/companion, as well as various patrons and a waiter in the café. An examination of the first reference to the companion and the terms used to describe the "person" reveals an interesting point. There are three long paragraphs at the beginning of the story before any reference is made to the companion. The narrative voice calls attention to the companion a second time in the journalist's saying "to his guest," "For God's sake, . . . let's have another drink." Near the end of the monologue the journalist observes, "Our glasses are empty again." And near the end of the story the narrative voice becomes omniscient and says, "His guest wished to say, 'Don't forget to invite me to your wedding,' but thought better of it." The "guest" is referred to in the succeeding sentence as "the shadow opposite," and the next-to-last paragraph begins, "His guest moved to the chair edge and watched the orchestra folding up for the night." The guest/shadow companion never speaks, and his/her presence is never acknowledged by anyone else in the café. The critical questions arise: why is there such a delay in suggesting the presence of an auditor, and why make the reality of such a person so nebulous? The only convincing answer to both is that Porter intended to make the very existence of the auditor/companion ambiguous. There is evidence within the story to support this theory.

First, the reference to the other person occurs only after the journalist has brought to light the essential conflict between the romantic ideal and the middle-class American one. He has talked about his own paradoxical life, working as a successful journalist at the same time that he still believes he loves best the romantic life of a poet. He also has revealed his idealized view of his relationship with Miriam, who represents the American bourgeois ideal as well as what Beals once called "the Puritan self-repression that warps our northern races."[58] In the next section, between the first reference to a companion and the suggestion of drinks, the journalist reveals the misery of his marriage with Miriam, focusing on her sexlessness and her inability to adapt to Mexican ways and disclosing a contrasting relationship he had had with an Indian woman before Miriam's arrival.[59] The next section outlines the chasm that opened between him and Miriam. The companion materializes in the monologue after the journalist has shown us the conflict between the two ideals, the romantic life and the bourgeois life. As the journalist explores the conflict, the unnamed, unheard companion becomes the "guest" and is called the same in the final reference. The "guest" never speaks; the omniscient narrator tells the reader only that the guest wished to say something but did not.

The most important descriptive label appended to the companion is, of course, "shadow," and taken together with the final statement that "it was like looking into a mirror" the word suggests that the journalist is talking to another part of himself, trying to bring the two opposing ideals into harmony. That the conflict is within him is supported by the reference to the journalist's parents, who exhibited the same American bourgeois ideals as Miriam, and by the journalist's fond memories of his mother.

Here the title of the story assumes its most significant meaning. While the title literally refers to the tree of the journalist's fantasy (the tree under which he dreams of idling his time writing poetry), the meaning of tree in its more universal symbolic sense cannot be ignored. The tree of knowledge, with its attendant meanings associated with the integration of sensual knowledge and transcendental knowledge, is implicit in the meaning associated with the journalist's romantic illusion. Significantly, the journalist never finds the tree of his fantasy, and intimates that now he never will.

It is safe to assume that neither will he grasp the other tree, or in more directly thematic terms, he will never be able to reach the knowledge that a reconciliation of warring ideals would bring. He will never be able to reach a level of objective understanding. His failure is hinted at in the development of the other important symbol in the story, the chalk line. When it first appears in the story, it is quoted as being Miriam's phrase, which she applied to "all sorts of situations."[60] Here it symbolizes Miriam's notion of the straight and narrow path of duty. When it appears again, it is the journalist's phrase, and it represents "one that she hadn't drawn for herself." It is the opposite of Miriam's; it is the journalist's symbol of diligence to the free, romantic ideal: "She was going to live again in a Mexican house without any conveniences and she was not going to have a modern flat. She was going to take whatever he chose to hand her, and like it. And he wasn't going to marry her again, either. Not he. If she wanted to live with him on these terms, well and good. If not, she could just go back once more to that school of hers in Minneapolis" (79).

The second attempt at marriage is doomed to failure, too. The sharp line the journalist draws on the tablecloth with a cheese knife fades into crosshatches as he keeps on drawing "with a relaxed hand." His resolution in time will fail; Miriam will have her wedding if not her modern flat. The "guest"—or the journalist's other self—knows this as he considers saying, "Don't forget to invite me to your wedding." We have no reason to believe that Miriam will like Mexico any better the second time than she did the first. If she has deluded herself into thinking that they were happy then, she will have to go through the shock and misery all over.

The end of the little story is heavily ironic, and the symbolism of that tree blooms fully. The journalist begins saying to "the shadow opposite," "I suppose you think I don't know," and pauses "not for an answer, but to give weight to the important statement he was about to make." He continues, "I don't know what's happening, this time . . . don't deceive yourself. This time I know." The emphasis on the word *know* hints at the tree of knowledge and his warning to the guest/shadow, "Don't deceive yourself," makes sense only if we regard it as a self-warning. The final statement confirms the story's theme: "He seemed to be admonishing himself before a mirror" (79).

The journalist and Miriam represent the two idealistic poles within the American experience. The diametrical opposition is Hester Prynne's conflict between her romantic spirit and her community's obedience to law; it is Huck Finn's floating freely and nobly down the river and responding to his obligation to go ashore occasionally—it is the call of the territory and the appeal of civilization's comfortable structure. Porter's story, highly Jamesian in its style and subtlety, is a comment not only on the Anglo-American expatriate community in Mexico in the twenties; it is also a comment on the historical tension within the American consciousness.

"Flowering Judas" presents an expatriated woman who joins the revolution looking for a replacement for her faith, but the revolution fails her on an elemental level. "Hacienda" is the extension of "Flowering Judas" in that a detached narrator, a further developed Laura, analyzes the decay. "That Tree," however, is a transitional story because it is only incidentally set in Mexico, and revolution is only an echo in the background. The central characters are expatriated Americans, but their dilemma has nothing substantial to do with revolution. It is a particularly American dilemma and represents Porter's return to native themes.

The disillusion that follows the investment of places and things with perfection is the primary theme of "The Leaning Tower," Porter's short novel written in Germany between the wars and focusing on some of the problems in modern society. Soon after "The Leaning Tower" was published, Porter sent a copy to a friend and told him that she first "took notes for this story in Bamberger-Strasse in Berlin during the fall in 1931. . . . The scene is the pension where I lived. It was Gene, naturally, who picked up the little tower and broke it . . . poor man. But it gave me the idea for the story and also its title."[61] She also comments in letters to Pressly about the real persons in the pension who were the models for some characters in the story.[62]

Because Germany is the setting for this work and because Germany is the destination of the ship of fools, the two works have been linked. "The Leaning Tower" has been considered by many to be a precursor to the novel. That is true of the temporal flavor of the works and partly true of the themes. The story is finally not about Germans and Germany; it is not merely an attack on the German people, an interpretation that probably was encouraged by Porter's remarks about the Germans she met in the thirties.[63] "The Leaning Tower" is really about the disillusion of ideals, and that theme is apparent in the first long paragraph of the story. The first sentence establishes the setting for the story's beginning, Berlin 1931, two days after Christmas. The second sentence provides the name of the protagonist, Charles Upton, and begins a series of descriptive words that suggest the air of the place and the times: "dull," "mysteriously oppressive," "dark, airless, cold"—these to describe Charles's hotel, managed by the "yellow-faced woman" and the "ill-tempered fat man." Charles recalls that once when he had supper in his too-expensive hotel room "small white worms had come squirming out of the liver sausage on his plate."

And so Charles escapes to the café across the street, which while dull, too, emits a look of "thrifty cheerfulness" and holds pleasant associations for Charles, who had spent the recent Christmas Eve there listening to the Berlin accent: "blunt, full of a wooden kind of clucking and quacking and explosive hissing" (436). In the midst of all this, Charles ought to be disillusioned, but he has not learned enough to have that perspective. "Rather determinedly," he begins "to persuade himself that he had not made a mistake. Yes, Germany was the right place for him, Berlin was the city, Kuno had been right and would be glad if he could know his friend was here at last" (437).

Thus ends the introductory paragraph. Faced with a reality that seems anything but ideal, Charles still clings to some other impression of Germany and Berlin. The next several paragraphs provide the source of the ideal, Charles's friend Kuno, with whom he had gone to school in a little Texas town and who talked "for hours about Berlin until Charles in his imagination saw it as a great shimmering city of castles towering in misty light" (439). Kuno died mysteriously during one of the family's visits to Germany when he was about fifteen. Charles, sitting in the café, thinks to himself that Kuno is responsible for his coming to Berlin instead of having gone to Paris or Madrid or Mexico.[64]

Charles has not been able to shed his superstitious valuation of Germany. Even though the Christmas carolers have been standing in "ragged shoes sunk in the slushy snow, starving and blue-nosed, singing in their mourning voices" and are joined by other beggars, alone, miserable, and war-mutilated, Charles is able to ignore the harsh reality by dropping "rather carelessly without counting, small change into the hats and outspread handkerchiefs of the men along the streets" and hears only the familiarity and the melodiousness of "Heilige Nacht," "O Tannenbaum," and "The Cradle Song" as they carry him back to childhood days when his parents had taken him to the German Singing Society in the Texas town. He is able to detach himself from the misery he sees (he steps into a doorway and furtively sketches a starving young man whose teeth stand out "in ridges under the mottled tight skin of his cheeks") and blends it into a larger picture of German society, which includes young people, "lean and tough, boys and girls alike dressed in leather jackets or a kind of uniform blue ski suit, who whizzed about the streets on bicycles without a glance at the windows. Charles saw them carrying skis on their shoulders, shouting and laughing in groups, getting away to the mountains over the weekend. He watched them enviously; maybe if he stayed on long enough he would know some of them" (442).

In addition to the beggars and the young people, Charles observes the group of prosperous middle-aged men and women who are the celebrated pig worshipers in the story: "The streets were full of them—enormous waddling women with short legs and ill-humored faces, and round-headed men with great rolls of fat across the backs of their necks, who seemed to support their swollen bellies with an effort that drew their shoulders forward" (442). They gaze "with eyes damp with admiration and appetite" at real pig products, sausages, hams, bacon, and small pink chops, and "at dainty artificial pigs"—edible ones of marzipan and chocolate and pink sugar—and toy ones, plush or mechanical. This scene often is cited as evidence of Porter's anti-German sentiment; that interpretation, however, is simplistic. The scene is instead a comment about Charles's ideal and the falseness of it.

Charles walks away from the "spectacle," which he thinks "revolting," and encounters the streetwalkers and sickly looking young men "with fresh wounds in their cheeks, long heavy slashes badly mended with tape and cotton" (444). He thinks that "nobody had told him to expect that," but still he does not understand disillusionment and continues to look for lodgings to replace the dull and expensive little hotel room. When he does find Rosa's boardinghouse, in spite of the room which is a monstrosity, "a hell of a place," he agrees to a three-month lease. All of Charles's experiences hereafter illustrate the illusoriness of ideals, their attractiveness and their subjectivity. If the ideal seems particularly far out of reach, malice can replace the yearning. Americans, for example, are seen as rich and comfortable and are envied or hated by some persons, like the hotel proprietor and even Herr Bussen, the brilliant mathematical student who is Charles's fellow lodger at Rosa's establishment.[65]

In some instances people have cherished things as symbols of perfect lives. Rosa clings to the cheap little replica of the Tower of Pisa as the tangible representative of what she remembers as an ideal time and place; Hans has idealized the dueling scar that represents the bridge to the honor and comfort he believes existed in the feudal past. Others have idealized the hairstyle and mustache of Hitler. It is again the mistaking of appearance for reality, the mistaking of tangible reality for intangible truths.

Rosa, in addition to having idealized the replica of the Tower of Pisa, also, like Granny Weatherall, has idealized orderliness. Twice the point is made. She unpacks Charles's belongings and arranges them "with an orderliness that exposed all their weaknesses of quality and condition" (453). Charles sees it as "a prime regard for neatness and a symmetrical appearance," a particularly female compulsion. Later Rosa laments to Charles, "Oh, how hard it is to have an orderly and peaceful life, a correct life of the kind I was accustomed to." She persists in trying to keep "straight" Charles's stacks of sketches and Herr Bussen's stacks of mathematical papers.

Even though Rosa cherishes the little plaster of paris tower, it is its link to a place (more of the imagination than of reality) which makes it an appropriate symbol of the ideal. It is place as ideal that receives the emphasis in the story. For Charles it was Germany and Berlin (for his father it was Mexico where "the horses have silver bridles"); for the barber it is Malaga; for Hans it is Paris; for Tadeuz Mey it is London.[66]

The illusion of the ideal is illustrated in Charles's conversation with the barber. "There is nothing in the Tiergarten at this time," said the little barber, sighing. "This is a dark place in winter. I lived in Malaga once, I worked there in a barber shop for a whole year—nearly thirteen months, in fact. The barber shops there are not like ours, they are very dirty, but there, flowers were in bloom outside, in December. There, they use real almond oil for their hair lotions—real. And they have such an extract of rosemary as you cannot find anywhere else." He continues, "In Malaga, I never wore my topcoat all winter. Ah, I hardly knew it was winter." He adds, "like a man talking about a homeland he had lost," "In Malaga . . . I never had a cough, though here I cough all the time." Charles's injection of reality, "I noticed the other day that Malaga froze stiff, too, this winter," is dismissed by the barber. "Well, yes," he says, "once perhaps, but only for a few days" (451–52). However, the application of this evidence to himself is lost on Charles. The subjectivity of ideals is illustrated in the differing opinions of the characters in the story and in the fact that each person fashions his own ideal according to his own desires and deprivations. Often it is simply the superstitious valuation of a place one has never been or of a place where one once was and now remembers selectively.

The fragility of the ideal is underscored in the plaster tower's crumbling under Charles's slight touch, and the tentativeness of things as ideal is suggested further in the bundles of money Rosa has kept from more prosperous days. She shows Charles a black box full of paper money: "These are five hundred thousand marks each—look. . . . One million marks each, these." As she drops the bundles on the table, "terror and awe" are in her face, "as if again for just a moment, she believed in the value of this paper as she had once believed" (477). Rosa knows that the bundles of money, once paper representatives of real gold, are now worthless. "Try now to buy a loaf of bread with all this, try it, try it!" she tells Charles. But she cannot apply that knowledge to her faith in the little plaster tower. After Charles breaks it, it reappears mended and "safely behind the glass of the corner cabinet." Charles thinks, "It was there, all right, and it was mended pretty obviously, it would never be the same. But for Rosa, poor old woman, he supposed it was better than nothing. It stood for something she had, or thought she had, once" (494). This small realization is the crux of the story, although Charles is not able to interpret it yet. The little leaning tower, "a curiosity," has some kind of meaning in his mind. "Well, what? He tousled his hair and rubbed his eyes and then his whole head and yawned himself almost inside out. What had the silly little thing reminded him of before? There was an answer if he could think what it was, but this was not the time" (495).

The answer is tied to Charles's being in Berlin and is to be found in a later stage of the initiation process that has brought him to Europe and to Germany. Charles is the naive and sincere young American would-be artist who is trying to find meaning not in his European past, like Henry James's Americans, but in his own superstitious ideal, which happens to be Germany. In the second paragraph, the narrative voice has revealed that Charles was "remembering Kuno in rather sudden, unexpected pictures, even seeing himself as he was then, and these flashes of memory came against still other flashes, and back somewhere in the dark of his mind was the whole story, whatever it was" (437). The whole story is about the integration of the ideal and the reality, combining Kuno's idealistic vision of Germany with the disillusioning reality and confirming that truth lies outside of both. Charles gains small truths that point him toward the larger truth. For example, soon after he agrees to stay at Rosa's for three months, he feels "a blind resentment all the more deep because it could have no particular object, and helpless as if he had let himself be misled by bad advice." By subconscious association, he links the bad advice to Kuno, against whom the resentment is directed, as his next·thought hints. "Vaguely but in the most ghastly sort of way, he felt that someone he trusted had left him in the lurch, and of course, that was nonsense, as Kuno used to say. 'Nonsense' was one of Kuno's favorite words" (454).

Charles has gained just enough knowledge, just enough experience, to be unable ever to go home again exactly as he was. He senses that his former state of innocence and naiveté is forever lost. "He felt young, ignorant, awkward, he had so much to learn he hardly knew where to begin. He could always go home, but that was not the point. It was a long way from home from where he stood, he could see that" (459).

Charles has seen all around him the sham of the ideal and the lengths to which people will go to preserve the ideal. He himself has experienced at an emotional level the disillusionment that comes from recognizing the falseness of one's idealistic illusion. His experience in Germany has been the catalyst for his partial awakening. He is too close to the experience to understand it fully; the reconciliation must take place later.

In treating Charles's initiation, Porter has used Germany of the thirties to illustrate the falsity of hopes or ideals; the problems in Germany, a microcosm of modern society, are seen as the result of conflicting ideals and the great disparity between the ideals of opposing groups of people. It is no accident that Charles dreams that Rosa's house burns down. Just when he thinks in his dream state that he and all the others have escaped, he hears "a loud and ghostly groan." If Germany is doomed because it is filled with hollow ideals, Charles intuits that his spiritual fate will be tied in some way to Germany's fate. At the end of the story, as he is preparing for bed and sleep, he is overwhelmed with a sense of "something perishable but threatening, uneasy, hanging over his head or stirring angrily, dangerously, at his back. If he couldn't find out now what it was that troubled him so in this place, maybe he would never know." That truth which awaits him is described as "an infernal desolation of the spirit, the chill and the knowledge of death in him" (495). He senses, without knowing precisely, that ideals fail. The death he intuits is the death of the dream and the impending world doom. However, his transformation of that intuition into full knowledge fails to take place. "The Leaning Tower" looks ahead to *Ship of Fools* and its blind voyage toward the homeland. It also links together the characters in Porter's earlier stories who have chased the illusory ideal, mistaking it for truth.

Chapter Four

Reconciliations

Throughout the canon, Katherine Anne Porter's characters exhibit more failures of insight than successes. "María Concepción," "The Martyr," "Virgin Violeta," "He," "Rope," "Magic," "The Jilting of Granny Weatherall," "That Tree," "The Downward Path to Wisdom," "A Day's Work"—none contains a single character who transcends shortsightedness or mere instinct to achieve an integrating perspective.

Some stories, however, have characters who find small truths that light the path ahead for the continuing journey. The unnamed narrator of "Theft" has a glimmer of understanding, even if that understanding is too slight to lead to any significant awareness; Laura in "Flowering Judas" confronts in a dream-vision a dark truth about herself that she still cannot express; the narrator of "Hacienda" and Carlos are aware of some truths, but the narrator is paralyzed in inaction and Carlos is regarded as a fool by all but the narrator; Miranda in "The Circus" and "The Fig Tree" intuits some elemental truths that she cannot transform into awareness, and later, at the end of "Old Mortality," she gains some truths through disillusion that she will have to integrate into a larger vision later in her life; and finally, Charles Upton of "The Leaning Tower" absorbs a formless truth that surely will crystallize later.

The stories that contain true reconciliations, by which Porter meant not only integration of seeming oppositions and apprehension of truth but also "catharsis, the purification of your mind and imagination—

through an ending that is endurable because it is right and true. . .[even if] tragic," are "Holiday" and two stories that feature Miranda, "The Grave" and "Pale Horse, Pale Rider."[1] "Holiday" is not a part of the Miranda saga, but it was written at the same time most of the cycle was being written, and the unnamed narrator in "Holiday" is much like Miranda. It is she who discovers an important and unifying truth.

Like her host family, the Müllers, the narrator in the beginning believes that an outwardly ordered life is a meaningful life. From the moment of her arrival at their farm she approves of their efficiency and orderliness. And on the basis of their physical likenesses, she wrongly assumes that the servant girl, Ottilie, has nothing in common with the Müllers: her wrinkled face is patternless, she cannot communicate through the structure of language, and she seems to have been the victim of reasonless forces.

As long as the narrator can view Ottilie as irrelevant to the Müller family, she is content. Gradually, however, she understands that truth is separate from visible order and logic. The knowledge she first reaches is subconscious, relayed to the reader in images and details. One of the first hints the reader has that Ottilie is indeed a Müller is the narrator's observing Ottilie's pale, slanted eyes, the one physical similarity that identifies the hereditary link.

Because the Müllers have relied on physical laws to order their environment, laws which apply equally to all physical creatures, they have never understood the ineffectualness of positivistic systems that deny the value of the human spirit. Although Father Müller has spoken to his dying wife lovingly and has become aware of the uselessness of his "hundert tousand tollars" in preserving life, he nevertheless is unable to draw any conclusion about the waste of his own life. Furthermore, he stands as the symbol of a spiritually empty, ritualized life.

The Müllers' dedication to outward form results in their inability to give sufficient love. This failure is strongly apparent in their attitude toward Ottilie. They never acknowledge that Ottilie is their own, and it is only when she shows the narrator a photograph of the child she had been that the narrator knows the truth. The narrator then tries to communicate with Ottilie, describing her attempts in images apparently derived from Whitman's "A Noiseless Patient Spider": "For an instant some filament lighter than cobweb spun itself out between that living center in her and in me, a filament from some center that held us all bound to our inescapable common source, so that her life and mine were kin, even a part of each other, and the painfulness and strangeness of her vanished" (CS, 426).[2]

In the knowledge that she and Ottilie are bound together by common humanity, or common divinity if she were to accept Whitman's transcendental view, the narrator then falsely supposes that with love and understanding Ottilie can be brought into the family orbit. In naming Ottilie Müller, Porter may have been alluding to St. Odilia, or Othilia, the patroness of Alsace. Said to have been the daughter of Adalricus, a Frankish lord, she was born blind but later miraculously received her sight.[3] The narrator blindly presumes that she can bring light into Ottilie Müller's dark and mysterious world in the same miraculous way.

When other family members leave to bury Mother Müller and Ottilie howls in a frenzy, the narrator mistakes the sounds as an expression of grief. She then determines that Ottilie must attend the burial of her mother. After considerable difficulty, the narrator gets Ottilie in the wagon and they set out for the grief-dissolving burial ceremony. Soon, however, as they lurch through the hot sun and green earth, to the narrator's great surprise Ottilie begins to gurgle with happiness. The narrator stops and ponders her mistake. Ottilie is a part of the world, but she is not a part of an observable order. She cannot be forced into it. She is inexplicable, the illogical effect of darkness.

The narrator acknowledges that they both are the fools of life, Ottilie for her absurdity when measured against the rationality of an ordered universe, the narrator for momentarily thinking that Ottilie is not absurd. She affirms the value of life, with all its diversities and oppositions and mysteries, when she says that because they have escaped death for one day at least, they will celebrate with a stolen holiday, "a breath of spring air and freedom on this lovely, festive afternoon" (435). The temporary freedom from death is also the freedom from the restrictions of an artificial order, not unlike those life-negating orders that have fascinated American writers from Cooper and Emerson and

James to Faulkner and Kesey. In discovering life's larger truth, which resides beyond regions and religions and art forms, the narrator is celebrating her soul's rebirth, on a day that surely is, in the true meaning of the title, a holy day.

The narrator of "Holiday" has grasped an important truth about the deceptiveness of imposed order. But Miranda of "The Old Order" gains her truth in smaller doses, in the early years usually as formless intuitions. Elemental truths of human nature—sexuality, lust, cruelty, hatred, and mortality—are yielded in "The Circus," "The Fig Tree," and "The Grave," with a reconciliation taking place only at the end of "The Grave," the last story of the sequence.[4] "The Source," "The Journey," and "The Witness" provide necessary background for the three stories in which awakenings to truth occur. An important point is made in "The Fig Tree" that ought not to be overlooked, even though it is not related directly to Miranda's later reconciliation. It has to do with the beneficent role that science plays in our search for truth. In a letter to the editor of the Washington *Post*, which had carried a story about scientists making a silk purse out of a sow's ear, Porter chided "merry little groups of scientists" carrying on "wild games on Cloud Nine and then telling fibs." She concluded, "It is better to acknowledge that only silkworms can make silk, only scientists can make synthetics, and only God can make a silkworm" (CE, 226–27). Elsewhere she is less whimsical and more explicit about the value and the limitation of science. In her essay "On a Criticism of Thomas Hardy" she says, "There were some powerful nineteenth century Inquirers, . . . of whom we need only mention Darwin, perhaps. Scientific experiment leads first to skepticism; but we have seen in our time, how, pursued to the verge of the infinite, it sometimes leads back again to a form of mysticism. There is at the heart of the universe a riddle no man can solve" (CE, 7). Great-Aunt Eliza's Inquiry leads her to the infinite as she cheerfully answers, "No one knows, Child," to Miranda's question of whether the "million other worlds" visible in Eliza's telescope are "like this one." It is close to the insight the narrator of "Holiday" gains.

Miranda's own search for truth will not come to successful fruition until the last paragraph of "The Grave." The full reconciliation does not take place at the time of Miranda and Paul's terrifying adventure.

The narrative voice says, "Miranda never told, she did not even wish to tell anybody. She thought about the whole worrisome affair with confused unhappiness for a few days. Then it sank quietly into her mind and was heaped over by accumulated thousands of impressions, for nearly twenty years" (CS, 367).

The memory is pulled abruptly out of its recess by a Proustian kind of association. A grown woman, "picking her path among the puddles and crushed refuse" of a Mexican market street, she halts suddenly as the episode of that far-off day leaps into her mind, evoked by the sight of a tray of dyed sugar sweets in the shapes of small creatures. The narrative voice says that Miranda is "reasonlessly horrified" and then that the "smell in the market, with its piles of raw flesh and wilting flowers, was like the mingled sweetness and corruption she had smelled that other day in the empty cemetery at home." She then remembers it as the time she and her brother found treasure in the opened graves and "upon this thought" the dreadful vision fades (367–68).

The important question of why the horrible vision fades almost as suddenly as it appears can be answered partially by examining the stages of her recollection of the episode. The most horrifying part of the past experience was the discovery of the dead and bleeding rabbits with the concomitant discovery of her own mortality and femaleness. The sensory experience of seeing the sugar sweets, colored and shaped like "birds, baby chicks, baby rabbits, lambs, baby pigs," attaches itself in her mind to the long-ago impression of seeing the "bundle of tiny rabbits" pulled from the flayed flesh of the mother. That part of the experience was surely terrifying because it amounted to confronting the very blackness of existence. It is only when she perceives the smell of sweetness mingled with the market's corruption that she remembers that she and Paul also found treasure in the opened graves. Only with the intervening twenty years can she regard the experience with a total perspective and know that in addition to the corruption of death and destruction which they discovered, they also found the sweetness of an affirmation of life, the other half of the truth that contained death.

The final meaning of the story is given point by the dominant symbol of the story, the grave. The grave, which once housed death, also yields truth and knowledge, the sustainers of the spirit. The cemetery containing the graves has been described as a place of "uncropped sweet-smelling wild grass," an image suggestive of Whitman's "Song of Myself," in which the child asks, "What is grass?" and the poet responds with a paraphrase of Homer, "It is the sweet uncut hair of graves." The metaphor hints at the power of death to nourish new life and provides a clue to the paradox that evolves by the end of the story.[5]

The truths yielded by the grave have been represented by the gold ring and the silver dove. The ring's only reliable meaning has been that of the temporality of the past social and economic orders; its evocations of superficial womanliness, evocations insufficient to lead to an essential truth, are finally submerged in the basic and terrifying truth of the dead rabbits. The silver dove is quite another matter. It is indeed partially linked with the small creatures Miranda and Paul capriciously have killed and thus stands as a reminder of their destructive natures, but equally important are two additional meanings. Universally the dove symbolizes the holy spirit and must be interpreted also as an affirmation of life over death. It is interesting that Porter supported this interpretation once when she directly addressed the symbolic meanings of the dove, without directly referring to "The Grave." In 1960 she participated in a panel discussion at Wesleyan College in Macon, Georgia, with Flannery O'Connor, Caroline Gordon, Madison Jones, and Louis D. Rubin, Jr. During the discussion Porter commented upon the dynamic and changing nature of symbols. "The dove begins," she said by way of example, "by being a symbol of sensuality, it is the bird of Venus, you know, and then it goes on through the whole range of every kind of thing until it becomes the Holy Ghost . . . the symbol would have the meaning of its context."[6]

The dove also remains the primary representation of art in the story. The silver dove is the essence of the dove that has been immortalized in art. Like the figures arrested in time on Keats's Grecian urn, the dove illustrates the most basic attraction art holds for the human consciousness; it represents immortality, and what Porter called "the substance of faith," and gives hope for a spiritual permanence that transcends death. Like the grave and the smell of sweet corruption, the silver dove intermingles meanings of life and death.[7]

The final vision, which constitutes an epiphany, is itself art. The child Paul, "in the blazing sunshine," lives in the center of Miranda's memory and is immortalized there; the story's structure, with its sudden leap into future time, dramatizes the memory within the present reality by the juxtaposition of a twenty-years-distant past with the present. One detail in Miranda's vision is particularly significant. Although we cannot be sure what insight Paul has gained, we do know that either he has acquired an essential awareness or Miranda thinks he has. There is an important contrast between the early Paul and the Paul in the final vision. At the beginning, when they discover the opened graves, the children look at each other with "pleased adventurous eyes" (362). At the end of the story Miranda imagines Paul as "turning the silver dove over and over in his hands" with a "pleased sober smile in his eyes" (368). That he is turning the silver dove over and over confirms both the dynamic process of knowing and also the perpetual yielding of new meanings by the work of art. But the important change is from "adventurous" to "sober." The pleasures of childhood in discovering "a new sight, doing something they had not done before," have given way to the sober pleasures Aristotle speaks of in the *Rhetoric*. It is the consummate pleasure derived from seeking and finding, of wondering—and finally knowing, which includes darkness, destruction, and death, to be sure, but also light and life.

The important distinction between adventure and sobriety must be seen as the distinction between adventure and experience, which Porter discusses in "St. Augustine and the Bullfight." She refers to Yeats's remarks about the unhappy or unfortunate man "whose adventures exceeded his capacity for experience," interpreting "capacity for experience" as "the faculty for understanding what has happened to one." She defines the difference between adventure and experience as this: "Adventure is something you seek for pleasure, or even for profit, like a gold rush or invading a country; for the illusion of being more alive than ordinarily, the thing you will to occur; but experience is what really happens to you in the long run; the truth that finally overtakes you" (92). She asks whether experience, "that is, the thing that happens to a person living from day to day," may not be "anything at all that sinks in? is, without making any claims, a part of your growing and changing life? what it is that happens in your mind, your heart" (CE, 93). The essay illustrates the theory that is implicit in "The Grave." Porter talks of her horrifying adventure at the bullfight, the full truth of which she did not face until years later, and then when she was reading St. Augustine's *Confessions* and suddenly saw her own adventure in that of the young fourth-century Roman student described by Augustine. She was able to transform the adventure into the experience of a truth that was "a commonplace of human nature."

"Pale Horse, Pale Rider" is a continuation of the quest of Miranda that has been traced in "The Old Order" and "Old Mortality." Its thematic core is the reconciliation of life and death, and it offers the most conclusive and positive philosophic view of any of the Porter stories. Appropriately it was the last Miranda story Porter wrote.[8]

The story begins with Miranda's sleeping consciousness and retrospectively traces the immediate events that have led up to the point at which the story begins, the climax in Miranda's struggle between life and death. The story is told in a structured stream-of-consciousness mode; although the imagery and details are highly symbolic, Miranda's reported thoughts are syntactically complete. Porter transfers the interest in the story from plot to theme; the reader knows almost from the beginning that Miranda will survive and that Adam will die. This knowledge is transmitted through Miranda's intuitive awareness, and thus there is no suspense about the outcome.

The story concerns Miranda's confrontation with death and the new awareness of death, and consequently of life, that she gains as a result of her experience. She is able to look at both with a new, transcendent perspective. The new awareness is presented through changing images and symbols. In the beginning of the story Miranda, in her dreamy state of consciousness, considers a journey she "does not mean to take" and wonders which horse to ride, Graylie or Miss Lucy or Fiddler. She decides upon Graylie "because he is not afraid of bridges," a metaphor for her state between life and death. Thus, she begins her race with death. Through sheer will, however, she stops the race, shouting to death in the person of "the stranger": "I'm not going with you this time—ride on!" (CS, 270). As Miranda tries to draw herself up out of the death-like sleep, the first word that enters her consciousness is *war*.

From there she thinks of her immediate past experiences, most of which circulate around her friends, the newspaper office, and people associated with the war: the Liberty Bond salesman, the Red Cross volunteers, and the wounded soldiers. Incorporated in these memories are those of the love affair with Adam, who dies of influenza he probably caught from her.

Death is presented in a number of images in the story, first as "that lank greenish stranger" who has been "hanging about the place" and has been "welcomed" by Miranda's grandfather, her great-aunt, her "five times removed cousin," her "decrepid hound," and her "silver kitten," all presumably dead. Miranda asks a timeless question: "Where are they now?" She examines the elegant stranger, sitting straight upon his own gray horse (with tarnished nose and ears) and dressed "in dark shabby garments that flapped upon his bones." His "pale face" smiles "in an evil trance" (270). Although the stranger looks familiar to her, she cannot place him; she nevertheless suspects that "he is no stranger" to her, a comment that reminds us of Porter's observation that "we are born knowing death." Thus far, death is presented in images of paleness, tarnished gray, and darkness. It is important to note, however, that the image of grayness in the figure of the horse Graylie also symbolizes the bridge between life and death.[9]

The account of Miranda's experiences at the newspaper office and at the hospital, and her experiences with Adam, are permeated with subtle reminders of the nearness of death to the living. Everything is remembered and acted out against the backdrop of the war, and three times a funeral procession is a part of that backdrop. When Miranda and Adam walk out together into "the fine fall day" they have to wait for a funeral to pass before they can cross the street. A little later they have to wait at a corner again and "hardly . . . [glance] at a funeral procession approaching." The third time a funeral passes, however, they watch together "in silence." The funeral procession so emphasized is a variation on the journey motif—it is literally a final journey to the grave but figuratively it is mortal life in its continual progress to death. The journey motif is reinforced with references to other means of transportation; when, for example, Miranda first becomes ill and thinks she is dying, her feverish mind conjures up a tall sailing ship moored nearby; and when she is in the hospital and fluctuating between life and death, in one of her half-lucid nightmares she thinks: "The road to death is a long march beset with all evils, and the heart fails little by little at each new terror, the bones rebel at each step, the mind sets up its own bitter resistance and to what end? The barriers sink one by one, and no covering of the eyes shuts out the landscape of disaster" (309). When it is apparent that she will live, she weeps "silently, shamelessly, in pity for herself" and thinks that "Dr. Hildesheim, Miss Tanner, the nurses in the diet kitchen, the chemist, the surgeon, the precise machine of the hospital, the whole humane conviction and custom of society, conspired to pull her inseparable rack of bones and wasted flesh to its feet, to put in order her disordered mind, and to set her once more safely in the road that would lead her again to death" (314). At the end of the story, after Miranda's return from near-death, after the armistice, after Adam's death, she prepares to leave the hospital and start on that journey again. To signify the recommencing of the journey Miss Tanner, the nurse, tells her, "Your taxicab is waiting, my dear" (317).

The state of death is regarded by Miranda from changing perspectives. When she first becomes ill she thinks of earthly places she would like to be ("I wish I were in the cold mountains in the snow"), and then she thinks of a jungle as the state of death to which the ship will take her. The images are dark and fearsome: "a writhing terribly alive and secret place of death, creeping with tangles of spotted serpents, rainbow-colored birds with malign eyes, leopards with humanly wise faces and extravagantly crested lions; screaming long-armed monkeys tumbling among broad fleshy leaves that glowed with sulphur-colored light and exuded the ichor of death, and rotting trunks of unfamiliar trees sprawled in crawling slime" (299). The image changes to a less horrifying one, however, as Miranda worsens. When she is taken to the hospital, its physical reality combines with the image of the physical place she longs to be, the cold mountains in the snow: "The white walls rose sheer as cliffs, a dozen frosted moons followed each other in perfect self-possession down a white lane and dropped mutely one by one into a snowy abyss" (308). The source of Miranda's equating death with a pleasant place of cold is perhaps an experience Porter described to Warren. She said, "Let me tell you something about poetry which will probably explain something. I read it first when I was about ten, and I cannot even think of it now without a rising of the hair: 'Fear no more the heat of the sun. . . .' remember that?"[10] The lines from *Cymbeline* (IV.ii) indeed refer to the assuaging power of death that is an escape from worldly pain and care, the heat of the sun symbolizing life in the physical world.

Whiteness becomes the image of death, as, for example, in the grotesque whiteness of the dead man removed from the bed next to hers. "The man on the springs was swathed smoothly from head to foot in white, with folded bands across the face, and a large stiff bow like merry rabbit ears dangled at the crown of his head." After the corpse is taken away by two living men, "a pallid white fog" arises "in their wake insinuatingly," and it is "fog in which was concealed all terror and all weariness, all the wrung faces and twisted backs and broken feet of abused, outraged living things, all the shapes of their confused pain and their estranged hearts" (308). Miranda already has thought that "this whiteness and silence" is only "the absence of pain," an image she would draw upon later when her father died. She wrote to her sister, "I'm glad he is free, darling, I feel only relief too, as if a beautiful white silence had fallen in all the places where he breathed such fury and bitterness."[11]

Miranda thinks of oblivion as "a whirlpool of gray water turning upon itself for all eternity." She concludes that "oblivion and eternity are curtains hung before nothing at all." Although she tells herself that "death is nothing to fear," she still cannot "consent." This unwillingness to consent is her will to live, "a minute fiercely burning particle of being . . . composed entirely of one single motive" (310–11). This "hard unwinking angry point of light" which is "herself" dissolves into a fine radiance that is removed from all physical life. Miranda thus enters the state of death that is pure spirit, stripped of the putrefaction of physical decay. The human beings she joyfully meets are "pure identities" of all the living she had known. She has no questions or desires but stays "in the quietude of her ecstasy," her "eyes fixed on the overwhelming deep sky where it was always morning" (311). Into Miranda's joy, however, enters a "small flick of distrust" because something, somebody was missing. With this realization she enters the netherworld of bitter cold and picks her way back to the world of pain and corruption, back to the living. It is Adam, of course, who is missing, then, from the land of the dead. When she wills herself to live to be with him, she rightly feels betrayed when she learns that during her own tenuous convalescence he has died. Her willing herself to live, however, to return from a place of joy to a place of suffering and pain, is motivated by her pure love for Adam and is a testament to the reconciling power of love.

During the long illness and the nightmare it encapsulates, Miranda has moved back and forth between life and death, existing in a twilight world that stands between. In an ironic reversal, her brief sojourn in a deathlike state was permeated with light and her return to the living is a return to a twilight world—always "just before morning, a promise of day never kept." She asks, "Shall I ever see light again?" And feeling like an alien, she also asks herself, "Is it possible I can ever accustom myself to this place?" (313). In her peculiar position, which she describes as having "one foot in either world," she is able to anticipate being more completely among the living, when "the light will seem real" and she will "be glad" when she hears that someone she knows "has escaped from death" (317).

But having seen the state of death, Miranda will never be completely the same again.[12] Here, gray, which Porter favored all her life in her clothes, takes on the final meaning of unifying death and life, the gray that results from being neither darkness nor light, or that becomes the gray that results from being both. Her transcendent state is symbolized in the gray suede gauntlets and the gray sheer stockings she requests. And her "silvery" walking stick symbolizes her renewed journey. Gray has been the controlling image of the story, moving from death to the between state to finally the transcendent state that unifies both life and death. The change is symbolized most dramatically in the tarnished gray of death's steed and the silvery color of her walking stick. The precious glow of the silvery color is gray made brilliant. Miranda's experience has led her not, as some critics would have us believe, to contemplation of suicide or to only a grim determination to keep on living, but rather to a universal truth that acknowledges the beauty of both death and life.

Two additional points must be made. First, Miranda in "Pale Horse, Pale Rider" is not an initiate in the traditional sense, nor in the way that she is in "The Old Order" and "Old Mortality." She is not naive and idealistic when the story begins. It is she, in fact, who strips away the insincere patriotism of the exploiters and is sickened by the emotional parasites the war has spawned. Her journey is not from innocence to experience but from a limited view of life and death to a transcendent one. Adam, her beloved, is another matter. He is both innocent and naive. Miranda thinks of him as "pure" and observes that there is "no resentment or revolt in him." When at the theater she is angered by the Liberty Bond salesman whom she calls "just another nasty old man who would like to see the young ones killed," she questions Adam: "They don't fool you really, do they . . . ?" Adam is surprised at Miranda's vehemence, and his pride makes him feel sorry for the salesman. He says, "Now what could the poor sap do if they did take him?" (294).

If Adam has a flaw, it is that pride in his youth and in his masculine beauty. "He had his uniforms made by the best tailor he could find," telling Miranda that "it's the least I can do for my beloved country, not to go around looking like a tramp" (279).

Later, when she sees Adam in an unguarded moment, he, like Christ, has lost his naiveté but not his goodness. His face is "set in a blind melancholy, a look of pained suspense and despair." Thus Adam must be sacrificed because of the world's sin. Miranda understands this. To her he is "flawless, complete, as the sacrificial lamb must be" (295). Adam represents twentieth-century man, perhaps, but more important, twentieth-century American man. He looks "like a fine healthy apple," and his hair is "the color of a haystack when you turn the weathered top back to the clear straw beneath" (280). When he walks with Miranda, he keeps her on the inside of the walk "in the good American style." He is a man of action, not a man of intellect; his roots are Calvinistic (he was born Presbyterian), and he represents ideal American manhood.

The war is the integrating touchstone of the story's themes. It is the war that has brought Miranda, the seeker of truth, and Adam, the innocent lamb, together. Significantly, when the war ends, Miranda is reclaimed by the living, but Adam is claimed by death. In abstraction, American innocence is sacrificed on the altar of modern social evil, and America will never be the same again. The poet, the singer, in the person of Miranda is left to tell the tale, as the song, to which the title alludes, says. The pale horse and the pale rider of the song are death and the way to death. Adam and Miranda sing some of it; both have heard Negroes sing it (he in a Texas oil field, she in a cotton field). Because it has a primitive source (she once commented about the truth of Negro music), it is closer to elemental truth. The song foreshadows Adam's death, as do many other images and symbols in the story, and prophesies Miranda's final role, that of the singer left to mourn. "Death always leaves one singer to mourn," she says. It is a role also that the narrator and Carlos are given in "Hacienda."

The relationship between the story and the author's own experience has been carefully detailed by Porter herself. But again, she has transformed the "adventure" into experience, as she consistently transforms the details of her life into art. On one level "Pale Horse, Pale Rider" is a love story set against a catastrophic war, the purity of Miranda and Adam's love measured against the inanity of a male-female relationship depicted by the young woman in a restaurant; Miranda and Adam's story is about disillusion and false hopes created in the tumultuous destruction by world forces. On another level it is the story of the American Adam who comes of age in the conflict between new world values and old world values and dies in the conflict. On a still more transcendent level it is the story of a unifying vision that reconciles life and death and gives everlasting new meaning to the journey from life to death. Miranda thus shares Ishmael's vision and role, and she repeats universally a statement that was made indigenously American in the nineteenth century.

In two of Porter's stories, "The Grave" and "Pale Horse, Pale Rider," there are scenes that might be described as showing an amalgam of time that in itself symbolizes the unity of things. In "The Grave" the adult Miranda is able to look into the past and to see again the child

Paul. In "Pale Horse, Pale Rider" a still more adult Miranda looks at Adam in the full flower of his beautiful manhood and sees his death. In both cases, timelessness transcends temporal boundaries and conforms to an uplifting vision that is so rare in Porter's fiction as to be startling and memorable.

Chapter Five

Ship of Fools

B y Katherine Anne Porter's own account, the execution of *Ship of Fools* occupied a large part of her long life. She dated the finished manuscript "Yaddo, August, 1941" and "Pigeon Cove, August, 1961," a circumscription of the twenty years in which most of the writing was done. But the real voyage that generated her account of a fictional one was taken in 1931, and she told an interviewer that some of the ideas of *Ship of Fools* were in her mind when she was five years old.[1]

Because some parts of the long novel were written concurrently with some of the stories and short novels, the long work naturally shares traits with many of the shorter works. Beyond that logical similarity, however, if everything Porter wrote was, as she declared, a fragment of a larger plan, then *Ship of Fools* must also fit into the thematic pattern. A careful reading of *Ship of Fools*, in fact, shows that it is the culmination of Porter's large theme. Her version of the quest theme, implicit in her other fictional pieces, becomes explicit in the only long novel. Recapitulating everything else she had written, *Ship of Fools* indeed represents the final stage of Porter's thematic and stylistic evolution. On the ship are versions of earlier characters she created or planned to create; in the narrative are scenes that mirror scenes from her other stories, short novels, and essays; themes treated in the shorter works are treated again in the long novel; and the prose medium of the long novel is a combination of stylistic techniques that served her well in the other pieces.

During the thirty years of planning and writing *Ship of Fools*, Porter came up with several different titles for the intended novel. "Promised Land," "The Land That Is Nowhere," and "No Safe Harbor" were at one time or another used as working titles.[2] But although those particular titles confirm her thematic intention in the novel, none seemed to satisfy her. She argued with her publishers for *Ship of Fools*, a title she preferred as early as 1946, finally convincing Little, Brown that it was the right one. She explained the choice in a note preceding the contents page of the published work:

> The title of this book is a translation from the German of *Das Narrenschiff*, a moral allegory by Sebastian Brant (1458?–1521) first published in Latin as *Stultifera Navis* in 1494. I read it in Basel in the summer of 1932 when I had still vividly in mind the impressions of my first voyage to Europe. When I began thinking about my novel, I took for my own this simple almost universal image of the ship of this world on its voyage to eternity. It is by no means new—it was very old and durable and dearly familiar when Brant used it; and it suits my purpose exactly. I am a passenger on that ship.

There are some important similarities in the two works, notably the names of the ships and the illusion under which both Porter's fools and Brant's fools suffer: the belief that they are journeying toward a better place when in fact they are sailing to death.[3] But critics have been quick to point out the differences between *Ship of Fools* and *Das Narrenschiff*, a work that traces the voyage of personified abstractions like those in Bunyan's *Pilgrim's Progress*. Porter, however, preferred to think of her novel as a "parable" rather than an allegory, and the truth is that Brant's work inspired Porter more than it provided a technical model.[4] It was the quest theme within the ship and voyage symbolism that appealed to her and that now makes sense in light of her other works, all of which illustrate the constant impetus toward truth and the great difficulty of reaching it.

As was true of most of her fictional works, Porter began with a real event and real people and changed them into something more in the artistic rendering. Often when students or critics asked about a symbolic meaning in a work, she was able to say, "But that was his name," or "But it really happened." In a lecture she delivered when she was eighty-two, she explained her method as "reportage, only I do something to it. I arrange it and it is fiction but it happened."[5] She did admit, however, that sometimes she later would see symbolism as having accrued to the fact, symbolism that she had not consciously planned but that was there all the time, organically.[6] That no doubt is true of the voyage that inspired *Ship of Fools*, the real voyage Porter took with Gene Pressly in 1931 from Veracruz to Bremerhaven. Even in selecting that event for a fictional account, she had to be aware of its symbolic possibilities.

Ship of Fools began as a shorter work Porter first called "Promised Land," fiction based loosely on the log she kept during the voyage to Bremerhaven. Having begun the story and put it aside in the early thirties, she briefly took it up again about 1936 but still was unable to develop it. In 1938 she reported to friends that as soon as she finished a critical essay on Katherine Mansfield she planned to return to "Promised Land."[7] At about the same time she began to think of this story more explicitly as a novel, and she also changed her working title to "The Land That Is Nowhere." Two years later she changed the working title again, this time to "No Safe Harbor," as she accepted an advance of $2,500 from Harcourt, Brace, who for many years had been hoping for a novel from her.[8] But by 1943 she feared she would never finish the novel, telling Glenway Wescott of the failure of her creative energy.[9] Nevertheless, three years later she wrote to Josephine Herbst that she felt ready to finish the novel, which she wanted to retitle "Ship of Fools."[10]

She described to Herbst the writing of the novel. It was a "one-draft" work, she said, two hundred and forty pages of which had been done in six months. She had worked for two months at Yaddo in 1940, two and a half months at a later time in the same place, and one and a quarter months at South Hill in 1943. By then the story had grown not only into a novel but a long and ambitious one.[11] In spite of her optimism, it was 1954 before she was able to engross herself again in the novel, but once more she was unable to sustain the flow. Finally, in 1960, she seriously undertook the completion of *Ship of Fools*. Having left Harcourt, Brace for Atlantic-Little, Brown, she finished the novel in June of 1961, and it was published on April Fool's Day, 1962.

The length of time Porter took to finish *Ship of Fools* can be accounted for in various ways. She always had difficulty keeping her creative energies alive for the completion of even her short stories and short novels, and the very length of *Ship of Fools* must have daunted her. Then, too, although she had planned or begun various novels in the past, it was the short story form that she had perfected and in which she wrote familiarly. The novel form was alien to her nature and method of writing, which she described as working at top speed between long intervals of dryness, a painful pacing she ascribed to "things form[ing] slowly, slowly" and her refusal to write "until it's absolutely ready to go."[12] Givner believes also that Porter had difficulty keeping track of the theme of the novel over the thirty years or so of its gestation. In a narrow sense that may be true, because Porter tended over the years to describe the novel's themes according to the world's concerns at the moment, but the large theme that pervades the shorter works pervades the novel as well, and that did not change.[13] In discussing *Ship of Fools* with Barbara Thompson, she said, "It's astonishing how little I've changed: nothing in my point of view or my way of feeling."[14] The proposed titles, serving as thematic indicators, show that Porter always was writing about illusions and false hopes in the search for truth.

By the time *Ship of Fools* appeared in 1962, Porter already had published portions of it separately. In fact, the subtitles of two of the three parts of the novel had been used as titles for two of the published pieces. Yet the novel has a structure and a unity appropriate to its form and its length, and the final, integrated work is indeed a whole entity rather than a pastiche. It is a mistake to think of it as a collection of episodes simply strung like beads on the device of a journey. Careful analysis supports *Ship of Fools* as a work as economically structured as Porter's jewel-like short stories and as pertinently developed. Its symbolism never subsumes the realism of its characters, but both work together to effect Porter's last presentation of her fictional theme.

Structurally, the novel is made up of three parts uneven in length, "Embarkation," "High Sea," and "The Harbors," with part 2 being by far the longest section. Part 1 is introductory, as its title implies, and part 3 is resolving. The development of character and theme appropriately occurs in the long middle section. All three parts cohere to the allegorical matrix of the voyage and are bound together by the development of the same characters and by the net of symbols and images woven into the narrative. What some critics have deplored as an episodic quality to the novel derives from a constantly shifting viewpoint. But rather than a distraction it in fact is crucial to the novel's theme. By and large the action of *Ship of Fools* takes place on the actual voyage from Veracruz to Bremerhaven, but the dozen or so pages that constitute the opening frame of the novel are particularly important—even can be compared with Ishmael's early narrative in *Moby-Dick* before the *Pequod* sails—because they establish the context of the embarkation. In describing the port of the departure and the society of the port, this section provides an index to the novel's primary themes, which Porter summarized as "betrayal and treachery, but also self-betrayal and self-deception—the way that all human beings deceive themselves about the way they operate."[15] Porter confirmed the significance of the opening pages when she told an interviewer that the scene in Veracruz contained in briefest form a synopsis of the thematic structure of the novel.[16]

Veracruz would have been the logical starting point for a trip from Mexico to Germany because it was the port from which most such transatlantic crossings began. It also had a distinctive social structure and an interesting history. It had been the center of the 1914 uprising and for a time was occupied by American troops. Anita Brenner said that in 1914 "the nightmare of Mexico was fact in Veracruz."[17] The aftermath of that revolution continued to be reflected in the Veracruz that Porter knew in the 1920s and from which she herself embarked in 1931. She no doubt saw in this particular port town a combination of ambience and social structure that later would tie in with her thematic purpose in the novel. Once again mining experience for symbolic usefulness, Porter focuses on Veracruz's class stratification, materialism, and cynicism, all against a background rich in the contrast of a faded revolution and the vivid colors of a tropical setting. She must also have been aware of the ironic usefulness of the name of the port town, which translates as the "true cross." A cold narrative voice calls it "a little purgatory between land and sea for the traveller," and the society of Veracruzanos depicted exists far from the religious ideal of self-sacrifice implied in the symbol of crucifixion, an image Porter effectively used in "María Concepción."

Unnamed Veracruzanos receive the attention in the opening frame. In the very first sentence they are described as being "very fond of themselves and the town they have helped to make." The narrator explains the fondness as so excessive as to constitute narrow-minded regionalism, a trait that later is fully developed as a major theme in the novel. Veracruzanos, the narrator says, "carry on their lives of alternate violence and lethargy with a pleasurable contempt for outside opinion, founded on the charmed notion that their ways and feelings are above and beyond criticism." In the two succeeding paragraphs the Veracruzanos are seen identifying "lavish" with "aristocratic," showing that for them wealth determines "good society," whose members maintain "a delicate balance between high courtesy and easy merriment." They refer to this balance as "civilized freedom," and furthermore think of the people in the capital as "polyglot barbarians of the upper plateau." To illustrate that the Veracruzanos' regionalism is not unique, the narrator observes that the inhabitants of Mexico City "obstinately go on regarding Veracruz as merely a pestilential jumping-off place into the sea" (3).

In the third paragraph the tone becomes more bitter as the people of Veracruz are shown in their "methodical brutality" to "the travelers who must pass through their hands to reach the temporary haven of some ship in harbor." Both the Veracruzanos and the travelers are isolated in their self-pride and hostility: "The travelers wish only to be carried away from the place, and the Veracruzanos wish only to see the last of them." But the Veracruzanos are also cunning exploiters who wish to keep the travelers long enough to extract from them "every possible toll, fee, extortion, and bribe due to the town and its citizens." The narrative voice provides also the objective view of Veracruz: "It is in fact to the passing eye a typical port town, cynical by nature, shameless by experience, hardened to showing its seamiest side to strangers," a view inconsistent with the Veracruzanos' image of themselves as "generous, warmhearted, hospitable, sensitive" (3).

The narrative telescopes to "a few placid citizens of the white-linen class." They are members of the old families and know all the intimate details of one another's lives. Juxtaposed to these representatives of the leisure class is "a small, emaciated Indian sitting on a bench under a tree." He is "a country Indian wearing weathered white cotton drawers and a long shirt, a widely curved old straw hat over his eyes. His feet with their ragged toenails and cracked heels, in sandals fastened with leather thongs broken and knotted together again, lay meekly together on the gray earth."[18] The class stratification is displayed: "The men at leisure on the terrace did not notice him except as a part of the scene, and he seemed unaware of them" (4).

The social scaling continues with an account of the quadriplegic beggar who comes to the terrace every morning to receive small copper coins from the leisure-class men, who regard him "as if he were a dog too repulsive even to kick." Indeed, in the social scheme he seems hardly human; "dumb, half blind, he approached with nose almost to sidewalk as if he followed the trail of a smell, stopping now and then to rest, wagging his hideous shock head from side to side slowly in unbearable suffering" (4). When one of the men offers him half of a squeezed lime, "he . . . [sits] back on his haunches, . . . [opens] his dreadful mouth to receive the fruit, and . . . [drops] down again, his jaws working." He is disregarded by not only the men who watch his progress across the street, "as they might a piece of rubbish rolling before the wind," but also by the Indian, who does not even turn his head. The descriptions of the working-class girls and the upper-class girls, both classes distinguishable by their clothes, further delineate class distinction.

Two paragraphs later the account of the accidentally murdered Indian servant boy points again to the class stratification in Mexico and is reminiscent of the revolutionary background of "That Tree," "Flowering Judas," and "Hacienda." In fact, the boy's death is similar to the Indian girl's death in "Hacienda." They both are victims of blind and insidious forces, and both are objects of exploitation by unscrupulous and detached officials.

In these early paragraphs Porter has treated the important subjects of social isolation, ruthlessness, self-pride, and regional biases, and she has depicted people who are confined to their stations without in the least understanding the human condition. She has suggested their in-humanity by animal imagery, a familiar device in her fiction. The Veracruzanos think of the "stranger passing through" as "a sheep bleat-ing for their shears," and the grotesque beggar is regarded as "dog" by the townsmen, imagery that expresses the contempt humans feel for one another. However, when the narrative viewpoint of the men wan-ders "to the familiar antics of creatures inhabiting the windowsills and balconies nearest them," real animals become participating characters in the scene. The creatures are a cat, a parrot, a monkey, and a dog, and they set up the references for a chain of images and metaphors that will operate throughout the novel. The "long gray cat" watches his enemy the parrot, who watches his enemy the monkey. The cat, though wary, has no fear of either one; he simply despises them. Only "the mangy dog" is able to send the cat clawing his way to safety. The dog, in turn, is a nuisance to the sleeping Indian, who plants a well-placed kick to the dog's lean ribs. The dog rushes back to the butcher's stand that he guards. The implied irony is that the dog at any moment could become the victim and the ware of the butcher. Thus, the safe harbor is an illusion, and the chain of fear and confrontation will continue.

In the conversation between the two unnamed Veracruz men, a younger one and an older one, animal imagery continues to illustrate the contempt humans feel for one another. When the viewpoint en-larges from that of the two men, who walk on, to onlookers who are left behind, the travelers arriving to meet ships are described as "birds of passage" who chatter in "ungainly tongues." The viewpoint changes to the waiters and the desk clerk at the hotel who see the travelers like "swarming insects" and "burros" and among them a "peahen," a monkey, a pig, and a flock of quarreling birds. The narrative voice describes a young man's profile as "like a willful, cold-blooded horse," and a bridegroom's mother clings to him "like a mourning dove." Thus, before they board the ship, many of the passengers have been seen in Veracruz as unnamed caricatures of animals, birds, and insects. The multiple viewpoints have provided the means by which Porter has illuminated the separateness and ignorance of humans. She continues to use the technique to develop the theme throughout the novel.

As the boarding passengers prepare to leave the port town and its inhabitants behind, the narrative focus moves to the ship and the imminent voyage. The name of the ship, the *Vera*, means "truth," of course, but it also is phonetically close to the name of the real ship on which Porter sailed, the *Werra*. In the allegorical context of the voyage, the ship's name is indeed appropriate. Although the voyage to eternity is the voyage of this world on its physical journey, ideally the soul's concurrent voyage ought to be a voyage toward truth. Most of the *Vera*'s passengers think of their voyage as a voyage toward amelioration, but ironically fail to see it as anything but physical. That struggle toward the illusion of something better provides the action of *Ship of Fools*.

Aside from the very general symbolism of the "ship of this world on its voyage to eternity," the voyage from Veracruz to Bremerhaven has additional meaning. Certainly the trip had personal significance to Porter, who regarded Mexico as her artistic launching point. It was Mexico that provided material for her first published fiction and where her apprenticeship to her craft ended.[19] But Germany was personally important, too. Although Givner says that the destination was accidental and was merely the result of convenience, Porter later described her trip to Germany as a "God-sent opportunity" and told her childhood friend Erna Schlemmer Johns that she had chosen Germany as the destination of her first European trip on Erna's "account."[20] So whatever Germany was to Porter in 1931 in fact, she later saw it as having been designedly significant. Like her character Charles Upton, she probably had an idealized view of Germany that grew out of her friendship with Erna. In retrospect, she must have felt that like Upton she had been attracted to an illusion.

Figuratively, the trip from Veracruz to Bremerhaven is the new world's returning to its cultural source. Porter always thought of Mexico as a part of America, as the new world, as she explained in a letter to the editor of the *Century* in 1923 (CE, 356). Carleton Beals explains more specifically why Veracruz was symbolic of the new world. "Vera Cruz was the New World," he wrote. "The tempo, the attitude of the folk, a certain rawness, a mongrel quality—all was subtly different from the Old World. There was something in common with even a sun-stricken, half-sleepy little city like Vera Cruz, there on a tropic sea, and the great bustling New York that stamped it as not of Europe, but of this our new world."[21]

Thus, while the trip to the old world seems to be a return to a cultural home, the voyager is unwittingly going to the center of chaos in the modern century. Perhaps Porter intended to show that Nazi Germany had held the moral destiny of modern times; more universally, though, the *Vera's* journey takes its meaning from its model, the archetypal quest. Twentieth-century interpretations of the quest have included the search for identity and the search for a refuge that constitutes a return to Eden. Porter regarded the search for identity as the search for truth, because to know oneself was to know humanity; to know less was to exist on only a physical level, a philosophy which has underlain her heavy use of animal imagery throughout her fiction. A classic humanistic view, Porter's philosophy is based on the premise that persons must first recognize their animal natures before they can understand their difference from animals and therefore know their humanity, a point she has explored fully in "The Grave." The search for a refuge is the equivalent of the psychological search for the father, an illusion that fails to yield truth. Both searches are alluded to in the early pages of *Ship of Fools* when it is clear that most of the passengers do not know themselves and most are joyously looking forward to a return to their homelands. Those who are not going home are going to places they mistakenly consider refuges from the world's chaos.

The absence of self-identity is implied in the protracted revelation of characters' names and in the heavy use of animal imagery, which suggests, in addition to the contempt humans feel for one another, soulless existence. By the time the ship slides out to sea, the reader knows only two names among the citizens of Veracruz and the ship's passengers and crew, those of the bulldog Bébé and Dr. Schumann, the ship's doctor. From various viewpoints are seen about half of the ship's passengers and "the crew of the big solid blunt-faced sailors moving about their duties," and through Dr. Schumann's eyes are seen a hunchback, a tall boy and a man in a wheelchair, a young Mexican woman with her baby and nurse, and a bride and groom. All the major characters except Dr. Schumann, but including the bulldog, have been presented first as "anonymous, faceless travelers," with their distinguishing traits largely those of animals. Dr. Schumann, however, is introduced and described at once:

> Dr. Schumann crossed the deck with the ordered step of an old military man and stood firmly planted near the rail, relaxed without slackness, hands at his side, watching the straggling procession of passengers ascending the gangplank. He had a fine aquiline nose, a serious well-shaped head, and two crookedly healed dark dueling scars on his left cheek. One of these was a "beauty," as the Germans call it, the enviable slash from ear to mouth perfectly placed that must once have laid the side teeth bare. Healed all these years, the scar still had a knotty surface, a wide seam. Dr. Schumann carried it well, as he carried his sixty years: both were becoming to him. His light brown eyes, leveled calmly upon a given point where the people approached and passed, were without speculation or curiosity, but with an abstract goodness and even sweetness in them. He appeared to be amiable, well bred and in perfect possession of himself. (16–17)

He is never described in animal images (except later by himself) because he is farther along on the human scale than any of the other passengers. A few pages later the difference between Dr. Schumann and the other passengers is clear. Unlike the others, he has had his identity all along; he knows who he is, and so do we. He illustrates the self-knowledge for which Porter praised E. M. Forster, of whom she said, he "lives in that constant state of grace which comes of knowing who he is, where he lives, what he feels and thinks about his world" (CE, 74). When the others investigate their cramped, airless quarters each discovers again what seemed to have been lost, his or her "identity." But the identity is name only. "Bit by bit it emerged, travel-worn, halfhearted but still breathing, from a piece of luggage or some familiar possession in which he had once invested his pride of ownership, and which, seen again in strange, perhaps unfriendly surroundings, assured the owner that he had not always been a harassed stranger, a number, an unknown name and a caricature on a passport" (21). So the passengers think they "know" themselves. "Soothed by this restoration of their self-esteem, the passengers looked at themselves in the mirrors with dawning recognition." For some, their knowledge of themselves will never exceed this superficial identity. Others reach higher levels of self-truth. From there on, the characters' names begin to unfold as they introduce themselves to one another or are introduced by the narrative voice. When part 1, "Embarkation," ends, the reader has met most of the major characters. La Condesa, Captain Thiele, the two Mexican priests, an Indian maid, Nicolasa, the remainder of the Zarzuela troupe, and Herr Graf with his nephew, Johann, are brought forward in the early pages of part 2.

As the *Vera*'s passengers set out on their voyage to the Old World, to Germany, inevitably, because they are mortal, they continue their voyage to eternity, to death, as Miranda in "Pale Horse, Pale Rider" learns. The degree to which each reaches or fails to reach one port of truth in the concurrent spiritual voyage makes up the interest of the novel. Through scene and picture, techniques James defined, Porter explores the complications within the human personality and human society that make the voyage as fulfilling or as unfulfilling as it is.

All the passengers have multiple opportunities for finding truth. Within themselves are the universal truths to be discovered, and the voyage itself ought to suggest to them metaphorically the destiny of life in this world. And yet most ignore the truth available to them and pursue illusions that they mistake for truth. The truth within includes primitive instinct, the potential for evil as well as the potential for love, and death.

Although some aspects of primitive instinct are pure and good, such as that exhibited in the childlike woodcarvings of the artist Etchegaray, other instinctive impulses are dark and destructive. As Porter shows in "Rope" and "Noon Wine," malice, hatred, and cruelty—the extreme of which is bloodlust—are elemental and must be acknowledged. Once acknowledged, they may dissipate in purification. Like the quarreling pair in "Rope," David and Jenny alternate between professions of love and exhibitions of hatred and cruelty. Remembering a scene that repeats itself in her dreams, Jenny sees a truth within her and David's relationship. It is a scene that Porter described once to Caroline Gordon the year before she sailed on the *Werra*. She tells of an experience she had on the way to Taxco:

> On that terrible and beautiful road, something like a Coney Island scenic railway magnified beyond all human reason, I saw an Indian man and woman beside the dusty way, engaged in killing each other with knives and

stones . . . his shaven head was gashed round and the blood streamed
down in his face which looked like the Indian Christ's in the country
churches; he was done for, his face showed it, but she was still screaming
and wild and furious . . . we rattled and bounded by in a whirl of dust and
gasoline fumes.

Porter had written in by hand, "With half a dozen bleeding knife
wounds in her stomach and breast" and "blood was . . . [running]
from a knife blade in her stomach."[22] By the time she used this scene
in *Ship of Fools* she was able to interpret it. The artistic rendering
changes it only slightly:

As the bus rolled by, Jenny saw a man and a woman, some distance from
the group, locked in a death battle. They swayed and staggered together in
a strange embrace, as if they supported each other; but in the man's raised
hand was a long knife, and the woman's breast and stomach were pierced.
The blood ran down her body and over her thighs, her skirts were sticking
to her legs with her own blood. She was beating him on the head with a
jagged stone, and his features were veiled in rivulets of blood. They were
silent, and their faces had taken on a saintlike patience in suffering, abstract, purified of rage and hatred in their one holy dedicated purpose to kill
each other. Their flesh swayed together and clung, their left arms were
wound about each other's bodies as if in love. Their weapons were raised
again, but their heads lowered little by little, until the woman's head rested
upon his breast and his head was on her shoulder, and holding thus, they
both struck again. (144)

Like Laura's in "Flowering Judas," Jenny's dream illuminates a truth
about herself. The faces of the fighting Indians change to hers and
David's, and she understands at once the destructiveness of their love.
She also understands the thin line between love and hate and the pu-
rifying effect of loosed hate. By extension, she understands that this
capacity for hatred, this lust for blood, is universal, that she and David
are as close to it as the primitive Indian couple she has seen first in life
and then in her dreams.

Mary Treadwell has a similar opportunity for understanding her
own dark impulses, but she fails to translate her experience into edifying knowledge. Having decided not to go to the gala planned by the
Zarzuela dancers, Mrs. Treadwell is amusing herself in her cabin play-

ing solitaire when quite unaccountably she looks in the mirror and begins "painting a different face on her own, as she used to do for fancy dress balls." The "mask" she creates is clownish but one of "unsurpassed savagery and sensuality" (462). She sees that she looks like one of the Zarzuela dancers, and soon regards her new face as "a revelation of something sinister in the depths of her character." Mrs. Treadwell has been a superficial person, living in a polite world of convention and materialism, of dancing schools and sedate manners. She has repressed her own sexual feelings, preferring arms-length dancing with her young German officer to kissing him. She enjoys "the floating lightness and the pleasant male nearness, no weight and no burden but only a presence." However, when he envelops her "wholly, waist, shoulders, arms," brings her "instantly under control," and kisses her "violently on her mouth, which was still open in speech," Mrs. Treadwell shudders "at the same unpleasant sensation of being bitten, of the blood being drawn by suction to her mouth that had revolted her in the past" (460).

With terrifying revelation, the mask symbolizes the violence of her repressed primitive sexuality, which surfaces when the drunken Denny, thinking she is indeed one of the Zarzuela dancers, accosts her in her cabin door. Her violence is murderous, illogical, and—the narrator's word—"unpremeditated." Having put on the savage makeup, Mrs. Treadwell has tapped a depth in herself that she had suppressed all her life. But the loosing of the violence and the bloodlust has been satisfying at the same time it has been frightening. Turning back into her cabin, she smiles "delightedly at her hideous wicked face in the looking glass," and in "joy and excitement, she . . . [snatches] off her blood-stained sandal and . . . [kisses] it." However, instead of absorbing the truth about herself, Mrs. Treadwell represses it, an act symbolized by her tossing the sandal through a porthole and saying, "*Bon voyage*, my friend." She restores the old identity of innocence and propriety by washing off the mask, tying an Alice-in-Wonderland ribbon in her hair, and slipping into "her white satin gown with the bishop sleeves" (466). Like Laura's in "Flowering Judas," her outward appearance projects a protective image of unapproachable chastity, and she is reminiscent of Rosalie Caden Evans, whom Porter described as

having "a timeless feminine coquetry tempered by that curious innocence which is the special gift of the American woman" (CE 417).

Mrs. Treadwell is not changed in any significant way by the experience, but remembers "illogically" the incident with Denny as a pleasurable one. When Jenny tells her the passengers' version of Denny's
encounter with "mysterious forces," an appropriate ironic label for
Mrs. Treadwell's dark impulses, she "suddenly and surprisingly . . . [laughs] out—not a loud laugh or an empty one—a small rich
trill of merriment, of pure pleasure." Her sense of propriety in control,
she drifts "away in her strange motionless walk as if she did not use the
ordinary human muscles" (482). She does not occupy an important
position at the end of the novel but is remembered by some of the
other passengers as having failed to make any connection with them.
Wilhelm Freytag recalls that she walked rudely away from him, and
Lizzi Spöckenkieker broods "on the way Mrs. Treadwell had simply
picked herself up and left the cabin as if she were going to take a turn
on deck, and had said no farewell—not even a little, simple '*Grüss
Gott*,' which costs nothing." Had she been able to make connection
with herself, Mrs. Treadwell might have found the filament that con-
nects to others.

Close to bloodlust is the potential for evil, and to recognize this
potential is an important step toward enlightenment. Closest to meta-
physical evil in the novel are the members of the Zarzuela troupe and
Ric and Rac, Lola's twins. But Porter makes it clear, again, that evil is
not an absolute and external force in the universe but resides within,
waiting to be tapped by a catalyzing stimulus. Once remarking that she
had had a "long standing fascination with the psychology of villainy,"
she supported the theory that evil has psychological causes.[23] She also
wrote that "the refusal to acknowledge the evils in ourselves which
therefore are implicit in any human situation is as extreme and un-
workable a proposition as the doctrine of total depravity" (CE, 185).

Ric's and Rac's adventures introduce and conclude the long middle
section, "High Sea." They are namesakes of comic-strip characters,
"two lawless wire-haired terriers" who seem to their idolators to be
"real devils such as they wish to be." They do a "kind of demon dance"
around Herr Graf in his wheelchair, and Frau Rittersdorf thinks that

"those indescribable twins" are outside "of human origins." To her they are "rather, little demons one expected to blow up with a smell of brimstone and disappear before one's eyes" (268). Frau Schmitt also regards the twins as indecipherable agents of universal forces: "Trouble went where they were, confusion and ill doings. Possibly," she thinks, "it had something dimly to do with the will of God, His great mysterious plans" (356). Other passengers share Frau Schmitt's views but without her equanimity. When the twins ecstatically watch passing whales, they are warily observed by other passengers: "Deeply, deeply not one of them but would have found a sympathetic agreement with all the others that overboard, the deeper the better, would have been a most suitable location for Ric and Rac. Any one of them would have been indignant if accused of lacking any of the higher and more becoming feelings for infancy; but Ric and Rac were outside the human race. They were outside undeniably, and they had known it for a good while; it was where they chose to be and they could more than hold their own" (330). Ric and Rac as purely evil creatures without the chance for redemption is the view of the other passengers rather than of an objective narrator. Ironically, this conclusion is reached in the whale scene, white whales at that; the *Vera*'s passengers have projected evil onto Ric and Rac with the same shortsightedness with which Captain Ahab obsessively regards Moby Dick.

Ric and Rac are indeed cruel and malicious, and the reader probably shares for a while this simple view of the twins. But in a crucial scene at the end of the long part 2 Porter places them in perspective. Ric and Rac have stolen La Condesa's pearls and thrown them overboard. Lola and Tito, the parents, are horrified when informed, but only because they themselves have been denied the chance to acquire the pearls by their own devious means and also because the twins may have exposed the intentions and methods of the burglarizing Zarzuela troupe. Enraged, Lola and Tito, trying to extract admissions of guilt from the pair, torture the twins by pressing their fingernails down and by turning their eyelids back. They also threaten to stick pins under their nails and pull their teeth out. When their parents are gone, Ric and Rac crawl "into the upper berth looking for safety; they lay there half naked, entangled like some afflicted, misbegotten little monster in a cave, exhausted, mindless, soon asleep" (360). The reader knows that the source of this evil is elemental, as "cave" and "mindless" imply. The cruelty of Tito and Lola and the withholding of love from the children have destroyed "everything worth saving in them," and they are doomed to soulless existences. Long ago they, like Stephen, traveled "the downward path to wisdom."

The elder members of the Zarzuela troupe present an additional aspect of evil. In addition to the fact that there was indeed a Zarzuela group on board the *Werra* with Porter, she would have been familiar with this kind of low musical comedy group in Mexico. They were popular with all levels of Mexican society at the time Porter was there. The January 1925 issue of *Mexican Life*, for example, carried an article about the popularity of the Zarzuela. "The backbone of the theatre . . . is the native musical sketch, known as the 'zarzuela,' a mixture of rather low humor, native songs and dances, and occasionally adaptations of modern jazz songs. If the jokes are rank, the dancing fair, and the singing good, the folks go home satisfied." The writer observed that the predominantly male theatergoing public ensured that the entertainment was "spicy."[24] The real Zarzuela troupe described in notes Porter made during her voyage seemed only to suggest dashed hopes to her. She built upon a generally seamy quality in their act to create the "evil" group on board the *Vera*.

Although we cannot know the source of their evil as we can that of Ric and Rac, the narrative voice leads us to believe that it was created in just the same way, that it is passed down, as is the hatred in "The Downward Path to Wisdom." Through Dr. Schumann's eyes, the reader is allowed to see the common source of evil. Distressed over the cruel notes the dancers have been posting, particularly the one about La Condesa, the doctor naively suggests to them that they change their methods and their manners, "at least for the rest of the voyage." They stare him down after he gets the impression "that he was gazing into eyes that had got misplaced: they belonged to some species of fierce beast peering out of a cave or ready to leap in a jungle, prowling and sniffing for blood; the same expression, only older, more intensely aware and ready, that had dismayed him in the eyes of Ric and Rac" (348). The doctor, who is more human than any of the other passengers, is not intimidated by this blatant evil but is "repelled and indignant at the immunity of such insolence." Their "chilling burst of laughter . . . [follows] him down the deck" as he puts them in proper perspective. He seems to know that he shares something with them. Relying on the language of his particular Christian perspective, he thinks, "Are we not all sinners?" (349).

The evil of the Zarzuela troupe takes on forms other than their cruelty to children and their deceptiveness. One form of their cruelty has special meaning in the context of American literature because it is the evil that intrigued Hawthorne and James. According to Givner, Porter absorbed the powerful influence of Hawthorne when she lived in Salem in the fall of 1927 and the winter of 1928; not only was she reminded of him whenever she left her lodgings, but she also read or reread all his works.[25] James shared Hawthorne's view of evil as the denial of free will when the sanctity of the human heart is invaded, a view which included biographers among the invaders. Porter often complained about the mischief done by "researchers," writing to Monroe Wheeler about "those greedy, grabby birds, the crows that swarm to the planted corn field—the *biophages*, as Montherlant called them according to Julian Green—and I have seen them at work in every situation of life for half a century."[26] She told Josephine Herbst that she did not "much believe in all this personal touch system between author and public." She said, "I do love a private life, and I should like the public to read my work. That is all they need to know about me." She goes on to describe the flood of biographies about Lawrence, who recently had died, as "a perfect, shameless hyena feast."[27] Explaining the problem as a problem of the times, she wrote to a student who had sent a copy of a term paper to her, "The real plague of the artist now, and I believe for the first time in human history is, that the people of the whole world are less interested in art of any sort than ever they were before and at the same time, perversely, I think, interested in the artist *himself*, his personality, his adventures such as they may be. Sometimes a cloudy half-formed theory wanders through my mind that people having been alienated from art, the love and understanding of it, find life a little dull and pointless and don't know why, and get some kind of vicarious satisfaction out of knowing personally, seeing, or hearing gossip about, those persons who seem to be leading such independent bold lives, working at something of no use to anybody just because they like to work at it."[28]

Hawthorne's and James's "villains" function within this moral sphere. This same invasion is what the Zarzuela troupe is guilty of, for they cunningly discern the secret shames and fears of their fellow passengers, and make them public in the form of notices posted on the ship's bulletin board. They expose Herr Baumgartner's alcoholism,[29] Herr Löwenthal's feeling of inferiority, David's and Jenny's fear of artistic inadequacy, Dr. Schumann's giving drugs to La Condesa, and Herr Glocken's Kafkaesque view of himself. Both James and Hawthorne pose the question of whether the artist himself enters into this kind of evil. Other passengers on board the *Vera* parallel the Zarzuelas' invasion of the human heart: Jenny with her caricatures of her fellow voyagers, and Frau Rittersdorf with her journal, as cruel as the dancers' notices, which in turn are little more than the public versions of Frau Rittersdorf's journal entries.

It is finally only Dr. Schumann who comes close to understanding the source and nature of evil as Porter saw it. When he speaks of "the seed of evil" and when he also voices his compassionate understanding, he is illustrating Porter's dual contention that "we are all naturally depraved but . . . all naturally redeemable, too."[30] Having already noted its universality, he later points out its appeal. "The gauzy glittering surface of gaiety lay lightly over the foulest pools of evil. Yet how dull life would be without the dancing and the music and the drinking and the lovemaking and all that ecstatic confusion!" (349). The subject of evil is the center of several conversations which allow the narrator to explore contrasting views and by implication to point to one that is supported within the text of the novel. One such conversation takes place among Herr Professor Hutten, Frau Hutten, and Dr. Schumann. The professor presents the intellectual view: "The problem of good and evil is by definition insoluble. Do they really exist, except as concepts in the human mind? Even if so, how and why did they originate? Philosophically, this is unanswerable. I ask it merely for the sake of the argument." Dr. Schumann says that for him it is not a philosophical matter but a theological one: " 'I rely on the teachings of the Church and I am sorry I cannot argue the matter. I am a poor sinner,' he said, good-temperedly and dryly, 'who needs divine help every day'" (294). Dr. Schumann then proposes his theory of evil by collusion. "Our collusion with evil is only negative, consent by default, you might say." Frau Hutten, surprisingly to her husband, voices support for Dr. Schumann, but it is soon apparent that she misinterprets Dr. Schumann's views. Her husband's theories always having seemed "so far removed, so infinitely above and beyond the actual," she speaks her own mind, perhaps for the first time: "I do know well there are many evil people in this world, many more evil than good ones, evil by nature, by choice, by deepest inclination, evil all through; we encourage the monsters by being charitable to them, by making excuses for them, or just by being slack, as Dr. Schumann says." In misrepresenting Dr. Schumann's position, she illustrates the difference between her level of spiritual development and that of Dr. Schumann. His view is one of compassion and of understanding that we all drink from the same well. He has said, "I suppose in our hearts our sympathies are with the criminal because he really commits the deeds we only dream of doing!" (294). Frau Hutten is like Mrs. Thompson, who fails to see her own relationship with evil.

Dr. Schumann's theory of evil has been much abused by reviewers' and critics' misinterpretation. Some have concluded that Frau Hutten is the explicator of Schumann's view and that he indeed is saying that we collude with evil when we do nothing about it, a seeming call for zealously punishing wrongdoers and promoting "good." What Dr. Schumann means, perhaps, is what Porter called the assistance of evil by apathy, a view she may have borrowed from Aquinas, who saw evil as the absence of good or the existence of good in insufficient degree. By apathy Porter means an inability to believe in anything, an inability to pity others and to offer help, a state that she consistently describes as evil. [31] Dr. Schumann's compassion places him outside the apathy, but Frau Hutten's inability to feel pity places her closer to the kind of apathy Porter is talking about. The inhabitants of the world of "Theft" are true members of the apathetic state, but Dr. Schumann is not.

One of the proofs of Dr. Schumann's humanity is his ability to face the evil in himself, evil as he defines it in his own moral code. When he discovers that the stewardess assigned to sit with the drugged La

Condesa has left her, he suffers extreme remorse at what he sees as his own evil. "His heart gave a perilous leap of rage when he thought of her abandoned there by that cowardly stewardess, and yes—yes, abandoned by him, who had caused her to be made helpless and then had left her to her fate. In this moment of possible danger he had not given her a thought. 'God help me,' he said, almost terrified at the evil he was discovering in his own nature" (316).

A little later he contemplates the same "evil." Dr. Schumann faces "an aspect of his character he had not suspected until that hour. He had lived on flattering terms with the delusive wickedness of his own nature; comfortable in the doctrine that no man may be damned except with his own consent, and that man's desire for redemption is deathless as his own soul; and when he does evil he knows what he is doing. How could he have wronged that unhappy creature so, when he had believed he meant only to help and comfort her?" (350). It is the articulation of the import of Laura's dream in "Flowering Judas." But while Laura was horrified that she had failed in her female role of giver of life, Dr. Schumann is horrified that he has failed in his physician's role of preserver of life. His progress toward humanity is illustrated well in his willingness to face evil in the universe and in himself—for they are the same—and to suffer in the knowledge of it. Frau Hutten's view, on the other hand, illustrates only the belief that evil is external to oneself and ought to be punished. It is a misinterpretation of Dr. Schumann to see his view as a didactic reformer's view that urges us to fight evil lest we collude with it. Frau Hutten's view allows for the fighting of evil with evil, with the weapons of malice, vindictiveness, and self-righteousness.

The last, and most important, dark truth is death, the discovery and understanding of which are important steps in Miranda's awakenings in "The Grave" and "Pale Horse, Pale Rider." Several characters in *Ship of Fools* illustrate different attitudes toward death. Death as a reality is brought up in the introduction when the younger man and the older man read about the death of a young Indian servant boy. They see it only as a political "mistake" and not as the inevitable conclusion to human existence. Soon after the *Vera* sets out, the subject of death reappears, this time in the conversation of Mrs. Treadwell and Frau

Schmitt, whose dead husband lies in a coffin in the hold of the ship. A Frau Schmitt grieves aloud, "Oh it smothers me to think of it," Mrs Treadwell thinks, "It is always death, . . . for this sentimental kind i can never be less than death." Although she continues thinking, "Tha death, there beside them at the table, death was what they had i common" (30), she does not understand the implication of her ow thoughts. It soon becomes apparent that rather than accepting death a the proper destiny of human beings, Mrs. Treadwell spends much c her time trying to escape it. During the voyage she has her forty-sixt birthday. Her age, she feels, is "a downright affront" to her aestheti sense, for she sees fat, perversion, gracelessness attending old age "She was half reclining in her deck chair, partly reading an old copy o *L'Illustration* in a comfortable drowse, partly thinking about her age which had never really worried her before, when without any warnin at all she felt Time itself as a great spider spinning a thick dusty we around her life, winding and winding until it covered all—the light i shut out and the pulse shrivels and the breath is slowly smothered off— Death, death! she said, and her fright was as simple and overwhelmin as her fear of the dark when a child" (253).

Mrs. Treadwell is like Miranda in "The Circus" or Miranda early i "Pale Horse, Pale Rider," who looks at death but does not accept it Mrs. Treadwell comes back to her subject again later. Examining he image in a looking glass, she wishes "there were not those lines from nose to mouth, deeper on the right side, or that small shadow of a fol under the chin. With those away she would have nothing to worry about for a long time; but they were there, and to stay and to grov deeper, and to be joined by other shadows and folds and lines markin every step of the long solitary journey towards old age." Concernec with appearance rather than reality, Mrs. Treadwell thinks of her agin face as a mask that could be wiped off to reveal her sixteen-year-ol heart. "'What is expected of me now, I wonder,' she asked herself a she had done at fourteen, almost in the same bewilderment. I stil dance as well as I did, still ride, still swim, still like doing most of the young things I did like—still, still—what a terrible word" (413). The reason that "still" is such a dreadful word to Mrs. Treadwell is that it essential meaning is stasis—and by extension, death, which is wha she really fears. Paradoxically, it is stasis that she wants. She wants time to have stood still and herself not to have aged. Aging is the process to death, and she rejects both. She refuses to grasp, again, an essential truth that is available to her.

Other important attitudes toward death are cited in the novel. On one hand there are the bride and groom, who like Miranda in the beginning of "The Grave" have not faced their own mortality. The young bride has been repelled by Herr Graf's "blessing" but repents at once of her "uncharitable" feelings. "She knew they were caused by her horror of age and ugliness and sickness and her fear of them, and her greater fear of death, which was the only alternative, the one possible escape from them. Feeling rather sensible and calm, and joyously well and immortal, she said in a dreaming voice, 'I hope we die young.' Her husband, in the privacy of the bow, slipped his arm around her and gave her a little shake. 'Die young? We'll never die. We're going to live together until the end of the world!' They laughed together for happiness, without a trace of irony" (439–40). They do not yet "know" that death is inevitable, and they are a long way from Miranda's integrating vision of life and death in "Pale Horse, Pale Rider." The bride sees death as only an escape from sickness and age.

That, too, is how Herr Graf himself finally views death. Ironically, as he silently first discourses on it, he seems to see it as a gateway to "immortality for the suffering bewildered soul." However, doubts insinuate themselves in Graf's musings. The notion of an afterlife, he considers, may have been created by man, who "loves himself so dearly he cannot relinquish one atom of himself to oblivion" (183). His faith vanquished, he finally prays not for grace or for encasement in God's eternal love but for total oblivion: "Drop from Your great nerveless hands darkness and silence, silence and stillness, stillness of dust buried under dust, the darkness and silence and stillness of the eyeless deeps of the sea" (444). Mrs. Treadwell's terrible vision of stillness has become Graf's prayer, and his imagining God's blowing out the candles of life mirrors Granny Weatherall's final surrender of hope. It is Herr Graf's private heresy that makes his messianic pronouncements terrifyingly hypocritical.

Again, it is Dr. Schumann who offers the proper view of death.

Before he embarked on this voyage, he reached the point of understanding death that Miranda reaches in "Pale Horse, Pale Rider." "My own death," he thinks, "I know it is of no importance, . . . especially my own if I have made peace with it" (113). His words are like Porter's own: "I have always believed," she wrote her sister, "that when Death really touches you, you know and recognize it and are tamed and ready, and perhaps even happy."[32] Although Dr. Schumann longs to live, he feels in the deep waves of the sea the power of "universal harmony." His whole being reconciles itself "almost completely to the prospect of death." Because he understands death and the source of evil, Dr. Schumann emerges as the character farthest along in the process of vision.

The greatest irony in Porter's world view as it is illustrated in her fiction is that human beings live in self-contained isolation and yet are unable to learn the truths about themselves. Not grasping the core of inner truth, they look outward and see only the surfaces of others. In *Ship of Fools* Porter particularly explores the causes and effects of isolation, a theme which is implied in her other works. She has pointed out that by nature humans are separate beings. She elaborated to Barbara Thompson, "We come together only at these pre-arranged meeting grounds: . . . at his destination each . . . [is] alone."[33]

Separateness, which makes humans strangers to one another, is a theme that pervades *Ship of Fools* and is implied in the title of the excerpt previously published as "The Strangers," in which the theme is developed. Although characters in her other works of fiction coexist without understanding one another in the least, only in "Noon Wine" and *Ship of Fools* does she develop the metaphor of stranger to its fullest philosophical and ironic proportions. As she uses the idea in the shorter work, it is ironic, for the people are revealed to be kin—rather than strangers—in their common, dark, human impulses. In *Ship of Fools*, however, the passengers not only see themselves as strangers to one another but prefer it that way. Early on, before the *Vera* embarks, the harried travelers coming together in Veracruz avoid making any connection among themselves, and as the voyage gets under way they continue to perpetuate the separation. Mrs. Treadwell observes that at least half of her fellow passengers do not salute each other, "not from distaste but from indifference" (139). As the voyage nears its end, Jenny says to David, "Everybody looks tired. It's just the same as we were in Veracruz, or in Havana. We all remember we're strangers and don't like each other" (400–401). And in fact, as the *Vera* pulls into the Bremerhaven harbor, the passengers who remain prepare to end their association: "Eyes met eyes again vaguely, almost without recognition and no further speech. They were becoming strangers again, though not suspicious and hostile as at first. It was a pleasant indifference to everything" (494).

Self-absorbed isolation combined with an arrogant pride explains many of the moral flaws seen in the passengers on the *Vera*. It lies behind class consciousness, narrow-minded regionalism, nationalism, religious intolerance, and sexism—in short, it expresses itself in the myopic belief in the superiority of one group of persons and in the wrongness and inferiority of others, a human inclination toward group identification that frightened Porter. She told Archer Winston that whenever she was tempted to "join up," she refrained because she was "afraid for her mental freedom."[34] Class consciousness as a theme is developed at some length in the introductory frame set in Veracruz, where it is seen as the reason for human indifference and cruelty to one another. During the voyage class consciousness is exhibited most vividly by Frau Hutten, who has spent her married life protecting her husband, the professor, and by Frau Rittersdorf, who has escaped from lower-class poverty. On one occasion Professor Hutten is holding forth in boring discourse on various theological subjects, and his wife recalls to herself "those many years when she had interposed herself, literally, bodily, between her husband and the seamy, grimy, mean, sordid, tiresome side of life that he simply could not endure" (291). Frau Rittersdorf's identification with a class is recorded clearly in her notebook: "The innumerable heterogeneous elements so freely mingled on the ship naturally have brought on a series of most sinister occurrences, the logical consequences of such lack of discipline, the insolence of the lower classes when allowed the least shade of liberty—" (382). Always conscious of the social class from which she had come ("the awful wallow of ignorance and poverty and brutish living") and of the one to which she had ascended (she wears "immaculate light-colored shoes and gossamer stockings"), she regards her future in the same terms, her worst fear being that she will fall back into a lower social level. Considering a taxi for her return to the ship, she is stopped by "an uneasiness" about spending money for the fare: "Such extravagances, she foresaw, would be preparing for her an old age of loneliness, a servile existence in middle-class houses, a superannuated governess on board and keep with an occasional holiday tip, putting up with insufferable children in common families no young, able woman would look at. . . . If Otto could have dreamed she would be left to such a fate, would he have gone with never a thought of her to a hero's death?" (384).

Class consciousness may be related to regionalism, only a smaller version of nationalism. William Denny is the passenger who is most provincial, although others exhibit the trait, too.[35] David detests "Denny's vulgar habit of calling all nationalities but his own by short ugly names; yet even for his own he had a few favorites—'cracker' for example, but that applied strictly to people of the state of Georgia; 'white trash' was another, specifically applied to persons of low social station combined with financial insolvency, and in general to anybody whose attitude towards him or his point of view he found unsympathetic" (275). Intolerant of every place, belief, or culture that is not his own narrow one, Denny longs for a return to Brownsville, "where a man knew who was who and what was what, and niggers, crazy Swedes, Jews, greasers, bone-headed micks, polacks, wops, Guineas and damn Yankees knew their place and stayed in it" (333–34).

Although Lizzi Spöckenkieker, like the other Germans on board the ship, is avidly nationalistic, she, too, makes regional distinctions. She tells Mrs. Treadwell, "Oh, you will never learn good German if you go only to Berlin. . . . Perhaps you cannot hear the difference, but for example, Frau Rittersdorf for all her airs and graces speaks a vile Münchener accent; the Captain speaks Berliner style, atrocious; the purser speaks Plattdeutsch, the worst of all except some of those sailors from up around Königsberg who talk like mere Baltic peasants!" (213–14).

Nationalism was a particularly real force in the thirties when Porter made her voyage, and she does treat it extensively in the novel. All those passengers who are longing for their homelands do so partly out of national pride, a sense that everything will be better once "home." The most rampant nationalism seen on the *Vera* is that of the Germans during the first hours of the voyage. At the Captain's table are the German passengers (with the exception of Herr Löwenthal), who think of themselves as "the chosen ones," and their self-contained society consistently arouses their good spirits.

One of the most complex characters aboard the *Vera* is Wilhelm Freytag. His personal conflict lies in the contradiction between his own German identity and his un-German wife. "He knew he was altogether German, a legitimate son of that powerful German strain able to destroy all foreign bloods in its own veins and make all pure and German once more; and the whole world had been for him merely a hunting ground, a foraging place, a territory of profitable sojourn until the day should come when he would go home for good, having never been away in his soul. Wherever he had been, he had felt German ground under his feet and German sky over his head; there *was* no other country for him" (134).

The Germany Freytag prizes is the vanished Germany of Captain Thiele's memory, the Germany "whose existence he admitted in his soul—that fatherland of order, harmony, simplicity, propriety" (427). The Zarzuela troupe try to exploit the German national pride, but they misinterpret it and are saved from public denouncement only by the powerful self-control of the Captain. At the fiesta they hold ostensibly in honor of the Captain, they toast "those two great martyred countries, Spain and Germany" and hope that "the old splendid order might be restored—the Spanish monarchy, the German Empire, in all their glory!" (429). The Captain's nationalism having become the pure nationalism of Nazism, he has no royalist sympathies and is inwardly enraged at the dancers' presumptuousness. [36]

It is, of course, this nationalism that explains the Germans' anti-Semitism. Freytag's intense nationalism, or Nazism, cannot accept the Jewishness of his wife, Mary. In an imaginary conversation he has with her, he says, "You are no longer a Jew, but the wife of a German; our children's blood will flow as pure as mine, your tainted stream will be cleansed in their German veins" (134). But he knows that his reasoning has no support in Nazi Germany, from which he runs as he runs from the truth. As he anticipates returning with Mary to Mexico City, he thinks to himself, "They would never see Germany again, except for a miracle. Mary must be his native land and he must be hers, and they would have to carry that climate with them wherever they went; they must call that climate home and try not to remember its real name— exile" (134). Freytag's conflict is that he loves his wife—or an idealized version of her—but hates her Jewishness. He is, in fact, strongly anti-Semitic at the same time that he knows he is indelibly tied to her. The contradiction is exemplified in his anti-Semitic actions and statements and in his Jewish sympathies. Assigned to the dining table of Herr Löwenthal, the only Jew on board the *Vera*, Freytag feels "his throat closing as if he might choke on his sense of injury; one thing certain, he would not sit at the table with that Jew. . . . No, he explained to himself as if arguing with a disapproving stranger, No, it is not because he is a Jew. It is because of what has been done to *both of us*. But he will never acknowledge that any wrong has been done to anyone but himself. The thought was like a flash of light in his mind—I have no prejudice against Jews—how could I? Mary is one, Mary—but why must he worry about this wretched little man, with his comic trade— he would just be a laughingstock anywhere" (262). Although he thinks that he will have his meals sent to his cabin rather than dine with Herr Löwenthal, Freytag reveals Jewish sympathies in his refusal to eat ham and in his penchant for "swine" and "pig" as derogatory epithets. As Freytag's inner conflict approaches tragic level, his name provides the clue to his role in the drama he has chosen. Meaning Friday, his surname has inescapable associations with crucifixion. Freytag's self-sacrifice comes about by his linking himself, however reluctantly and to some extent involuntarily, to the fate of his Jewish wife.

In spite of some token protestations, few of the other German characters are ambivalent toward Jews. Although Herr Rieber says that he is not an anti-Semite, declaring that he is very fond of the Arabs, among whom he once lived, he goes on to explain that he is "anxious only that the German nation, the bloodstream of our race, shall be cleansed of their [the Jews'] poison" (230). Rieber and Lizzi represent the anti-Semitic mentality of Nazi Germany. Lizzi tells Mrs. Treadwell about Rieber's opinion of Jews, an opinion she supports. Rieber, according to Lizzi, "is part of the movement to restore German publishing, more especially in the trades and professions; it has been almost destroyed by the Jews." Lizzi describes the Jews in her business, "lingerie," as being "everywhere, making prices, cutting prices, tampering with fashions, bargaining, cheating, trying to control everything and everybody" (213).

Although Professor Hutten's views seem in contrast to those of Rieber and Lizzi, his honest feelings eventually surface. At first his opinions seem merely those of the intellectual or academic, but he cannot hold onto his detachment very long. At first he defines Jewishness as "a state of mind," but on the following day he is more candid. He nods toward Freytag and Löwenthal and tells the Captain, "Such as *They*, . . . such as They should have special quarters on ships and other public conveyances. They should not be allowed the run of things, annoying other people" (246). The Captain, who sees himself as an official representative of Nazi Germany, is uncompromising: "Let me say at once that if I had my way in the matter, . . . I should not allow one even on board my ship at all, not even in the steerage. They pollute the air" (247).

German nationalism is formulaic and structured; it has its own code and set of rules. It also is racist. However, an equally insular and uncompromising viewpoint is presented by Herr Löwenthal himself. With disdain for his persecutors, he contemplates his "inescapable destiny as Jew" and "his chosenness."[37]

With the exception of Denny, who is the supreme bigot, the Americans on board the ship seem more nearly free from such intense nationalistic and racist feelings. David deplores Denny's bigotry in general, Jenny seems to make few superficial judgments about people, their religions or races, and Mrs. Treadwell counters Lizzi's diatribe against the business dealings of Jews with, "Isn't all business low? . . . Doesn't everybody cheat?" (213). She establishes an objective position when she replies to Lizzi's question of whether she likes Jews. "Not particularly," says Mrs. Treadwell, "should I? Is there something about them?" Lizzi reacts indignantly with "Oh, you Americans who go through the world and never understand anything!" (214–15).

Only Dr. Schumann, however, has an actively transcendent view. Answering Frau Rittersdorf, who has asked him, "What do you think about Jews?" Dr. Schumann says, "I have nothing to say against them. I believe that we worship the same God" (230).

Anti-Semitism or pro-Semitism is grounded in race more than it is in religion, but it is tied to religion also. In addition to Judaism, Lutheranism and Catholicism are represented among the passengers and crew of the *Vera*. In almost every instance, religious faith requires an intolerance of other religions. Löwenthal is willing to socialize with the other passengers "so long as they keep off the subject of religion— his religion, for he did not admit the existence of any other; all religions except his own were simply a lot of heathens following false gods" (335). The Lutheran purser does not care "what happened to Catholics, their mummery was their own business. . . . That Bolshevik—those Catholics! Let them all kill each other—a good thing!" Others have no religious faith themselves and so scorn all religions. Arne Hansen expresses the strongest feelings: "If I believed in a God I would curse him. . . . I would spit in his face. I would send him to his own hell. Oh, what a foulness is religion!" (332).

One of the reasons religions are despised is that they are seen as attachments to politics. The fat man in the cherry-colored shirt hates Catholicism because he sees it as an arm of oppressive paternalistic government, while the fat man himself is hated by Lutheran and Catholic alike as a Bolshevik, an abolisher of religion. The fat man is finally brutally beaten because he says the word "freedom" in front of a priest. Cruelty and malice, rather than love and forgiveness, are the more common feelings of both the "godly" and "ungodly" aboard the *Vera*. Dr. Schumann is the only religious person among them who tolerates the religious rights of others.

A final example of insular pride and shortsightedness explored in *Ship of Fools* is sexism. It is built into German nationalism, which is based on patriarchal authority, and into formal religions, which incorporate the subservience of women. Various characters throughout *Ship of Fools* express the view of male superiority. David is the first. He considers Jenny to be "out of place" as a painter because "there had never been a really great woman painter, nothing better than some superior disciple of a great man" (77). Jenny has had to contend with such a sexist attitude most of her life. Her family has considered her alleged pursuit of art simply "desertion": "They couldn't be fooled for a moment with all that nonsense about wanting to paint, to be an 'artist.' A young woman of good family leaves her home and place for only one reason: she means to lead a shameless abandoned life where her relatives and her society cannot restrain or punish her. Artist indeed! What was to stop her painting at home in the back garden?" (186– 87).[38] David's sexism is confirmed later when he interprets Freytag's self-possession in Jenny's presence as proof of his "professional expertness of a born handler and trainer of women" (452). The observation probably tells more about David than Freytag, but indeed Freytag's sexism already has been confirmed in a scene at which David has not been present. Jenny has been dancing with one of the Cuban students when Freytag favors her "with a very German, superior smile" and asks, "Tell me, you should know this, do all women prefer thugs, and *maquereaux*, and guttersnipes at heart? What is this strange feminine taste for lowness? *La nostalgie de la boue?*" (436).

Near the end of the novel, when the passengers are disembarking, both David and Freytag are seen in a bond of sexism that is stronger than the sexual jealousy each has experienced in rivalry for Jenny's attention. "David offered his hand and Freytag gave it a good manly shake. Their eyes met, and though their faces were entirely impassive Jenny saw a curious expression pass between them—the merest flicker of a glance like light on water, but it chilled her blood. It was the wordless affirmation of pure male complicity, complete understanding from far depths of instinctive being, safe from all surface movements and perplexities of events, sympathy and a secret alliance, from which she was excluded by natural law, in their unalienable estate of manhood" (496).

The Captain's authority is patriarchal in general but also decidedly sexist. Suffering under the prattle of several German matrons at his table, he takes in "their unbalanced female emotions, their shallow, unteachable minds, their hopeless credulity, their natural propensity to rebellion against all efforts of men to bring order and to preserve rule in life" (176). Later he is offended at Mrs. Treadwell's "unfeminine frankness" about her age.

Others show their sexism in different ways. Herr Graf recalls having to combat the modesty of women in order to carry out God's directive to him. When his family and friends had told him that it was not decent for an Indian woman to let a man see her having a baby, he "had gone in boldly, pushing them aside, asserting a man's authority over them, and they gave way before him as God meant them to" (182). Herr Rieber provides one of the comedy scenes in the novel when he tries to assert his male supremacy over Lizzi. Finally getting Lizzi in the proper place for his amorous attack, he embraces her violently but meets unexpected resistance. As she pushes him backwards, he tries to "reverse the unnatural posture of affairs" and "to roll into the proper position of masculine supremacy." Unsuccessful, Rieber considers his predicament: "He must not for a moment admit discouragement. After all, this was only another woman—there *must* be a way, and he would find it. He thought with some envy of the ancient custom of hitting them over the head as a preliminary—not enough to cause injury, of course, just a good firm tap to stun the little spirit of contradiction in them" (284–86).

Neither is Dr. Schumann exempt from sexist attitudes. Struggling with his love for La Condesa, he allows himself "a brief vengeful meditation on the crockery-smashing sex, the outraged scullerymaid, the exasperated housewife of the lower classes, the jealous mistress—the sex that brought confusion into everything, religion, law, marriage; all its duplicities, its love of secret bypaths, its instinct for darkness and all mischiefs done in darkness" (237).

The relationship between Herr Professor Hutten and Frau Hutten is the most expanded example of sexism in the novel. Their marriage is based on the "main conviction . . . that a wife's first duty was to be in complete agreement with her husband at all times, no matter on what questions, from the greatest to the smallest" (295). Regarding women as "children," the professor explains the "doctrine":

> A woman's loyalty must not, cannot ever be, to her own sex, but to her men—to father, to brother, to son, finally above all and before all, to her

husband. They have no understanding of true friendship in the high noble sense as it exists so naturally between men; they are incapable of it, they are born rivals and not to be trusted with each other. There is always something tainted, hysterical, in the associations of women; nor can they be admitted to the great hermetic male society, for they have no reverence for the Truth, nor for sacred rites. (296)

The tragedy is that Frau Hutten acquiesces to this view of women. Although she sometimes privately rebels against the simple distortion, she recalls that she has read this doctrine in a number of books by respected writers, has heard it from ministers of the gospel and from her own father. "In the end, she was bound to admit that this bitter judgment was just another of those great truths she was by nature unfitted to grasp" (296).

This "great truth" is accepted also by Frau Schmitt, who likes always "to see the man taller than the woman," and by Frau Rittersdorf, who thinks it "unbecoming to the dignity of a man to submit to amorous persecutions from any woman, no matter how irresistible her charms. More properly," she concludes, "the other way about, for the crown of womanhood was suffering for the sake of love" (155). Mrs. Treadwell accepts it insofar as she accepts rules of decorum that are based on predetermined notions of womanly behavior, and Frau Lutz wishes that her husband would assume his rightful place as master. It is evident in the relationship among the members of the Zarzuela company as well. Only Jenny seems to see the horror of such limited vision.

The smugness of a narrow-minded belief in the exclusive rightness of one group of persons, whether determined by class, region, nationality, religion, or sex, points to one difficulty in reaching an enlarged vision. But other obstacles compound the difficulty. Assuming that outward order is the same as inner order, humans follow or cling to systems. Among the systems treated in the novel are those Porter dealt with elsewhere in her fiction, those of politics, religion, philosophy, and social decorum. Political systems are first apparent in the early pages of part 1 in the revolutionary background to Veracruz. The Indian boy's death is being exploited by ruthless government leaders: "An immense, honorable funeral was being planned for his remains, as a martyr to the great cause of liberty and justice; ample material compensation as well would be extended to his grieving family. Already two truckloads of floral offerings had been provided by voluntary contributions from every labor union in the city; there would be five bands to play funeral marches and revolutionary songs from the Cathedral door to the graveside, and it was expected that every working man and woman able to walk would be in the great procession" (7). The naiveté of the workers is also implied in the conversation of the two factory owners, one of whom remarks to the other that management also has a means to fight strikes: "They don't seem to realize that this kind of thing can be made to work both ways." The other says that the striking workers "don't even know they are just fighting for a change of masters" (7–8).

The conflict between revolutionary and establishment politics glimpsed in Veracruz surfaces during the voyage, primarily in the steerage among the 876 persons being deported back to "where they came from." The establishment is represented by the Catholics, and the revolutionary point of view is essentially socialist, as indeed they were in the Mexican revolution. Other political viewpoints are related to the two central ones, with Nazism being the extreme expression of the status quo principle of establishmentarianism. Nazism, predicated on a devaluation of human life, does not, Porter shows, lead to the high places of human happiness as its advocates and practitioners believe it will. The foundations of Nazism are delineated by Captain Thiele throughout the narrative. As Captain of a German ship, he believes that he belongs "to a larger plan . . . [and fulfills] his destiny in his appointed place as representative of the higher law; if he failed in his duty—and the very foundation of his duty was to exact implicit obedience from every soul on the ship, without exception—why, then the whole structure of society founded on Divine Law would be weakened by so much. He could not face such a moral catastrophe, and he need not. He would not" (174). It is difficult to uphold "the Divine Law" because of "the perpetual resistance of the elemental forces of darkness and disorder against the very spirit of civilization—that great Germanic force of life in which—and the Captain began to feel a little more cheerful—in which Science and Philosophy moved hand in hand ruled by Christianity" (216).

Immediately after these lofty thoughts, however, the Captain displays his low regard for human life and the inefficacy of the systematic "force of life." "Gazing downward" into the steerage at the passengers whom he earlier has seen as "heaps of refuse," he despises "these filthy cattle, as he should." He wonders even whether they are "lower than four-footed animals." The Captain cannot imagine himself "on any side except that of established government," and he often revels "secretly in the notion of lawless murderous fury breaking out again and again at any time, anywhere—in some place he could not even fix on the map, but always among people whom it was lawful to kill, with himself at the center, always in command and control." The Captain, "from his eminence of perfectly symmetrical morality," is "a man who steered by chart and compass, secure in his rank in an ascending order of superiors so endless the highest was unknown, invisible to him" (426–27).

Nazism is life-negating in the strongest sense and leads away from truth rather than toward it. Another version of the Captain's fantasy of legalized killing is offered by Frau Rittersdorf, who writes in her notebook, "Query, whether it would not be a benefit to the human race if there were a well-enforced law providing that all defective children should be given the blessings of euthanasia at birth or as soon afterwards as it might become evident that they are unfit?" (352).

Although Porter probably intended the reader's sympathy to go to the oppressed people in steerage, their systems no more ensure life than does that of Captain Thiele and Frau Rittersdorf. The steerage people feel murderous toward one another with only difference of politics as provocation.

The person who best presents systematic philosophy is Herr Professor Hutten, the dry, detached academic who may be a development of the academic in "The Martyr." Although it is difficult to put a label on his particular system, it is consistent in several points. But he does not practice his own doctrine. His words are meaningless, not at all from the heart. On the one hand, he expresses tolerance and optimistic faith in the redemption of everyone: "Generally," he says, "I have found that even the most unenlightened obstinate man may be approached, persuaded, won over to right feeling and irreproachable conduct if only you first demonstrate to him your own intention of dealing honorably with him in every smallest particular" (290–91). On the other hand, the Cuban students, who call him and his wife "meat-balls," elicit an expression of contradictory philosophy from him. He tells his wife they are "mere ragamuffins, naturally stupid, and stu-pidity is always evil, it is not capable of anything else." He is dismayed at his own words, which no doubt represent heartfelt emotions. "Sure-ly he did not believe that any human being, no matter how sunk in sin, was irredeemable? What had come over him? He could not imag-ine, but he could not deny either that this strange point of view struck him powerfully as revealed truth. There was such a thing as incurable love of evil in the human soul. The professor tasted such bitterness in his mouth he wondered if his gall bladder had emptied itself suddenly on his tongue" (342). After this "revelation" he changes his viewpoint to one of modified positivism. Although he now sees the students as "a lamentable example of naturally base minds incapable of the higher understanding" and "unable to endure . . . the very thought of no-bility or greatness," he incorporates his old philosophy in his consoling conclusion that "they will be given their lesson, in time" (343). The most consistent aspect of Hutten's philosophical "system" is that he adulates great thinkers: Nietzsche, Schopenhauer, Kant, Goethe, Shakespeare, and Dante, one suspects in that order. He has built his ideas on the sepulchers of the past and depends not on his own insights but on the codified ideas of others.

Hutten's "philosophy" is largely theological in its concern with the nature of good and evil and the role of man in relation to God. But it is not ritualistic, as is the Catholicism or Lutheranism held by other passengers. In their blind obedience to the codes and laws of a particu-lar religion, the "godly" on board the *Vera* seem not to find God at all. Their insularity and arrogance are tied to theological hatred and lead only to malice, cruelty, and disdain rather than to love.[39] The most spectacularly religious person is Herr Graf, and his religion not only is hollow, as we have seen, but is a sublimation for his own repressed sexuality. Only Dr. Schumann, whose religion seems to serve him rather than he it, approaches the heart of sacred teachings. But even Dr. Schumann discovers that the rituals of religion, if not in touch with true emotions, are useless. When he has confessed his love for La Condesa to Father Garza, the priest's admonitions and directions change "nothing" and mean "nothing." Elsa Lutz makes the same discovery when she searches the Bible for help. "It's no use," she babbles, "nothing helps. I can't find anything in it that tells me how to live . . ." (484).

The other "system" that Porter deals with in *Ship of Fools* is that of social decorum, a theme that has interested her throughout her fiction. Many of the characters not only make judgments about one another based on a code of social propriety but also follow such a code as a way of life. Mrs. Treadwell is the character who best represents the theme. Her very name is significant: Treadwell. The kind of name found in Restoration comedy (appropriately based on manners), it suggests the care with which the lady walks. Moreover, she has her feet planted firmly in the physical world. Superficial, proper, decorous, she avoids life's dark truths available to her. She is a foil to Mary Champagne, Freytag's wife, who is not grounded in the physical world at all but is an illusion that the reader sees through Freytag's eyes; the name they share is again an ironic reminder of their own distance from a divine ideal, as is the María shared by María Rosa and María Concepción. Mrs. Treadwell is also a foil to La Condesa, who flouts all social codes.

Mrs. Treadwell was a pampered child, living in luxury, which she mistook for love. The result of that childhood of boarding schools and nurses is that she has existed without being able to make a human connection. She cannot remember the name of her boarding school roommate, she made a bad marriage, and when her parents were killed in a car accident she did not return for the funeral. She disembarks without saying anything to her fellow voyagers.

Mrs. Treadwell spends her life searching for meaning in a place that is idealized to the point of being an illusion. Her ideal is Paris, as Germany is for many of the passengers, Switzerland for some, Spain for others, Brownwood for William Denny. Her waking dreams focus on the rosy adventures she will have in Paris. She prays, "Oh God, I'm homesick. I'll never leave Paris again, I promise, if you'll let me just get there this once more" (212). Paris, in fact, is heaven to Mrs. Treadwell. "What she wanted to hear, God let her live to hear again, was Parisian in every street and alley and *place* and park and terrace in Paris, all of it, from Montmartre to Boulevard St. Honoré to St. Germain to Ménilmontant; from the students on Mont-Ste.-Geneviève to the children in the Luxembourg—the speech of Paris, and in every accent from the Haute Savoie and the Midi to Rouen and Marseille." She wishes she might "sleep the voyage out or be dead drunk all the way" (214). The hollowness of the ideal is conveyed in a kind of dream Mrs. Treadwell has near the end of the voyage, a dream that ought to foreshadow the dashing of her hopes for happiness in Paris: "A small deep wandering sensation of disgust, self-distaste came with these straying thoughts. She remembered as in a dream again her despairs, her long weeping, her incurable grief over the failure of love or what she had been told was love, and the ruin of her hopes—what hopes? She could not remember—and what had it been but the childish refusal to admit and accept on some term or other the difference between what one hoped was true and what one discovers to be the mere laws of the human condition?" (481).

Such places as Mrs. Treadwell's Paris or an idealized Germany are illusions of perfection. The Edenic myth of a perfect place from which one came and to which one continually seeks to return underlies the illusion. It explains why Mrs. Treadwell is "homesick" for Paris and why others have invested their memories of "the homeland" with Golden Age qualities that are contradictory to the apparent reality. The illusiveness of the ideal is confirmed at the end of the novel when the *Vera*'s German passengers are lining up to disembark and to "escape to life once more": "For a moment all the faces were raised, eyes searching out the roofs of the town, filled and softened with generous feelings—their hearts beat freely and their stomachs trembled with the illusion of joy; all mysteriously entranced as if they approached a lighted altar, they prepared to set their feet once more upon the holy earth of their Fatherland" (494). It is a particular illusion Porter has treated in "The Leaning Tower."

An interesting contrast, which again shows the difference between Dr. Schumann and his compatriots as well as most of his other fellow voyagers, is his notion of "home." Dr. Schumann looks like the idealized German toward which the student Hans, of "The Leaning Tower," aspires. With an aristocratic bearing and a beauty of a dueling scar, he is admired by his countrymen: "The highest kind of German good breeding, they could see, with the dignity of his humane profession adding still more luster; and his fine scar, showing that he had gone to a great university, that he was brave and coolheaded: so great a scar so perfectly placed proved that he had known the meaning of the *Mensur*, that measure of a true German. If he seemed a little absent, thoughtfully silent, that was his right; it belonged to the importance of his duties as ship's doctor" (40). Even the Captain, who thinks highly of himself, regards the doctor as an equal. But the doctor does not have what James called a "superstitious valuation" of Germany. He recognizes the universality of the human condition ("I have seen all this before, over and over, only never until now did I see it on a ship" [197]), and moreover he knows that truth is within rather than without. Instead of thinking of Germany as "home," he thinks of his own body as "home": He longs "so deeply . . . to stay safely within himself, a place he knew as home, he could not control the warm wave of excitement that ran all through him as if he had drunk hot spiced wine" (113).

Porter treats still other illusions in the novel. There is, of course, the illusion of visible order, which she has explored in "The Jilting of Granny Weatherall" and "Holiday." The Huttens, Frau Baumgartner, and Mrs. Treadwell are "orderly," as the Zarzuela dancers are "disorderly." But Captain Thiele is the person in the novel who most exemplifies order. In one sense he is Nazi Germany, and he remembers the Germany of his youth, the one to which Nazism would return, as "the fatherland of order" (427). The ideal of orderliness is at the heart of the nationalism that is Nazism. The Captain tells Frau Schmitt, "To put people in their proper places and keep them there cannot be called severity, nor defense. It is merely observing and carrying out the natural order of things" (248). Unlike Dr. Schumann, Captain Thiele has no vision or insight into the truth of things. Visible order does not ensure inner order, or truth, as Granny Weatherall tragically discovers, but as he and others do not. The value on patterns and orderliness reflects a desire to structure the chaos that is life.

The most elaborate illusion in the novel is Mary Champagne, Freytag's wife. The reader knows her only through Freytag's thoughts and
conversations, which reveal more about him than they do about her.
Near the end of part 1 Freytag's story emerges: "He, a German of a
good solid Lutheran family, Christian as they come, against terrible
opposition from both families, against his own better judgment,
against all common sense and reason, had married a Jewish girl with a
beautiful exotic name, Mary Champagne" (63). A strange name for a
Jewish girl, it is explained: "The family had come from wherever Jews
did come in the Middle Ages, and had dropped Abraham ben Joseph
or whatever it was, named themselves for the district and settled down
for a few hundred years. Some of them turned Catholic or married
Gentiles and were kicked out, and changed their names once more
and became really French; but Mary's branch were diehards and they
started roaming again, through Alsace into Germany, God knows why.
Pretty poor judgment it seemed to him. But they kept the fine French
name they had picked for themselves. And they all made a point of
broad-mindedness and liberality, and mingled socially with Gentiles, if
they were of the right class and would still have them" (63).

If Freytag's account is accurate, the choosing of a name by Mary's
family was the creation of an illusion, a false front that belied the
truth. While champagne is indeed the name of a district, its common
referent is the effervescent wine of the region. Champagne clouds the
reason and distorts reality, as Mary's family has done and as Freytag
himself continues to do. Herr Rieber, for example, in a highly comic
scene, relies on champagne to get Lizzi in a properly receptive mood
for his amorous advances; the purser carries the illusion still further by
refusing to use the French word to describe the German bubbling
wine—he insists on "Schaumwein," which sounds suspiciously like
"champagne." Porter also may have been alluding to Marie of Champagne, the daughter of Eleanor of Aquitaine, who introduced the system of courtly love into northern France. Marie is remembered as
having impressed upon Court society Chrétien de Troyes, who declared that his romances, which became the representatives of the
chivalrous and courtly ideal of twelfth-century society, owed their existence largely to Marie of Champagne. Her name became synonymous

with the courtly love ideal and is an effective choice for that of Freytag's wife.[40]

The Mary Champagne that Freytag describes is a model of gentility and beauty. "She is a little golden thin nervous thing, most beautiful and gay in the morning, she is innocent, innocent, she makes life charming where she is, when she talks it is like a bird singing in a tree!" (258). She is amusing and "has a knack," he tells Mrs. Treadwell, "for making everybody around her comfortable." "Life," he adds, "goes on better wherever she is." The telling comment by the narrative voice is "And for a moment he was reassured by the sound of his own words." The truth is that a more balanced view of Mary occasionally creeps into Freytag's thoughts, and it reveals the disparity between the idealized Mary and the real Mary. Once feeling hostile toward Jenny, he consoles himself with imagining Mary's reaction to her: "Mary would size her up in a glance, and dispose of her in a phrase—some shrewd and murderous flick of the tongue that need not be in the least true, or even near the mark, but it would be deadly and would make him ashamed of his interest in such a girl" (412).

Moral definition is made difficult by the unwillingness or inability of persons to face the available truths within their own natures. Porter believed that pure art and pure religion, and sometimes science, could light the way to inner truth, but such purity was rare. In *Ship of Fools* only Dr. Schumann's religion seems to be pure, and the examples of art seem lost on most of the *Vera*'s passengers. The primitive art of the woodcarver in the steerage is appreciated only by David, Jenny, and Dr. Schumann among the passengers on the higher deck.

Beyond art and religion but closely linked to them lies the greatest illuminator, love. The potential for love exists within as surely as does the potential for evil, but like evil it has to be tapped—or "learned," as Porter says. The theme of love is the most pervasive one in the novel, and it is tied securely to Porter's large design. Many of the characters talk about love, even philosophize about it, but few understand what it is. Porter said that "it is hardly possible to exaggerate the lovelessness in which most live, men and women: wanting love, unable to give it, or inspire it, unable to keep it if they get it, not knowing how to treat it, lacking the humility, or the very love itself that could teach them how to love: it is the painfullest thing in human life."[41] Love is noticeably scarce in the early pages set in Veracruz, where malice and cruelty characterize the port society. One of the first to discuss it is Elsa Lutz, who yearns for it without knowing what it is. She describes her dilemma to Jenny: "My father, all my life, told me to believe in love, and to be loving, and it would make me happy; but my mother says it is all just make-believe. Sometimes I wish I knew—" (66). Jenny looks at Elsa's double chin, oily skin, and gross ankles and understands in a flash the human condition: "And inside, there groped blindly, the young innocence and the longing, the pained confused limited mind, the dark instincts winding upon themselves like snails" (67). Elsa's story, published separately earlier as "The Prisoner," is Violeta's story of being caught between two unreconciled ideals, as the title suggests. Jenny later sees that Elsa on the one hand confuses lust with love, probably the result of her mother's views, or idealizes it as her father does. When she sees obviously romantic films, like Rosaleen O'Toole she accepts them as real. As she recounts the plots carefully to Jenny, saying how "sweet" and "beautiful" the stories were, they stand revealed as fairy tales.

Freytag has romantic notions about love not very different from Elsa's. Love as Freytag describes it is always related to his wife and is as much an illusion as his wife. When Freytag talks to Jenny about love, "flowers" creep into his sentences as "life, death, even eternity" are mentioned: "bread and wine, with the perpetual recurrence of hopeful mornings with no evil memories and no remorses" (168). Jenny's honest reaction that Freytag's words seem "sick and sentimental and false" (168) reflect Porter's already established view of romantic love.[42] Freytag's declarations of profound love for the elusive Mary Champagne have a hollow ring in view of his amorous attentions to both Jenny and Mrs. Treadwell. For all her unwillingness to face her own inner truths, Mrs. Treadwell is able to recognize the truth about Freytag: "She did not trust Freytag for a moment, he was obviously a born scene-maker" (259). Freytag is an illusion-maker, the habitual actor, always onstage, setting up props, and providing lines for the characters he creates, including the one that he himself plays.[43]

According to their concepts of love, the passengers seem to fall into several groups: those who separate sex from romantic love, such as the Huttens and Freytag, and those who hopelessly confuse them, such as Elsa. There are also those who, like Johann, Denny, David, the Cuban students, and Mrs. Treadwell, recognize lust but fear even the word *love*. Moreover, there are those who call lust love, like Herr Graf and the Zarzuela members. Only Jenny and Dr. Schumann (and perhaps La Condesa) understand the integrating relationship between sexual and spiritual love that gives the lie to the romantic notions of Freytag and Elsa.

Male-female love relationships or attempted relationships aboard the *Vera* are numerous. There is the perverted sexual love of the Huttens and the Baumgartners, the sheer animal pleasure of the newly married Mexican couple, the playful antics of Herr Rieber and Lizzi, the sexual contracts labeled "love" by the Zarzuela dancers, and the idealized love for a dead or absent mate, illustrated by Frau Rittersdorf, Frau Schmitt, Señora Ortega, and Freytag. The two relationships which are developed most fully during the *Vera*'s voyage and which concurrently develop the primary theme are the relationships between Jenny and David and between Dr. Schumann and La Condesa. One is a failed relationship, and one is not.

The names by which Jenny and David address one another—"Jenny angel" and "David darling"—are superficial because neither loves the other in a profound or adoring way. When Jenny and David are first seen, they are unnamed but obviously in conflict, staring "at each other like enemies." Even their choice of voyages had been the compromise of a quarrel. They continue fluctuating between bickering and coming together with "angel" and "darling" on their lips, but the bickering lasts longer than the harmony. They in fact spend much of the voyage in argument. The cause of the disharmony between the two of them, however, lies more with David than with Jenny, because David is in disharmony with himself. He has rigid ideas about art, love, sex, and politics, in contrast to Jenny's fresh and unrestricted responses. In Porter's view it is the contrast between life and death, and the most important step Jenny takes in her own process of vision is to recognize David's life-negating characteristics. It has the illuminating power of Isabel Archer's recognition of Osmond's "evil eye," of his "faculty for making everything wither that he touched." The reader should have reached this conclusion about David early on, but Jenny reaches it during a scene with Freytag, with whom she compares David:

> That's one thing about David. He'll never be mooning around about love to any other woman. He won't even talk about it to me. David hates love worse than I do, even. You've got a roving eye and the sidelong approach. If you belonged to me I wouldn't trust you any further than I could throw you by the ear. I can always trust David. David is going to be mean and tough and stubborn and faithful to death. We aren't going to kill each other because I mean to get away before that happens. But we'll leave dents in each other. When I get through with David, he'll know the difference between me and the next woman, and I'll be carrying David like a petrified fetus for the rest of my life. She felt empty and sick and tired enough to lie down. (169)

Somewhat later she wishes "with the quiet fury of a high fever" for a place to spend a few nights with Freytag, to signal "the abandonment of a dream" (307).

Even David has a flash of insight into a half-truth. Denny has told David that he would put Jenny "out of circulation" if she belonged to him. David responds: " 'Well, she doesn't belong to you,' and added, with a stroke of lightning revelation, 'She doesn't belong to anybody, not even to herself.' He heard this with some astonishment, then felt instantly he had crossed a line into a new truth and was even then looking back calmly on the old false hopes" (438–39). David's new truth consists of knowing that one person cannot own another, in much the same way that Porter explained the impossibility of fully knowing someone else. David is wrong, however, in thinking that Jenny does not belong to herself. She belongs to herself more than does any of the others, except Dr. Schumann. Although both Jenny and David know that their love affair is over, neither is ready to let go. David has said, "We've crossed a line, it's all over, why can't we say so and let go?" Jenny replies, "Does it have to be a wrench? Do we have to break bones? I wish we could let it come of itself, when we are ready for it—when it won't hurt so much! We'll get used to it gradually—" (478). Right before they disembark, it is Jenny who poses the question:

"David, we aren't going to spend our lives together, why are we going on with this?" He reminds her: "Don't you remember? We aren't ready yet" (496).

The love affair between Dr. Schumann and La Condesa is different. Its unfolding leads to Dr. Schumann's greatest and most painful awakening. From the moment of her appearance on board the ship she is an enigma and an affront to all Dr. Schumann's values. Through her, however, he learns about himself. The real person on whom her character was modeled is described by Porter in her log as a mad woman being deported back to the Canary Islands.[44] But again, Porter was able to build upon a fact for the amplification of her theme. Although Porter makes La Condesa's madness uncertain, even ambiguous madness was highly useful in the character of Dr. Schumann's beloved. Madness, like love, is inexplicable and irreducible, and cannot be placed in a pattern.

La Condesa's presence is known before she herself appears. Gossiping with Jenny, Freytag tells about "a mysterious stranger aboard, a real political prisoner, being deported from Cuba, it was said, in connection with the student riots that led to the closing of the University—to be confined in cabin for the whole voyage, finally to be put off the ship at Santa Cruz de Tenerife" (87). She is said to be a Spanish countess, "and to the Captain . . . that alone makes all the difference possible" (87). A little later Elsa overhears one of the Cuban students talking about *La Cucaracha Mystica*. "The mystical cockroach himself," he says, "the queen of insects, is on board this ship, the very figure of rampant idealism. I saw her. She is here, pearls and all, a prisoner" (103).

When she first makes her appearance in the dining room, the students greet her with elaborate, mocking respect, and everyone in the room turns to stare at her. Dr. Schumann's tone and glance are "dryly professional." But when he sees La Condesa again, he becomes "very thoughtful." He observes "with a good deal of moral disapproval" that whenever she saw a man alone, any sort of man so long as he was young, . . . whether sailor or officer or passenger, she backed him into a corner, or against a wall, or rail, and somehow managed to pin him there, standing before him and talking always in the same intimate way, as if she were imparting some agonizing secret with which they would be bound to sympathize." He is "shocked deeply" at her stroking her own breasts and thighs, patting the faces of her listeners, and laying her hands upon their hearts—this nevertheless with a "grief-stricken" face and a "grave and hopeless" tone. Although Dr. Schumann tries to explain such behavior to himself from the standpoint of his professional experience as a sign of "innate perversity" in older persons, "especially women," he begins to intuit something of the mystery of La Condesa. Still observing her, he thinks, "At the very bottom of life there is an unanswerable riddle" (115–16).[45]

When Dr. Schumann responds to her request to see him in her room, he discovers that she is addicted to drugs. When he sees her making erotic gestures to the Cuban students, he concludes "with resignation, and a great temptation to give her up, to make no further attempts to help her." But in spite of his intentions he begins to love her. Frau Schmitt sees it in his eyes before he himself knows it, but it is La Condesa who declares her love first: "Not so much you, perhaps, though you are very nice, but I love what you are" (200). When she asks him whether he loves her, he says, "No, . . . not at all. Not at all if I know in the least what love is." When he faces the truth of his love for her, he faces the reasonlessness and illogic of pure love, its incapacity for pattern, something Porter, whose long history of liaisons with unlikely male partners, could understand. La Condesa flouts "the principles of . . . [Dr. Schumann's] whole life," his religious views, which include fidelity to the marriage vows, his regard for propriety, and his notions of femininity. He prays for help: "Mother of God, be my refuge!" But his head clears "as if the demons had fled," only when he acknowledges that "he had loved her from the first before he admitted it was love" (237–38).

La Condesa is the agent of Dr. Schumann's progress toward truth. His progress is like Laura's in "Flowering Judas" but goes further. Laura's dream at the end focuses on the death of Eugenio, to whom she had given drugs to ease his boredom. When he takes an overdose, her guilt, symbolized in her dream, arises from her abetting his death rather than nurturing him into life, a role that contradicts her natural one of female. Dr. Schumann's agony arises for much the same reason; having continued to provide drugs for La Condesa, and having fallen in love with her, he has violated all the principles of his religion, his society, and his profession. Before she leaves the ship he tells her, "I have not loved you innocently, . . . but guiltily and I have done you great wrong, and I have ruined my life" (369). All that he gives her is a prescription for drugs and a note to a doctor so that she will not be allowed to suffer. After her departure, when he faces his truth, he suffers "the psychic equivalent to a lightning stroke." He sees his recent actions as symptomatic of his "moral collapse." "He had refused to acknowledge the wrong he had done La Condesa his patient, . . . he had tormented her with his guilty love and yet had refused her—and himself—any human joy in it. He had let her go in hopelessness without even the faintest promise of future help or deliverance. What a coward, what a swine" (373).

In reaction to his new truth, he tries to get a message to La Condesa with his office address and his telephone number, the address of the International Red Cross headquarters, and a request that she write to let him know where a letter might find her at all times. He renews "his anxious inquiries for her health" and asks that a reply be sent before the ship sails. The message is a professional one, that of a guilt-ridden physician inquiring after a patient he has improperly treated. His action has been foreshadowed all along in his single identification as physician; we know him only as "Doctor" and never with a given name. His message deserves no reply from La Condesa and receives none. The purser tells the doctor that Madame had read the doctor's letter in the presence of a police agent, whom she had thanked, and "said there was no answer" (375). Afterwards Dr. Schumann dreams the dream of the betrayer:

> In his waking sleep La Condesa's face floated bodiless above him, now very near, peering into his eyes; then retreating and staring and coming again in ghostly silence. The head rushed away into the distance, shrunken to the size of an apple, then bounded back, swollen and white like a toy balloon tossed upward by a hand, a deathlike head dancing in air, smiling. Dr. Schumann in his sleep rose and reached up and out before him and captured the dancing head, still smiling but shedding tears. (469)

The head's asking him, "Oh, what have you done?" and "Oh, why, why?" is the equivalent of Eugenio's calling Laura "murderer." Unlike

Laura, he does not awake afraid of the darkness that contains the truth, but holds "the head tenderly between his spread palms and. . .[kisses] its lips and . . . [silences] it; he goes "back to bed with it" where it lies "lightly on his breast without smiles or tears, in silence, and he [sleeps] . . . on so deeply he . . . [does] not know it . . . [is] a dream" (469–70). His going to bed with it symbolizes his absorption of the truth and his acceptance of the suffering that accompanies it.

Although the love affair of Dr. Schumann and La Condesa is the most catalytic relationship in the novel, a more pervasive form of love treated by Porter is that tied to the dominant symbol of the journey, parental love with its major representative, maternal love. Although parental love is treated in various relationships, mother love and mother-child relationships receive the strongest emphasis. Real child-parent relationships are exhibited in the Lutzes and Elsa, the Baumgartners and Hans, and Tito and Lola with Ric and Rac; family relationships are remembered by Mary Treadwell and by Jenny. Perversions of the father-child relationship are seen in some others. When Johann and Herr Graf are first seen, for example, it is as a parody of father and son: "The dying man in the wheel chair" is "being pushed along like a baby in a carriage by the tall angry-looking boy" (73). The image is reinforced later when Herr Graf remembers a hospital in Mexico where the nurses fed him warm milk and cool fruit juices "through a glass tube . . . as if he were a baby again." The image is ironic because only Herr Graf's frailty prevents him from asserting himself physically over Johann. Like Lawrence's sexually repressed sadists, the dying man thinks that not so long ago his hands would have had the strength to thrash Johann "as he deserved." He muses, "For such as he there was only one remedy—to mortify the flesh until the hard knot of the will was reached and dissolved—ah, a task he might have done so well, and would have so delighted in" (180–81).

The oppressed, cruel Johann does not feel fatherly toward his uncle, and himself becomes the baby when he finally grasps Concha. To her he smells "like a clean baby." When his uncle gives him the money he wants, Johann's hard heart momentarily melts and he treats his uncle kindly: "He fought this new strange feeling as he undressed the little skeleton carefully as he had been taught, without immodest exposure in the change from dress to nightgown, lifting the arms one at a time and laying them down gently, pulling the gown over the swollen knee joints and lifting the limp body in his arms as if it were a child's, straightening the limbs, and tucking in the blanket lightly. 'There you are,' he said, in a husky voice" (443).

As Johann dashes off to buy Concha's services, he seems at first to have been saved from the darkness by an act of love. But it soon becomes clear that there are other ways to "mortify" and "thrash" without the hands. Johann resists "the softening of his heart towards his uncle, though he could not deny it. He argued with himself that his uncle had done for him only what he should have done long ago, and without waiting to be asked, much less threatened. Johann thought almost in despair, 'I'll never get rid of this—never—'" (444). Herr Graf has laid on Johann a burden of guilt, the consequences of which are more terrifying than any mortification of the flesh.

Mother-love is love idealized in the Queen of Heaven, who in the Christian mythos Porter draws upon bears the mortal god who must be sacrificed to show God's love for humankind. The maternalism theme can be explained partly by Porter's own relationship to a maternal ideal; the mother who died when she was two remained an elusive figment of her dreams all her life.[46] Givner claims that it was the void Porter was trying always to fill. For her, maternalism was elemental; it was of the earth, it was nature itself. It was nourishment, and it was life. Her Mexican experience added another dimension to her concept, as she regarded the Earth goddess Xochitl, who provided food for nourishment and drugs for forgetting. On the ship the symbol of elemental and perfect maternalism is provided by Señora Ortega and her newly born son: "Folded together, mother and baby slept as one in soft animal ease, breathing off sweet animal odors, cradled both like unborn things in their long dark dream." The obsessive yearning for mother-love, which Porter knew firsthand, is illustrated by Señora Ortega's Indian maid, Nicolasa, who often hears her dead mother's voice while she sleeps. The voice says, "'Nicolasa,' . . . very tenderly as if she were a child again" (131).

Other mother-child relationships fall short of the ideal, ranging from the simple yearning for an absent mother's love to a false, deluding substitute for maternalism. Porter shows that the absence of mother-love accounts for moral perversions. First, there are husbands and wives whose unequal relationship depends on the wife's mothering the husband. To protect him from the seamy world, Frau Hutten has carried her husband's books, paper parcels, suitcases, string bags, "and even pushed a market cart before her like a baby carriage" (291). Frau Baumgartner is an unwilling and stern mother to her husband, who always plays the child. Frau Rittersdorf remembers her dead and idealized Otto as if she were his mother.

The most perverse mother-child relationships in the novel are those of Frau Baumgartner and Hans and of Frau Hutten and the bulldog Bébé. Frau Baumgartner does not want to be the mother substitute for her husband, but she is compelled into that role because of his irresponsible and childlike behavior. Consequently, she turns her relationship with her son into something other than what it ought to be. Her maternity is oppressive. When Hans and his father begin their merrymaking in anticipation of the Zarzuelas' party, his mother's voice with the "familiar warning note in it" chills "the back of his neck" and stops him "in his tracks." "Come and kiss me," she says. After a particularly nasty and hate-filled scene between the two parents, Frau Baumgartner goes trembling to Hans and offers to tell him a story. Her unhealthful and unnatural attachment to her son is implicit: "Once upon a time there were a little brother and sister who lived in the Black Forest. His name was Hansel—Hans, like you; and hers was Gretel, like me; and one day they were wandering in the woods, picking flowers, when there came an old witch . . ." Later when the parents come together in sensual reconciliation, they fondle Hans instead of each other, and he feels "imprisoned" by them and looks "like any other lost, unhappy neglected child" (456–58).

Frau Hutten and Bébé apparently are modeled on Porter's sister Mary Alice ("Baby") and a bulldog Baby once owned. When the unnamed Huttens are first seen, Frau Hutten's relationship with the white bulldog surfaces. In response to Jenny's "That's a sweet dog," Frau Hutten declares in anthropomorphic pathos: "Oh, my poor Bébé, he is so good, . . . and so patient, and I am only afraid sometimes he may think he is being punished, with all this." She pours "a little beer on her handkerchief and . . . [wipes] his big face tenderly, and almost tenderly, she . . . [ignores] the unsightly, improperly dressed American girl" (15). Frau Hutten's inhumanity and anthropomorphism are clear. Professor Hutten treats Bébé with his customary academic detachment, but his wife has found in the bulldog a substitute child and an outlet for her pent-up maternalism. When the seasick Bébé is recovering, Frau Hutten feeds him a very good meal. "The dear blessed one," she says, "with his so fine instinct and feelings, eating his food humbly face downward like any animal; it is a great pity. He is too good for that" (78).

When Bébé is thrown overboard by Ric and Rac and is saved by the artist Etchegaray, who dies doing so, the distraught Frau Hutten is concerned only with Bébé. As the nearly drowned dog is laid on the deck, she kneels beside him, weeping loudly "like a mother at the graveside of her only child" (315). When Dr. Schumann finds the Huttens, they are bowed "like a sculptured Pietá over the prostrate form of Bébé." They have been oblivious to Etchegaray's sacrifice, and when told by Dr. Schumann, they show again their inhumanity; they suspect Etchegaray might have hoped for a reward, and only seconds later cannot remember his name. Ironically, it is Frau Hutten who is aggrieved at Ric and Rac's calling her and her husband "meatballs" because she is "only tired of the unkindness of people to each other" (342). She does not understand love, either human or divine, and she does not understand herself.

Porter goes a step further and blames some characters' moral blindness on incomplete relationships with their mothers or fathers. David has told Jenny "that his mother had not been able to keep him after she was deserted by his father—he had a nasty younger brother who cultivated asthma as a means of getting his mother's whole attention—and she had turned him over to be brought up by three dreadful, sour-smelling old great-aunts" (147–48). Just as David's fear of love is blamed on his mother, Johann's cruelty is implicitly blamed on his "hard-hearted" mother; Captain Thiele's sense of discipline is rooted in a beating his father gave him at age three when he had put his toe over the edge of a grass plot that bore the sign *Verboten* (428); Ric and Rac have been the creation of their parents; and Mrs. Treadwell's loveless childhood has formed many of her moral limitations.

In addition to the maternal ideal as nurturer, mirrored in Señora Ortega and her baby son, other aspects of the ideal are suggested in the story La Condesa tells Dr. Schumann about her sons. She explains why she allows the students to treat her disrespectfully; when Dr. Schumann says they should treat her with the regard due a mother, she is amused. "Do not all boys speak disrespectfully of women of any age?" she asks, laughing. "I am not their mother! If I were, they might have better manners, better family, better minds, more imagination, and I think, I am almost certain, they would be somewhat better-looking, too. No, I am attached to them because they were schoolfellows of my sons, my charming young madmen who must go running off after something they called the Revolution!" The woman on whom Porter based La Condesa's character was clearly mad, and in the log kept during the real journey Porter explains that the countess had no real sons but was mother to the revolution. If La Condesa is not mad, she at least is addicted to drugs, and so her words are always suspect. What is important, however, is that she extends maternal love to the irreverent students in the name of an ideal.

The real world is not an ideal one, and humans have to react to reality. Of all the characters on the ship, Jenny seems to have looked clearheadedly at her own family (vaguely unspecified in roles and relationships) and to transform her family experience into knowledge. She has placed them in proper perspective. She thinks, "Ah well, the family can get under your skin with little needles and scalpels if you venture too near them: they attach suckers to you and draw your blood from every pore if you don't watch out. But that didn't keep you from loving them, nor them from loving you, with that strange longing, demanding, hopeless tenderness and bitterness, wound into each other in a net of living nerves." Having gone beyond the other passengers, Jenny has a view of family that is elevated over mere absorption of influence. "She had spent years of strategic warfare trying to beat those people out of her life; then more years trying to ignore them; to forget them; to hate them; and in the end she loved them as she knew well she was meant in simple nature to do" (186). Jenny's words are much like Porter's words in a letter she wrote to Albert Erskine while she was visiting her family in Texas. She says, "I'll be glad when I am out of this, if one is ever out, really. I imagine one has a family for all eternity, in one way or another there they are, all those people of a blood bond."[47]

It remains, finally, to understand the symbolism of the *Vera*'s voyage that makes up *Ship of Fools*. The journey, framed by Veracruz and Bremerhaven, begins in the new world and ends in the old. Although it is a reversal of the mythic voyage of Columbus from the old world to the new, from cultural stasis to new-day hope, it is not Whitman's passage to India. Porter expands the irony fully: returning to the old world should have been a movement to the world of spirit, but Henry Adams's nightmare of the dynamo has replaced the world of art and religion, and the end of the voyage is, in fact, a state of moral decline.

Thus, Herr Glocken, the hunchback passenger whose name means bell and suggests time's tolling and whose being is grotesque (his face lined with fathomless wrinkles like Ottilie Müller's), is an ironic symbol of the guardian to the gateway of knowledge. Like the fig tree, the hump on his back is regarded as lucky, here by the Zarzuela dancers, who miss his symbolic link to life's mysteries.

Most of the characters on the *Vera* end the voyage as they began it, unaware and inhuman. Throughout the voyage Porter gauges the characters' progress with images of animals, dolls, fetuses, hunger, cold, poverty, and blindness. The animal imagery is especially heavy in part 1 in the opening frame, when it is useful in showing humankind's insensate animal cruelty to itself and its state of spiritual unenlightenment. Although it is sustained throughout the novel, other images are added to it in a terrifying picture of failure.

More negative images are those that refer to imitations of living things or to dead things. The Zarzuela company, themselves unnatural and malicious, create many imitations of life. At their fiesta the dining room is decorated in lace paper flowers and a stuffed dove and is engulfed in "an almost lethal cloud of synthetic rose scent." They parody everything from the Viennese waltz and the nobility (they call Amparo and Concha "doña") to Life itself, as their final "Viva!" ironically underscores.

Several characters are described in images of dolls—nonliving, but horrifyingly realistic, imitation humans. Lizzi is described as a "jointed doll" (464), a young German officer who dances with "waxlike smoothness" is "inhuman looking as if he were poured into a mold" (434), and David's face is viewed by Frau Schmitt as "like a wax face with blue marble eyes" (388). Falling short of birth as humans, some characters are seen as fetuses. The Cuban medical students "haven't been born yet," Frau Rittersdorf is as "pale as unborn veal" (289), and Jenny thinks that she will carry David all her life like "a petrified fetus."

The failure of spiritual birth is conveyed in still other ways. Images of poverty, defining spiritual impoverishment, are presented in the opening pages. When the travelers come together in Veracruz, although some are in circumstances "modestly comfortable," the narrative voice emphasizes that "each . . . [suffers] from insufficiency in his own degree." Herr Glocken's fear of poverty is symbolic of his fear of life. He tells David, "I have had no life—I only exist! And I have no existence coming except old age, and if I am not careful, I shall die under a bridge, or in a pauper's hospital." When David points out that perhaps he also shall die that way, Glocken concedes, "Maybe," for "no man knows his end!" In words reminiscent of Thoreau's visionary rationale for going to Walden Pond, Glocken concludes, "But you will not have to die in despair because you never had courage to live!" (276).

For some, hunger is the image that suggests the undernourishment of the spirit. The most grotesque example is the purser, who like Rubén the martyr is "enormously fat and getting fatter all the time—hunger gnaws at his vitals night and day" (249). Jenny also thinks that hunger is in David's "bones, in his soul" (148). In contrast, Dr. Schumann eats "with the moderation of an abstemious man who could hardly remember when last he had been really hungry" (40).

An extensive network of images lies in the idea of coldness, connoting death. David is more often associated with the image than any other character; there often is "cold" or "cold fire" in his eyes; he practices "dull excesses" in "cold yet sensual enjoyment," and he often watches Jenny "coldly."

The most dramatic image in the novel begins building midway the voyage, after animal imagery has been developed fully and after many characters have had—and passed up—opportunities for discovering truths about themselves or their fellow voyagers. It is the image of blindness, which has been central to other Porter stories. Lizzi first sets up the image when she says rhetorically to Freytag, "How could we have been so blind," referring to the passengers' thinking Freytag was the Jew instead of Freytag's wife. Because Lizzi's blindness of spirit already is evident, her question is ironic. The image is also ironic when Denny evokes it in telling Herr Glocken that perhaps he is near-sighted, when in fact they symbolically both are. David frequently is described as blind or nearsighted, a characteristic which, added to the heavy aura of animal, hunger, and death imagery, suggests the lack of fulfillment of his spiritual journey. Others, too, however, reinforce the idea that lack of vision is pervasive in the *Vera*'s microcosmic society. The stewards, for example, stumble "blindly" about their duties, and Elsa smiles "blindly" at her father. Porter has relied heavily on light and sight imagery throughout her stories and short novels, and it is no less significant here as it reaches its culmination in the long novel. Until the gangplank is lowered and the last passengers prepare to descend, the German band on board the ship plays *Tannenbaum*. Among them is a gangling young boy, a trumpet player, who represents the next generation of Germany. He looks as if he has "never had enough to eat in his life" and has never had "a kind word from anybody." His hunger symbolizes his spiritual impoverishment, and the lack of love will have destroyed everything worth saving in him. He stares with "blinded eyes" at the town and whispers to it, "*Grüss Gott, Grüss Gott,*" the German greeting, "as if the town were a human being, a good and dear trusted friend who had come a long way to welcome him" (475–76). The reader knows by historical hindsight, if nothing else, the significance of the illusion. It is the novel's last false hope, and the narrative ends with it.

The journey is thrown into larger perspective if one recalls a minor character in "Flowering Judas," the blind boy who plays a reed flute in the marketplace and whom Laura stops daily to hear. His real blindness suggests his reliance on spiritual sight, and his primitive musical instrument identifies the purity of his music, qualities Laura subconsciously is drawn to as a means of inspiration in the dry revolutionary air.[48] By contrast, the metaphorically blind Aryan youth who plays nationalistic music on his clarion instrument has no spiritual sight and is a long distance from elemental truth.[49] The blind boy of "Flowering Judas" reminds us of an ideal distant to even the beginning of the voyage in Veracruz. It has not been a voyage from innocence to experience but rather from cynicism to illusion.

If one were to view the conclusion of *Ship of Fools* in isolation, or some characters or events during the voyage in isolation, then a pessimistic interpretation of Porter's intention would be supportable. The critics and reviewers who reviled her dark novel of despair and human indignity would be proved correct. But Porter expressed dismay, and sometimes outrage, at what she saw as critics' failure to understand what she had said. She told Caroline Gordon that not one critic or reviewer had understood, and she later insisted that there was goodness and dignity on board the *Vera*.[50] Porter's description, however, is borne out in a more careful consideration of the total voyage and all the characters, for during the voyage two characters, Jenny Brown and Dr. Schumann, make significant gains toward truth. The voyage, with all its failures and complications, comes close in spirit at least to the *Odyssey*, which Porter greatly admired.[51]

In illustrating Jenny's and Dr. Schumann's progress toward truth, Porter has created a wide range of possibility: youth, age; male, female; old-world and new-world. Jenny and Dr. Schumann never come together during the voyage and only incidentally observe one another. They travel parallel roads, even if Jenny does not reach so far as Dr. Schumann. Jenny has not felt the extraordinary effects of pure and reasonless love as Dr. Schumann experiences it and as does Miranda in "Pale Horse, Pale Rider," but she has recognized what it is not, and she has faced that truth. She will be receptive to its transforming power when she does find it because she is not burdened with false hopes in systems, patterns, and ideals.

Dr. Schumann has made peace with death and has grasped the essential meanings of good and evil and love and hate. In contrast to

Jenny, he is a person who has found life's meaning while living in the very midst of a life-negating system as well as life-negating times. The two of them represent Porter's most affirmative statement, and her final statement. In showing their dynamic processes of vision, she shows the possibility for human dignity in the chaos that is the twentieth century.

Chapter Six

Style and Theme

R obert Penn Warren observed that "the more we steadily inspect the work of Katherine Anne Porter, the more we see the inner coherence—the work as a deeply imaginative confrontation of a sensibility of genius with the *chiaroscuro* of modern civilization."[1] That coherence Warren cites is made up of Porter's central philosophy and style, both of which grew out of her experience but have defied easy categorizing.

Porter's heritage and geographical roots are in the border South, but she is not a regionalist writer in the way that Wolfe and Faulkner, for example, are. She explained her difference as resulting from her nomadic life. "I do feel," she said, "an intense sense of location and of background and my tradition and my country exist to me, but I have never really stuck to it in my writing . . . since I have never lived just in one place."[2] It is that sense of belonging to something larger than region that accounts not only for an indefinable characteristic in Porter's fiction but also for her having escaped identification with beliefs and groups. And in spite of a Southern setting in the Miranda cycle and a backcountry setting in "He," "Noon Wine," and "The Jilting of Granny Weatherall," Porter never builds into the setting a regional myth like Yoknapatawpha; one finds Northeastern settings in "Theft," "The Cracked Looking-Glass," and "A Day's Work"; Mexican settings in "María Concepción," "Virgin Violeta," "The Martyr," "That Tree," "Flowering Judas," and "Hacienda"; and an unspecified rural setting in "Rope" and "The Downward Path to Wisdom." There is more evidence in her work of the influence of Henry James, Hawthorne, Flaubert, Joyce, and Dante than there is of Southern or Southwestern writers.[3] She also was inspired by numerous other writers representing a breadth of thought, and she acquired a Catholic world view that transcends the individual parts which contributed to her development as a writer.

Porter's individuality lies at the heart of her refusal to be confined. Lodwick Hartley pointed out that it was Porter's "pervading dislike of dogma and authoritarianism" that "effectually prevents her acceptance of anything like neoclassical ideals in literature. Yet it leads her neither into a form of nineteenth-century Romanticism nor into sympathy with any of the various revolutionary schools of literature that have flourished so profusely in the twentieth century."[4] The avoidance of dogma and authoritarianism led Porter to a pervasive theme and to a style consistent with it.

The grand theme of her work has been all along the search for truth, which is knowledge, to be sure, but finally life itself. Throughout the stories and the novel she has created characters struggling both toward truth and against it, and she imaginatively conveys the agonies of the human struggle while showing the tragedy of the failures and the glory of the successes. She depicts life's complications and contradictions that often are embedded in the darkness of human nature, and she presents characters who foolishly try to find structure and simplicity through systems and orders that are superficial and meaningless; it is the grand illusion that offers the false hope. *Ship of Fools* is the externalization of the theme that was developed in fragments for forty years.

Rejecting orthodoxy on so many fronts, Porter insisted on an aesthetic integrity that depended on precise language and an unflinching facing of truth while refusing embellishment and insincerity. Her pure style is the medium of the honest vision and also the symbol of it.[5] While her style has been analyzed astutely from critical perspectives, it has been no better summarized than in a nostalgic letter from Porter to her sister Gay, who was planning a family reunion. Porter wrote: "And I suppose now you will be together at Magic Valley, a hellish name for a no-doubt beautiful spot. Who named it, for God's sake? Why didn't you call it the Orange Grove or the Orchard or the Place in the country and let it be?"[6] Such insistence on absolute honesty in language is the foundation of her aesthetic.

Porter's personal life was full of failures to make lasting connection with others, and sometimes full of self-deception; she created fictions for herself that often were as artistic as those in her stories. But when it came to art, she looked clearly and courageously. She always had a strong sense of her own vocation as artist, and she had firm ideas about the artist's role in society; for her the artist was not prophet, reformer, or politician. "It is not the artist's business," she told Bill Hale, "to divine the future, unless he has the faculty of divination and happens also to be an artist."[7] Describing the artist as "sublimely superfluous," she says that artists' work is rediscovered when people want a "fuller record of the past" or when they want "light . . . on the present predicament," but sometimes only when the work seems "again fresh and beautiful and new."[8] She says that the artist "tells fewer lies than other men, though his reasoning may be faulty."[9]

She finally saw the only acceptable mission of the artist as that of the truth-teller, no matter the cost in pain. She told Caroline Gordon, "I sprained my soul" writing *Ship of Fools*, and one has the undeniable feeling that the same might be said of most of the stories.[10] The artist who looked deeply enough at life to create Granny Weatherall's death, Mr. Thompson's despair, and the pain of Miranda, Stephen, He, and Laura, suffered likewise in the process. The process of creation provided Porter's own process of vision.

Notes

Introduction

1. See E. R. Richardson, *Bookman*, 72 (October 1930): 172; and Louise Bogan, *New Republic*, 64 (22 October 1930): 277.
2. See P. B. Rice on *Pale Horse, Pale Rider: Three Short Novels* in *Nation*, 148 (15 April 1939): 442; and Orville Prescott on *The Leaning Tower and Other Stories* in *Yale Review*, 34 (Autumn 1944): 190. Rice, while praising Porter's "polish," goes on to say that he is less certain of her "depth," and he regrets that her themes are "miscellaneous." Christopher Isherwood, writing in *New Republic* (98 [19 April 1939]: 312), says that while Porter "has no genius," she has "much talent."
3. See Richard Sullivan in the *Chicago Sunday Tribune*, 26 October 1952, p. 4.
4. See M. M. Liberman, "The Responsibility of the Novelist and the Critical Reception of *Ship of Fools*," *Criticism*, 8 (1966): 377–88.
5. A substantial bibliographical essay on Porter and her work is available in Joan Givner, Jane DeMouy, and Ruth M. Alvarez, "Katherine Anne Porter," *American Women Writers: A Critical Reference Guide from Colonial Times to the Present*, ed. Lina Mainiero (New York: Frederick Ungar, 1979), 201–31.
6. She told Barbara Thompson, "The truth is, I have never written a story in my life that didn't have a very firm foundation in actual human experience—somebody else's experience quite often, but an experience that became my own by hearing the story, by witnessing the thing, by hearing just a word perhaps." See "The Art of Fiction XXIX—Katherine Anne Porter: An Interview," *Paris Review*, No. 29 (1963): 103.

7. See Rice, 442.
8. Porter used the "fragment" metaphor as early as 1923 when she wrote to the editor of the *Century:* "My stories are fragments, each one touching some phase of a versatile national temperament, which is a complication of simplicities" (CE, 356).
9. KAP to Caroline Gordon, 30 September 1964, McKeldin. In reviewing Nance's book, Gordon says that Porter's work "seen as a whole, exhibits a characteristic not found in other short-story writers." That characteristic, according to Gordon, is the unity of the short stories, which she says comprise a *Comédie Humaine* in short stories. See "Katherine Anne Porter and the ICM," *Harper's,* 229 (November 1964): 146.
10. See Wilson, "Katherine Anne Porter," *New Yorker,* 20 (30 September 1944), 64–66. Porter's relationship with Wilson was an interesting one. She mentioned to Barbara Thompson that Wilson had said she often was "silly and irrelevant" (p. 109), and she told Robert Penn Warren that "Bunny Wilson finally broke down and admitted that in all these years he had never read anything of mine, looking upon me as just another lady-author, and not being a girl-poet, he couldn't bother" (the last clause is mine, of course). KAP to Warren, 22 December 1944, Beinecke.
11. Caroline Gordon saw illogic in Nance's theory, for which insight Porter praised her (KAP to Gordon, 5 November 1964, McKeldin). See Gordon, "Katherine Anne Porter and the ICM," 146–48. See also William L. Nance, *Katherine Anne Porter and the Art of Rejection* (Chapel Hill: University of North Carolina Press, 1964), 11.
12. James William Johnson, "Another Look at Katherine Anne Porter," *Virginia Quarterly Review,* 36 (Autumn 1960): 610–11.
13. June 10, 1953, in "Ole Woman River: A Correspondence with Katherine Anne Porter," CE, 282.
14. Thompson, 94.
15. See "On a Criticism of Thomas Hardy," CE, 7.
16. "Three Statements about Writing," CE, 459.
17. "Ole Woman River," CE, 282.
18. Thompson, 113, 100–101.
19. See "The Future Is Now," CE, 200.
20. Letter of 2 June 1953, in "Ole Woman River," CE, 278. She also said, "Maybe that is why art is so endlessly satisfactory: the artist can choose his relations, and 'draw by a geometry of his own, the circle within which they shall happily *appear* to do so [from Henry James]'" (CE, 248).

21. KAP to Donald Sutherland, 2 June 1953, in "Ole Woman River," CE, 278.
22. "A Wreath for the Gamekeeper," CE, 23.
23. See "On a Criticism of Thomas Hardy," CE, 4–6, 8.
24. Introduction to Edward Schwartz, *Katherine Anne Porter: A Critical Bibliography* (New York: New York Public Library, 1953), 9.

Chapter One. The Inner Darkness

1. "The Future Is Now," CE, 199–200.
2. Katherine Anne Porter, "Children and Art," *Nation*, 124 (2 March 1927): 234.
3. See "Quetzalcoatl," CE, 421.
4. Thompson, 99.
5. 7 July 1965, McKeldin.
6. One of several creditable accounts of the Mexican Revolution from 1919 through 1936 is John W. F. Dulles's *Yesterday in Mexico* (Austin: University of Texas Press, 1961). For an overview, see Robert E. Quirk, "Revolutionary Mexico," in *Mexico* (Englewood Cliffs, N.J.: Prentice-Hall, 1971), 81–104.
7. Obregón was elected president in 1920, after he and two other leading generals, Plutarco Elias Calles and Adolfo de la Huerta, revolted against Carranza, who was killed in the ensuing conflict. In 1923 De La Huerta led an unsuccessful revolt against Obregón, and in 1924 it was Calles who was elected president. Obregón was reelected president in 1928, but was assassinated several months later. The Congress made Emilio Portes Gil president, and he was followed in 1932 by Abelardo Rodríguez and in 1934 by Lázaro Cárdenas. In 1932 the National Revolutionary party projected a six-year program for a system that by definition tended toward socialism and included a labor code, public works, distribution of land, socialist education, and the seizure of foreign owned oil lands. Cárdenas put the program into effect in 1934, but by then the character of the revolution had changed. See Dulles, 86–92, 262, 402, 539, 551, 598, and 608.
8. See Katherine Tyler Burchwood, *The Origin and Legacy of Mexican Art* (South Brunswick and New York: A. S. Barnes, 1971); Justino Fer-

nández, *A Guide to Mexican Art; From Its Beginnings to the Present*, trans. Joshua C. Taylor (Chicago: University of Chicago Press, 1969); and Alma Reed, *The Mexican Muralists* (New York: Crown, 1960).

9. A readable and detailed account of the history of Mexico's archaeological sites is Peter Tomkins's *Mysteries of the Mexican Pyramids* (New York: Harper & Row, 1976).

10. See Tomkins, 210–11.

11. The notes must have been written within two months of Porter's arrival because she mentions on the same page that she was moving that afternoon to 20 Calle Del Eliseo, which is her first known address in Mexico City and the return address on a letter to her family in December 1920. Notes and letter at McKeldin.

12. *Outline* was published in a limited edition by Young & McCallister in Los Angeles. She described to Hank Lopez her involvement in the exhibit in "A Country and Some People I Love," *Harper's*, 231 (September 1965): 58.

13. She credits "[William Hickling] Prescott, Alexander von Humboldt, [Adolph] Bandolier, Madame Calderon de la Barca, [H. H.] Bancroft, [Vicente] Rivas [*sic*] Palacio, [Albert] Reville, Nicholas Leon; . . . Dr. Atl, Licenciado Ramón Mena, and Don Manuel Gamio" as her sources (p. 2).

14. She several times described the writing of "María Concepción" in seventeen days and seventeen nights. See, for example, John Dorsey, "Katherine Anne Porter on . . . ," *Baltimore Sun Magazine*, 26 October 1969, p. 16.

15. In the *Outline* she identifies William Niven as among those who offered "invaluable aid in gathering, classifying and interpreting the materials" for the *Outline*. She calls Niven "the indefatigable digger who has brought out of the earth an extraordinary volume of relics from buried cities" (p. 2).

16. Niven (1850–1937) would have been nearing the end of his active career when Porter met him. His publications include "Ometlan: A Prehistoric City in Mexico," *American Antiquarian*, 19 (1897): 187–90; *Prehistoric Ruins in Mexico; Interesting Discoveries by Professor Niven* (Boston 1900); and *Novedades arqueologicas . . .* [with Ramón Mena] (Mexico 1921). See "Professor Niven Dead; Archaeologist, 86," *New York Times*, 4 June 1937, p. 23, col. 1.

17. 31 December 1920, McKeldin.

18. Porter said that "María Concepción" was set about ten miles out of Mex-

ico City." KAP to George Sessions Perry, 5 February 1943, Harry Ransom Center.

19. CE, 495–96.
20. See Allen Tate, "A New Star," *Nation*, 131 (October 1930): 352–53.
21. See Thomas F. Walsh, "Identifying a Sketch by Katherine Anne Porter," *Journal of Modern Literature*, 7 (1979): 551–61; and "Xochitl: Katherine Anne Porter's Changing Goddess," *American Literature*, 52 (May 1980): 183–93.
22. CE, 395.
23. For a better understanding of the events behind the filming of *Que Viva Mexico*, see Marie Seton, *Sergei M. Eisenstein: A Biography* (1952; rpt. New York: Grove Press, 1960), 187–42. Porter names Eisenstein among persons whom she entertained at dinner (KAP to Malcolm Cowley, 17 June 1931, Newberry), and she later said that during this three-day visit Eisenstein was "sick with a fever" (KAP to Cowley, 22 July 1931, Newberry).
24. On one of the blank front pages of a gift copy of "Hacienda" published in a separate edition by Harrison of Paris in 1934, Porter provided a "Key to Cast in the order of their appearance." She does identify the above models for the major characters. The copy, inscribed to "Rhea" and dated 1967, is in the Porter Collection at the Harry Ransom Center.
25. Robert L. Perry comments upon the hint at incest in "Hacienda." See "Porter's 'Hacienda' and the Theme of Change," *Midwest Quarterly*, 6 (Summer 1965): 403–15.
26. Dated Salem 1928, Beinecke.
27. The planned story was to be called first "The Never-Ending Wrong" and later "The Man in the Tree" (undated notes, McKeldin).
28. See *The Haunted Castle: A Study of the Elements of English Romanticism* (New York: E. P. Dutton, 1927), 263–64.
29. I explore James's use of the grotesque in "Henry James and the Grotesque," *Arizona Quarterly* 32 (Winter 1976): 293–300.
30. "Holiday" was published December 1960, but Porter told Thompson that she wrote the first version in 1923 (p. 112). For an account of the three versions of the story, all of which are in the Porter Collection at the Harry Ransom Center, see the preface to *The Collected Stories* (p. v.). The story apparently was based on a visit Porter and her sister made to a farm of a German family. See KAP to Gay Porter Holloway, 5 March 1928, McKeldin. An astute analysis of "Holiday" is found in George Core's "The Best Residuum of Truth," *Georgia Review* 20 (Fall 1966): 278–91.

31. KAP to Josephine Herbst, 5 May 1928, Beinecke.
32. Porter described the writing of "Rope" in this way: "I was once washing dishes in an old fashioned dishpan at 11 o'clock at night after a party and all of a sudden I just took my hands up like that and went to the typewriter and wrote the short story 'Rope' between that time and two o'clock in the morning. I don't know what started me. I know I had it in mind for several years but the moment came suddenly." See "Recent Southern Fiction: A Panel Discussion," *Bulletin of Wesleyan College* 41 (January 1961): 4.
33. Undated, McKeldin.
34. The inspiration for the story apparently was a childhood memory of Glenway Wescott. See Joan Givner, *Katherine Anne Porter: A Life* (New York: Simon & Schuster, 1982), 339–40.
35. She told Thompson that "people *can* be destroyed; they can be bent, distorted and completely crippled" (p. 96).
36. She went on to say that "his own remarkable memory of his experiences and feelings and states of mind as a child is naturally the source—his children are deliciously Jamesian, subtle and intelligent as he was, and as more children are than most adults seem to be aware of: James's children live in a strange world, as James did in childhood, and continued to do so all his life: a world of wonder and mystery which he labored steadily and with perfect concentration to understand and explain" (8 October 1942, Beinecke). She might have been describing her own Miranda, a fact which illustrates how closely she adhered to her model.
37. Sister M. Joselyn, "Animal Imagery in Katherine Anne Porter's Fiction," in *Myth and Symbol,* ed. Bernice Slote (Lincoln: University of Nebraska Press, 1963), 101–15. Sister Joselyn examines "Flowering Judas," "Pale Horse, Pale Rider," "The Leaning Tower," "The Circus," "The Downward Path to Wisdom," and *Ship of Fools* for animal images that serve as major devices of characterization, definition of conflict, establishment of tone, and dramatization of "value judgments." See also Johnson, 610.
38. Porter describes her writing of "Noon Wine" in " 'Noon Wine': The Sources," CE, 467–82. Porter says that the characters in the story are purely imaginary, but Givner has traced the models for the Thompsons and Helton (*Life,* 73–75).
39. Thomas F. Walsh, in "Deep Similarities in 'Noon Wine,' " *Mosaic,* 9, No. 1 (1975): 83–91, interprets the story as a doppelgänger story; he draws upon Otto Rank's theory of the double explained in *The Double*: *A Psychoanalytic Study* (1914; trans. Harry Tucker, Chapel Hill: University of North Carolina Press, 1971). Walsh sees a double relationship between

Helton and Thompson and between Thompson and Hatch but does not see them as a three-level relationship. Other critics have treated one or the other double relationship but have not explored both fully. See, for example, Frederick J. Hoffman, *The Art of Southern Fiction: A Study of Some Modern Novelists* (Carbondale and Edwardsville: Southern Illinois University Press, 1967) and D. F. Kepler, *The Literature of the Second Self* (Tucson: University of Arizona Press, 1972).

40. Porter may have been basing the character of Thompson partly on her father, who once had been a Sunday School superintendent, and whom she described to her nephew Paul as having begun "with a good lively mind, wonderful looks, spirits, the kind of young man who would have been welcome anywhere he wished to go." But, she writes, "he discovered absolutely not one glimmer of talent for anything, not a trace of a capacity for attention and direction of his energies, no imagination; and as he grew older his vices got possession of him: rages and resentments and petty mischief." She speaks also of his "idle motiveless mind." KAP to Paul Porter, 20 June 1957, McKeldin.

41. Walsh points out some similarities between Bartleby and Helton in "Deep Similarities in 'Noon Wine,'" 87.

42. "Halifax" was the family's name for a real place they went for camping excursions. At an early age Porter saw the fictional possibilities for the place; several times she recalled having written a "nobble" when she was six which she called "The Hermit of Halifax Cave." See Dorsey, 18, and Roy Newquist, "An Interview with Katherine Anne Porter," *McCall's* 92 (August 1965): 138.

43. James William Johnson was the first to suggest that in the "weep, weep" motif Porter was alluding to Blake's poem "The Chimney Sweep." See "Another Look at Katherine Anne Porter." Other critics have built upon that suggestion and explored the notion further. George Hendrick says flatly that "The Fig Tree" has as its literary background Blake's Songs of Innocence and Songs of Experience, even though, he concedes, Porter "goes far beyond the chimney-sweep poems" and "the borrowings are completely integrated into her own fictional world." Hendrick, *Katherine Anne Porter* (New York: Twayne, 1965), 62–63. Although it is true that Porter later planned to write an essay on Blake for the *Yale Review,* she was unable to complete it (KAP to Robert Penn Warren, 29 September 1944; KAP to Warren and Cinina Warren, 5 July 1945, Beinecke). Aside from the obvious link in the poems' and the story's treatment of the state between innocence and experience and the use of "weep," much of the source and influence argument seems strained. Givner points out that

Porter would have known about the tree frogs and their peculiar sound when she lived in Bermuda. See *Life*, 196–212.

44. Notes and letter to Gordon, 28 April 1963, McKeldin.

45. In a letter to Herbst, Porter says that she finished "The Fig Tree" and sent it to *Harper's* (letter dated Salem 1928, Beinecke). Givner thinks that the story was not finished until the following year, when Porter was in Bermuda. The story Porter mentioned to Herbst no doubt was a version of the later "The Fig Tree," which she probably revised after it was rejected by Harper's. Although the first version apparently centered on the grandmother rather than Miranda, the title suggests that the theme was the same.

46. Givner cites Porter's marginal notes in her books to show how closely she linked femininity with fertility. See *Life*, 92.

47. Plato in the *Theaetetus* (155d) reports Socrates's assertions that "wonder is the feeling of a philosopher and philosophy begins in wonder." Aristotle in the *Metaphysics* says, "It is owing to their wonder that men both now begin and at first began to philosophize; they wondered originally at the obvious difficulties, then advanced little by little and stated difficulties about the greater matters, e.g., about the phenomena of the moon and those of the sun and of the stars and about the genesis of the universe (982b). Translations above from *The Works of Plato*, ed. Irwin Edman, trans. Benjamin Jowett (New York: Modern Library, 1956), 499; and *The Basic Works of Aristotle*, ed. Richard McKeon, Oxford translation (New York: Random House, 1941), 692.

Among Porter's papers at the McKeldin Library is correspondence with Yale professor Francisco Aguilera, whom she calls a "silly fraud," but she says cryptically that she was "deceived all the same." In a telegram he addresses her as "Miranda." It was apparently Aguilera to whom she referred in a letter to Jean Thompson Tenenbaum (18 July 1950, UCLA Library). She wrote: "The name *Miranda* which stands for my shade haunting the lively scenes of family legend was given me by an early love who began his first letter thus: 'Ariel to Miranda: Take / This slave of music for the sake / of him who is a slave to thee.' What more would I ever need as christening for an alter-ego?"

48. Mary Alice Porter Breckenridge to KAP, 19 February 1914, McKeldin.

49. She quoted to Warren lines she said she had translated many years earlier: "The heart has to reason what reason does not know." She calls it "a great truth in any language." KAP to Warren, 15 September 1975, Beinecke.

50. See Ray B. West, Jr., "Katherine Anne Porter: Symbol and Theme in 'Flowering Judas,'" *Accent*, 7 (Spring 1947): 182–87.

51. See Thompson, 102–104, for example; and "Why She Selected 'Flowering Judas'" in *This Is My Best*, ed. Whit Burnett (New York: Dial Press, 1942), 539.
52. See "Recent Southern Fiction: A Panel Discussion," 13.
53. Walsh points out that, intentionally or not, in the sketch Porter was confusing the attributes of Xochitl and Mayahuel, the authentic goddess of pulque. Walsh believes that Porter "chose Xochitl's name because in Nahuatl it means 'flower' and Xochimilco means 'place of flowers.'" See "Xochitl: Katherine Anne Porter's Changing Goddess," 185.
54. See KAP to Eugene Pressly, 23 January 1932, McKeldin.
55. Undated notes, McKeldin.
56. KAP to Matthew Josephson, 7 January 1931, Beinecke.
57. See Dulles, 106–108, 166–67. Among Porter's papers in the McKeldin Library are six pages of typed notes (in Spanish and English) of petroleum data, facts from which she probably drew for her essays about Mexico.
58. The oil companies were defended by some persons, like Joseph Hergesheimer and Evelyn Waugh, but Porter, B. Traven, and Carleton Beals were among the writers who protested the methods of the oilmen and their devastating effect on the cultural revolution in Mexico. See Drewey Wayne Gunn, *American and British Writers in Mexico, 1556–1973* (Austin: University of Texas Press, 1973), 78. In her essay "Where Presidents Have No Friends" Porter explains that "Oil should . . . [have been] Mexico's greatest asset, but the Guggenheims and Dohenys have made of it a liability almost insupportable to the country." She goes on to describe the Doheny interests as the "most implacable of all Mexico's interior enemies" and "the source of eternal unrest." See CE, 410. Porter's correspondence for nearly a decade shows a continuing interest in the oil problems in Mexico.
59. KAP to family, 31 December 1920, McKeldin.

Chapter Two. Systems and Patterns

1. "On a Criticism of Thomas Hardy," CE, 6.
2. See Gunn, *American and British Writers in Mexico*, 4–5, 9–12, 28, 32–33, 39, 50, 78–79, 90, 105, 146, 171, 182, 199–200, 255.
3. Frank Tannenbaum, *Peace by Revolution: An Interpretation of Mexico* (New York: Columbia University Press, 1933), 3.
4. In undated notes (McKeldin) she describes her father's refutation of the

virgin birth as evidence of his agnosticism, which may account in part for her resistance to religious dogma. Late in life she explained her concept of God as "some measureless absolute merciless Power" and insisted she was not an atheist. She said, "I believe totally in something I have never heard or read or thought in words." KAP to Robert Penn Warren, 15 September 1975, Beinecke.

5. 13 August 1930, McKeldin.

6. See KAP to Robert Penn Warren, 16 October 1953, Beinecke.

7. See KAP to Paul Hanna, 29 May 1921, McKeldin. In explaining to Archer Winston why she would not have become a Trotsky sympathizer, she asks, "Why . . . should I have rebelled against my early training in Jesuit Catholicism only to take another yoke now?" See "The Portrait of an Artist," *New York Post*, 6 May 1937, p. 17.

8. McKeldin.

9. Extending the abuses of religious power to other religions, she pointed out in a review of George F. Willison's *Saints and Strangers* that "we are descended from the Puritans, who nobly fled from a land of despotism to a land of freedom, where they could not only enjoy their own religion but prevent everybody else from enjoying his." See CE, 141.

10. When she was eighty-six Porter used imagery reminiscent of that in this story when she wrote to Warren that she believed in something. She said, "I don't fight, or weep. I just wait, hoping to see [underlined twice]— someday." KAP to Warren, 15 September 1975, Beinecke.

11. Givner points out that Porter's father was superintendent of the Indian Creek Methodist Church Sunday school when he was married to Alice. See *Life*, 68. Perhaps her father's pattern provided some of the inspiration for the characters of the Thompsons and for the theme of ineffectual religion.

12. As she often did, Porter could have drawn the essential idea from biblical passages, for example, "When I waited for light, there came dark" (Job 30:20); "Mine eyes fail while I wait for my God" (Psalms 69:3); and "We wait for light but behold obscurity" (I Samuel 51:59). That Porter equated light with truth and life is reinforced in her book-length essay "The Never-Ending Wrong," in which she describes the tower light that failed at the moment of Sacco's and Vanzetti's electrocution. "At midnight, this light winked off, winked on and off again[,]" corresponding "to the number of charges of electricity sent through the bodies of Sacco and Vanzetti" (p. 44). Porter also uses the image in "Pale Horse, Pale Rider" (CS, 311).

13. KAP to Gay Porter Holloway, 1 April 1920, McKeldin.
14. Givner says that Porter got the story from a maid who once worked in New Orleans (*Life,* 197).
15. Porter's landlady at 75 Washington Place in Greenwich Village was Madame Katrina Blanchard. See Givner, *Life,* 160.
16. Porter referred to this story as "a nice dirty story." KAP to Gay Porter Holloway, St. Valentines, 1942, McKeldin.
17. Porter explained her heavy use of religious symbolism as having come out of her "deep sense of religion" and her "religious training." See "Recent Southern Fiction: A Panel Discussion," 12.
18. Leonard Prager points out the wasteland and inferno images in the story. See "Getting and Spending: Porter's 'Theft,' " *Perspective* 11 (1960): 230–34. For additional supporting interpretations of "Theft," see Joan Givner, "A Re-reading of Katherine Anne Porter's 'Theft,' " *Studies in Short Fiction* 6 (Summer 1969): 463–65; William Bysshe Stein, " 'Theft': Porter's Politics of Modern Love," *Perspective* 11 (Winter 1960): 223–28; Carol Simpson Stern, " 'A Flaw in Katherine Anne Porter's "Theft": The Teacher Taught'—A Reply," *CEA Critic* 39 (May 1977): 4–8; and Joseph Wiesenfarth, "The Structure of Katherine Anne Porter's 'Theft,' " *Cithara* 10 (May 1971): 65–71.
19. In the Thompson interview Porter said that she read "all at one blow, all of Dante" soon after she was thirteen. See Thompson, 89. Givner quotes Erna Schlemmer Johns as saying that Porter read Dante when she was eleven or twelve at their house (*Life,* 61). In an interview with Newquist, Porter tells of reading Saint Augustine's *Confessions* when her superiors would have her read Saint Thomas Aquinas (p. 89); she wrote to Genevieve Taggard in 1926, asking for books she could not get in Mexico. She includes the *Confessions* of Saint Augustine, saying she lost her copy which she had had for ten years (KAP to Taggard, 3 June 1926, McKeldin).

   Porter mentions Dante in a letter to Eugene Pressly, 18 November 1932 (McKeldin); and she praises the nobility of Dante, Sir Thomas More, St. Francis, Erasmus, and the Prince in *War and Peace* in a letter to Robert Penn Warren and Cinina Warren, 22 December 1946, Beinecke.
20. *City of God* (xv. 1), trans. Marcus Dods (New York: Modern Library, 1950).
21. KAP to Eugene Pressly, 18 November 1932, McKeldin.
22. KAP to Paul Porter, 20 June 1957, McKeldin.

23. KAP to Cinina Warren, 22 December 1946, Beinecke; KAP to Albert Erskine, 4 January 1947, McKeldin.
24. KAP to Josephine Herbst, 23 January 1946, Beinecke.
25. KAP to family, 31 December 1920, McKeldin.
26. Thompson, 97.
27. KAP to family, 31 December 1920, McKeldin.
28. KAP to family, 31 December 1920, McKeldin.
29. Notes, dated 1920, McKeldin.
30. McKeldin.
31. KAP to Paul Hanna, 29 May 1921, McKeldin.
32. KAP to Robert McAlmon, 5 February 1934, McKeldin.
33. Thompson, 97.
34. "Eudora Welty and 'A Curtain of Green,'" CE, 287.
35. Thompson, 104.
36. See Mark 14:15 and Luke 22:12.
37. Laura's movements through the city traverse the greater Mexico City area. All the landmarks and streets have revolutionary significance and stand as a reminder of how far from the ideal Braggioni and the current revolutionaries have fallen. The Zócolo means "foundation," and is at the center of the old city and surrounded by the National Palace. Here once stood the halls of Montezuma. It also is the center of the independence celebration every year on September 15. Chapultepec Park also has a long history in the social evolution of the city. See Leopold Batres, A Historic Guide to Mexico City (Mexico: Imprenta Mundial, 1935). Porter may have been referring to the Chapultepec Park footpath known as the Avenida de los Poetas rather than the Philosopher's Footpath.
38. See Thompson, 104; and "Why She Selected 'Flowering Judas,'" in Whit Burnett's This Is My Best, 539.
39. Notes at McKeldin. Mary is Porter's friend Mary Doherty, who is mentioned in Gunn, p. 171. See also Carleton Beals, Glass Houses: Ten Years of Free-Lancing (Philadelphia: J. B. Lippincott, 1938), 243; Beals, The Great Circle: Further Adventures in Free-Lancing (Philadelphia: J. B. Lippincott, 1940), 324; and Peggy Baird, "The Last Days of Hart Crane," Venture, 4 (1961): 36–38. Yúdico was Samuel Yúdico, a minor revolutionist.
40. See Dorsey, 19–20.
41. KAP to Peggy Cowley, 30 January 1933, McKeldin.
42. KAP to Paul Hanna, 19 April 1921, McKeldin.
43. KAP to Genevieve Taggard, 3 June 1926, McKeldin. Porter also com-

plained about *New Masses* and "literature as social criticism" (KAP to William Harlan Hale, 3 September 1932, McKeldin), and she lamented to Pressly about Josephine Herbst's "going for Communism" (5 August 1935, McKeldin). In a letter to Robert Penn Warren and Cinina Warren she suggests America do some clearing out of Nazis and Fascist organizations (20 June 1940, Beinecke). Many years later she wrote to Warren that she had never been sympathetic to the literary politics of the *Partisan Review*. She says that she "cannot learn to trust the judgment in any matter of any one who was ever a Trotskyist" (KAP to Warren, 22 July 1963, Beinecke). In the same year she wrote to Mary Doherty about the effective Communist sabotage of exploiting honest grievances for their own causes (30 August 1963, McKeldin). It was the point upon which she attacked Rosa Baron and others in "The Never-Ending Wrong."

44. See CE, 203–204.
45. "On Communism in Hollywood," CE, 208.
46. See "E. M. Forster," CE, 72.
47. (Pittsburgh: The University of Pittsburgh Press, 1957; rev. 1962), 98.
48. KAP to Ernestine Evans, 3 October 1930, McKeldin.
49. See Perry, "Porter's 'Hacienda' and the Theme of Change."
50. See KAP to William Harlan Hale, 8 July 1932, photocopy in the Beinecke, transcription in the possession of the author.
51. One of the *corridos* mentioned in the story illustrates the theme of the inevitability of change. Andreyev sings "La Sandunga" "in his big gay Russian voice," and the Indians shout "with joy and delight at the new thing his strange tongue made of the words." Andreyev cannot preserve "La Sandunga" because it is indigenous to the Mexican people; it changes to something else when he tries to claim it.
52. Note that Betancourt bases his secret formula on seven methods, just as his model, Best-Maugard, based his method of painting on seven ancient designs.
53. In the margin of her copy of Hendrick's *Katherine Anne Porter* at the McKeldin Library Porter identifies Carlos as Castro Padilla, as she also does in the key to the cast of characters in the gift volume of *Hacienda* at the Harry Ransom Center. In a letter to Monroe Wheeler she said that Padilla had written the song "La Norteña" for her (7 July 1965, McKeldin). Although Padilla may have written a song especially for Porter that he called "La Norteña" and never published, a very popular "La Norteña" of the 1920s was written by Eduardo Vigil y Robles expressly for a play set in northern Mexico. See Claes af Geijerstam, *Popular*

Music in Mexico (Albuquerque: University of New Mexico Press, 1976), 87, 90.

54. Porter describes the *corrido* and praises it in "Corridos," *Survey*, 52 (May 1924): 157–58.

55. Porter described a group of Rivera's disciples who eventually turned on him, "each one battling to create and put over his own personality." She names the "Good ones" in the group: David Siqueiros (later she retracts the praise), Xavier Guerrero, and Abraham Angel. KAP to Robert McAlmon, 5 February 1934, McKeldin.

56. Porter's earliest memory of being in Mexico included the awareness of Díaz' power. See Newquist, 140.

57. In the same year her revised version of "Hacienda" appeared, Porter described the state of the revolution when she left Mexico in 1931 as having "exploded" and being "empty of initiative," phrases that capture the tone of resignation in the story. KAP to Robert McAlmon, 5 February 1934, McKeldin.

58. Joseph Wiesenfarth addresses the themes of social approval and order in "Negatives of Hope: A Reading of Katherine Anne Porter," *Renascence*, 25 (1973): 85–94.

59. Porter said that Calvin put into action the idea "that God somehow rewarded spiritual virtue with material things." See "Recent Southern Fiction: A Panel Discussion," 16.

60. Dorsey, 25.

61. Interview with Señora Soledad Guzmán, 20 August 1981, Mexico City.

62. KAP to Malcolm Cowley, 5 November 1931, Newberry.

63. Porter's description of Mrs. Whipple's brother and his family is like her memory of her own relatives as "a mean selfish lot who descended on Sunday and ate up all the fried chicken." See KAP to Gay Porter Holloway, 13 November 1961, McKeldin.

64. According to Givner, the story was based on a family's quarrels Porter heard through the air ducts at her apartment on Perry Street in New York. See *Life*, 303.

65. Thompson, 98.

Chapter Three. Ideals

1. 5 June 1948, CE, 111–12. Porter told John Dorsey about having told a Spaniard in Mexico that Alexander (the model for Adam Barclay in "Pale

Horse, Pale Rider") was the only man with whom she ever could have spent her life. The Spaniard had replied, "Just think, now he can never disappoint you." Porter says, "It does seem an awfully high price to pay to keep one's illusions, doesn't it?" (p. 16).

2. Porter often called people she loved "Angel." See, for example, her letter to Eugene Pressly of 23 January 1932, which she signed "With my true love, angel . . ." (McKeldin); a letter to Albert Erskine dated 28 March 1938, in which she calls Erskine "my angel" (McKeldin); a letter to her sister Gay, 13 November 1961, which she closes by calling her sister "angel" (McKeldin); and a letter to Robert Penn Warren, whom she addresses as "Angel" (KAP to Warren, 24 January 1966), Beinecke.
3. KAP to Robert McAlmon, 5 February 1934, McKeldin.
4. See "Where Presidents Have No Friends," CE, 414.
5. See Lopez, *Conversations with Katherine Anne Porter* (New York: Little, Brown, 1981), 64.
6. Lopez, *Conversations with Katherine Anne Porter*, 63.
7. Notes at McKeldin. See also Carleton Beals, *Glass Houses*, 2.
8. See "The Guild Spirit in Mexican Art," *Survey* 56 (1 May 1924): 174–78; and "These Pictures Must Be Seen," *New York Herald Tribune Books*, 22 December 1929, p. 5. In the acknowledgment to the *Outline* she says that Rivera and other painters "contributed the fruits of their studies to my understanding of Mexican art . . . [and] have helped me to form my point of view and to place my sympathies."
9. KAP to Ernestine Evans, 3 October 1930, McKeldin.
10. "Rivera's Personal Revolution in Mexico," *New York Herald Tribune Books*, 21 March 1937, p. 7.
11. KAP to Mary Doherty, 30 August 1963, McKeldin.
12. McKeldin. At the time Porter wrote the notes, Lupe was very much alive. Porter was imagining her death in childbirth as an artistic conclusion to the story.
13. In an early letter (undated but probably 1923) Mary Doherty comments to Porter that she has just seen her story "The Martyr" in *Century*. She says she recognized "peculiarities of at least three persons in it . . . Yudico's sentimental fatness; the comic-tragedy of J. R." (Joseph Retinger), and her own "capacity for eating Lubens chocolate almond wafers or grapes in the face of all disaster." Doherty to KAP, McKeldin.
14. In "These Pictures Must Be Seen," Porter remarks that Rivera's "followers have for him a warmth of adulation little short of worship." *New York Herald Tribune Books*, 22 December 1929, p. 5.

15. See Bertram Wolfe, *The Fabulous Life of Diego Rivera* (New York: Stein and Day, 1963), 9–10, 78, 182–92, 241–42, 244–45, 248–52, 397.

16. Monotes is mentioned by Edward Weston in *The Daybooks*, vol. 1: *Mexico* (Rochester: George Eastman, 1961), 19, 45, 520; and Witter Bynner, *Journey with Genius* (New York: John Day, 1951), 28–29. Bynner points out that Monotes was owned by the brother of Orozco and that young Miguel Covarrubias was often there.

17. See Wolfe, 196–213.

18. "From a Mexican Painter's Notebook," *Arts*, 7 (January 1925): 21. See also KAP to William Harlan Hale, 8 July 1932, photocopy in the Beinecke, in which she comments at length about bourgeois taste in art.

19. Note to John Herman in KAP to Josephine Herbst, 20 February 1931, McKeldin.

20. " 'It Is Hard to Stand in the Middle,' " CE, 46.

21. Wolfe, 134–38.

22. Givner implies that the publishers omitted "The Martyr" as well as "Virgin Violeta" and "Theft" (*Life*, 221), but Porter told Jean Thompson Tenenbaum that the omission was her decision because she had not been satisfied with either "The Martyr" or "Virgin Violeta" after she saw them in print. See KAP to Tenenbaum, 18 July 1950, UCLA Library.

23. Givner says that Porter's marginal notes in Henry Charles Lea, *History of the Inquisition of the Middle Ages*, vol. 1 (New York: Harper, 1900), 400, show her sensitivity to the church's attitude to women and her resentment of antifeminist tendencies of church fathers and individual priests. See *Life*, 101.

24. Paul Porter to Mrs. K. R. Koontz, 23 March 1909, McKeldin.

25. See Newquist, 139. She also wrote the introduction (signed "Hamblen Sears") to *What Price Marriage* in which she cites paternalistic and sexist attitudes that have accounted for women's "slavery" (p. 10).

26. See "Mr. George on the Woman Problem," *New York Herald Tribune Books*, 29 November 1925, p. 11.

27. KAP to Gay Porter Holloway, 29 March 1956, McKeldin.

28. Henry Schmitt summarizes the main elements in the Carillo regime as socialism, feminism, art, and indigenism. See "American Intellectual Discovery of Mexico: 1920–1930," *South Atlantic Quarterly* 77 (Summer 1978): 357.

29. McKeldin.

30. Lopez, *Conversations with Katherine Anne Porter*, 83.

31. Notes hand-dated 1921, McKeldin.

32. The program is from the Teatro del Plantel, Consulado num 85, Colonia Anahuac, D.F., McKeldin.
33. 5 June 1948, CE, 109–10.
34. "The Necessary Enemy," CE, 184.
35. "The Necessary Enemy," CE, 184–85.
36. "A Wreath for the Gamekeeper," CE, 20.
37. Ibid.
38. "Marriage Is Belonging," CE, 188.
39. Givner, *Life*, 173.
40. KAP to Josephine Herbst, 5 May 1928, Beinecke. See also Joseph Wiesenfarth, "Illusion and Allusion: Reflections in 'The Cracked Looking-Glass,'" *Four Quarters*, 12 (1962): 30–37.
41. Porter may have had in mind a drama called *The Happy Prince*, in which she acted the part of a swallow and which she called "the silliest play I ever saw" (KAP to Jean Thompson Tenenbaum, 18 July 1950, UCLA Library).
42. See Givner, *Life*, 48.
43. The model for the convent school was the Thomas School in San Antonio, which Porter attended for one year. See Givner, *Life*, 79–85. See also KAP to Mrs. Thomas F. Gossett, 6 December 1965, Harry Ransom Center.
44. Porter had a long interest in Holbein. See, for example, KAP to William Harlan Hale, 8 July 1932, photocopy in the Beinecke.
45. Marginal notes in Porter's copy of Hendrick's *Katherine Anne Porter*, McKeldin.
46. Actually the widely quoted passage appears in the essay's letter of dedication (to Thomas Le Gros, of Crostwick Esquire). Browne explains his purpose. He says that the burial urns, whose history he traces, "silently" express "old mortality, the ruines of forgotten times, and can only speak with life, how long in this corruptible frame, some parts may be uncorrupted; yet able to out-last bones long unborn, and noblest pyle among us." *Works*, ed. Geoffrey Keynes (Chicago: University of Chicago Press, 1964), I, 131. Porter's personal library, preserved at McKeldin, contains a copy of a 1921 edition of Browne, *Religio Medici and Other Writings*, which includes "Hydriotaphia."
47. *Outline of Mexican Popular Arts and Crafts*, 4.
48. Notes for the novel are among papers at McKeldin.
49. KAP to Eugene Pressly, 18 November 1932, McKeldin.
50. The account of the journalist's artistic friends was added in the revision.

51. Porter had considerable disdain for people like Miriam and Kennerly, who ate only clean, bland food, and she used this eating habit as a symbol of a self-righteous, puritan attitude. Among her unpublished notes is a gleeful account of cooking a spicy dinner for some New England acquaintances and of their being bedridden the following day "with acute pains in the tum" (hand-dated 1925, McKeldin).

52. See Gunn, *American and British Writers in Mexico*, 76–101, 123–44, 188.

53. *Glass Houses*, 181. KAP to Carleton Beals, 16 January 1926, Carleton Beals Collection, Mugar Memorial Library.

54. Carleton Beals to his mother, May 1924, Beals Collection. I am indebted to John A. Britton for supplying information about Lillian and Carleton Beals.

55. Ibid.

56. Ibid.

57. See Hendrick, 48–49; Mooney, 50.

58. *Mexico: An Interpretation* (Philadelphia: J. B. Lippincott, 1923), 214.

59. In her review of Beals's *The Stones Awake: A Novel of Mexico* (Philadelphia: J. B. Lippincott, 1936), Porter hints at the identification of an Indian woman in the novel, whom Beals must have known in real life. She says, "No doubt he has worked faithfully from a model" (the journalist in the story once lived with an Indian girl before Miriam's arrival). See "History on the Wing," *New Republic*, 89 (18 November 1936): 82.

60. In the first version the phrase is not Miriam's but is used only by the journalist, first to describe Miriam's adherence to a virtuous marriage.

61. Porter goes on to explain that "one of Virginia Woolf's last essays had this title, and I think it was published in 1940, or a little earlier. I can't help it, I had it first, and it can't be changed; this story is about the Leaning Tower that since then has fallen on all of us" (KAP to George Davis, 1 June 1943, Olin Library, Cornell University).

62. See KAP to Eugene Pressly, 26 January 1931, and KAP to Pressly, 26 December 1931, McKeldin.

63. See "They lived with an Enemy in the House," *New York Herald Tribune Weekly Book Review*, 4 March 1945, p. 1; KAP to Josephine Herbst, 29 April 1945, Beinecke; and KAP to Paul Porter, 5 June 1948, CE, 113.

64. The character Kuno Hillentafel was probably based on Porter's childhood friend Erna Schlemmer (Erna Glover Johns), but his name was drawn from that of Porter's brother-in-law Kuno Hillendahl. See Givner, *Life*, 59–62.

65. Herr Bussen was the name of a hotel clerk in one of Porter's hotels in Berlin. Among her notes is a message from him that H. von Goering "belled" (McKeldin).

66. Compare "Old Mortality," in which Harry tells of going to Mexico where the horses had silver bridles. Porter's father presumably provided this description, but it corresponds to her recollection of a trip to Mexico when she was a child. See Newquist, 140. According to Givner, Tadeuz Mey is modeled partly on Joseph Retinger, a Polish-American with whom Porter had a love affair in the twenties. See *Life*, p. 152.

Chapter Four. Reconciliations

1. See Thompson, 101.

2. Porter acknowledged having read Whitman when she said she had read only four of Whitman's poems. See Givner, *Life*, 465–66.

3. See Donald Atwater, *The Penguin Dictionary of Saints* (Baltimore: Penguin Books, 1965), 257.

4. In a letter to Charles Pearce, editor at Harcourt, Brace, Porter suggested that "The Grave" might stand alone. "For it really is the first step towards the future out of the past Miranda has lived in all her childhood" (31 May 1934, McKeldin).

5. Wescott talks of the tomb-womb symbolism of medieval allegory, from which Porter may have drawn support if not inspiration. See "Katherine Anne Porter Personally," *Images of Truth* (New York: Harper & Row, 1962), 25–58. She also suggested something of the same relationship when she wrote to Pressly of going to her mother's grave and of the grave's being the center of life (KAP to Eugene Pressly, May 1936, McKeldin). The notion that out of death emerges life would be developed fully in "Pale Horse, Pale Rider." See also Cleanth Brooks, "On 'The Grave,'" *Yale Review*, 55 (1966): 275–79.

6. "Recent Southern Fiction: A Panel Discussion," 13.

7. Introduction to *Flowering Judas* (1940), CE, 457.

8. Porter told Dorsey that the events in "Pale Horse, Pale Rider" were exactly as they happened to her, except for the fact that they "didn't happen quite so fast" (p. 16).

9. Charles A. Allen analyzes the use of gray as image in several of Porter's stories. See "Katherine Anne Porter: Psychology as Art," *Southwest Review*, 41 (1956): 226.

10. KAP to Robert Penn Warren, 27 February 1947, Beinecke.
11. KAP to Gay Porter Holloway, St. Valentine's 1942, McKeldin.
12. Porter described to Barbara Thompson her experience that provided the inspiration for the story: "I knew what death was, and had almost experienced it. I had what the Christians call the 'beatific vision,' and the Greeks called 'the happy day,' the happy vision just before death. Now if you have had that, and survived it, come back from it, you are no longer like other people" (p. 97). She told Jean Thompson Tenenbaum that the date of the illness was October 5, 1918 to January 1919 (KAP to Tenenbaum, 18 July 1950, UCLA Library).

Chapter Five. Ship of Fools

1. See Lodwick Hartley, "Dark Voyagers: A Study of Katherine Anne Porter's *Ship of Fools,*" *University of Kansas City Review,* 30 (Winter 1963): 83–94.
2. See Donald Brace to KAP, 11 December 1940, McKeldin; KAP to Glenway Wescott, 27 December 1943, McKeldin; KAP to Josephine Herbst, 23 January 1946, Beinecke.
3. See Robert N. Hertz, "Sebastian Brant and Porter's *Ship of Fools,*" *Midwest Quarterly,* 6 (1965): 389–401; Daniel Curley, "Katherine Anne Porter: The Larger Plan," *Kenyon Review,* 25 (1963): 671–95.
4. She said that she did not "think much of the allegorical as a standard." See Thompson, 113.
5. She also wrote in "My First Speech" that "it is necessary to know and to remember what I was, what I felt, and what I knew then, and not confuse it with what I know or think I know now. So, I shall try to tell the truth, but the result will be fiction" (CE, 433).
6. Porter said, "Symbolism happens of its own self and it comes out of something so deep in your own consciousness and your own experience that I don't think that most writers are at all conscious of their use of symbols. I never am until I see them. They come of themselves because they belong to me and have meaning to me, but they come of themselves. I have no way of explaining them. . . . And I suppose you don't invent symbolism." See "Recent Southern Fiction: A Panel Discussion," 12. Porter also told Thompson, "I never consciously took or adopted a symbol in my life" (p. 107).
7. See Givner, *Life,* 310.

8. See Donald Brace to KAP, 11 December 1940, McKeldin.
9. KAP to Glenway Wescott, 27 December 1943, McKeldin.
10. KAP to Josephine Herbst, 23 January 1946, Beinecke.
11. Ibid.
12. See Dorsey, 18.
13. In 1942, when Porter was preparing an "apology" for the novel that became *Ship of Fools*, she wrote, "There are a good many references, events, and scenes, which now appear almost suspiciously 'timely' and the theme has a more sinister meaning than it seemed to have when the book was begun." Incomplete draft, Harry Ransom Center.
14. Thompson, 112. Porter also told James Ruoff and Del Smith that *Ship of Fools* ended exactly the way she originally had planned it. She said that she wrote the last three pages of the novel first and kept working toward that conclusion. See "Round Table: Katherine Anne Porter on *Ship of Fools*," *College English*, 24 (February 1963): 396–97.
15. Thompson, 113.
16. Dorsey, 23.
17. Anita Brenner, *The Wind That Swept Mexico: The History of the Mexican Revolution, 1910–1942* (Austin: University of Texas Press, 1971), 47.
18. The source of the image of the peon probably was an experience Porter described soon after her arrival in Mexico: "I met a ragged peon coming toward me with that steady, dog like trot they have, putting one foot exactly before the other at every step, which gives them an indescribably animal like swing. A wide band about his forehead supported the weight he carried on his back, and his hands were clasped at the back of his head, pulling forward perceptibly, thus saving the muscles of his neck a little. This is no doubt the first method of carrying known to primitive man. We passed, his patient eyes following the ground in a line before him, as though they were drawing a path for his blackened, calloused feet with their great ragged toe nails." Notes, November 9 and 10 [1920], McKeldin.
19. See Newquist, 138.
20. See Givner, *Life*, 243.
21. See Beals, *Glass Houses*, 174. Henry C. Schmidt traces the notion of "Americana Mexicana" as New Jerusalem to Puritan dreams of expansionism. The Enlightenment, he believes, encouraged the spirit of New Worldism, and unity of the Americas was sought as a foil to a corrupt Europe." See "The American Intellectual Discovery of Mexico in the

1920's," 335. See also Gunn, *American and British Writers in Mexico*, 14–52.

22. KAP to Caroline Gordon, 13 August 1930, McKeldin.

23. See Givner, *Life*, 134.

24. See "Shall We Go to the Theatre, Dearie . . . ?" *Mexican Life*, January 1925, p. 12.

25. Givner, *Life*, 195–96.

26. 7 July 1965, McKeldin.

27. 16 October 1935, McKeldin.

28. KAP to Jean Thompson Tenenbaum, 18 July 1950, UCLA Library.

29. Herr Baumgartner's character or name may have been inspired by the proprietor of a popular German restaurant in Mexico City in the twenties. See *Mexican Life*, March 1925, for advertisement of "La Germania."

30. See "Recent Southern Fiction: A Panel Discussion," 16.

31. KAP to Robert Penn Warren and Cinina Warren, 22 December 1946, Beinecke; KAP to Albert Erskine, 4 January 1947, McKeldin.

32. KAP to Gay Porter Holloway, St. Valentine's 1942, McKeldin.

33. Thompson, 113.

34. Winston, 17.

35. Givner thinks Denny may have been based on Porter's first husband, J. H. Koontz. See *Life*, 249.

36. The distinction between the two idealized views of the German past is explained in a journal entry Porter made: "A young poet . . . said, 'Oh, don't read Rilke. He belongs to the old romantic soft-headed Germany that has been our ruin. The new Germany is hard, strong, we will have a new race of poets, tough and quick, like your prize fighters' " (CE, 443).

37. Porter may have been basing the character Löwenthal partly on Walter Lowenfels, with whom she corresponded in the early thirties and knew when she was in Europe. In undated notes (McKeldin) she identifies Lowenfels as Cronstadt in Henry Miller's *Tropic of Cancer*, which Miller left for her with the concierge at her hotel. See Henry Miller to KAP, 22 November 1934, Harry Ransom Center. Also see Lowenfels's obituary in the *New York Times*, 8 July 1976, p. 34.

38. See Newquist, 139, for the similar description by Porter of her father's words to her. She also complained to Warren about sexist attitudes toward her by William Carlos Williams and Sherwood Anderson, "both of them saying in effect they had looked upon me as a pretty girl making a career

in literature via S.A. These simple lads never seemed to realize what they were saying" (22 December 1944, Beinecke).

39. See CE, 3–4.

40. See William George Dodd, "The System of Courtly Love," *Courtly Love in Chaucer and Gower,* Harvard Studies in English, I (Boston: Ginn, 1913), 1–20; and Sidney Painter, *French Chivalry* (Baltimore: Johns Hopkins University Press, 1940), 95–148.

41. "Orpheus in Purgatory," CE, 53.

42. She told Newquist, "God knows I'm not for all moonlight and roses" (p. 139).

43. Freytag may be partly modeled on Joseph Retinger. In a letter to Paul Hanna (29 May 1921, McKeldin) Porter said, "I thought him [Retinger] singularly free from intellectual malice. Otherwise a lover of mysteries that did not mystify: a perverse sense of the dramatic. . . . He has drama-tised his adventures and himself until life is now only a fog in the midst of which he moves fevered with visions."

44. See KAP to Caroline Gordon, 28 August 1931, Princeton University Library. She includes the following description: "A Cuban woman about fifty years old, with short curled white hair and a waxy smooth face, follows various persons about, backs them into corners, and talks for two hours at a time, making strange desperate gestures, thumbs turned in flat to the palms. She leans forward and peers at the person she is talking to, as if she were communicating some dark important secret. She is very slender and was a tremendous beauty not so long ago. She tells every one the same: that her husband was killed fighting for the revolution in Cuba, that her sons are fugitives persecuted by the government. Her eyes are very dry and bright, she talks with a crying, complaining voice, eternally about her children who are lost, who have no place to rest, and how the government officials laughed at her when she went to them asking them not to persecute her children. Now they have exiled her to Tenerife: it seems she is not married at all, nor ever was, but it is true that she has been very active helping the revolutionary students, and is being sent away, and her mind is unhinged. Cuba is her murdered husband, and the students are her children."

45. These words are from Porter's essay on Thomas Hardy, where the com-ment continues, "God may be the answer." See CE, 7. Dr. Schumann's thoughts continue, "And it is just there, . . . where man leaves off, that God begins" (p. 116).

46. In undated notes (McKeldin) Porter says that when she was two she knew her mother was dead.
47. KAP to Albert Erskine, 28 March 1938, McKeldin.
48. Porter used the blinded eyes image also in "Fiesta," CE, 398.
49. She must have envisioned the youthful Aryan trumpeter as a "Hitler child," which she considered a "horror." See KAP to Josephine Herbst, 16 October 1933, McKeldin.
50. In a letter to Warren she talks about the blindness of reviewers and says, "Not one of them has hit anywhere near what that book is 'about.'" KAP to Warren, 22 July 1963, Beinecke. She also told Newquist, "Of course, there's nobility and there's goodness and love and tenderness and feeling and emotion [in *Ship of Fools*]" (p. 139).
51. KAP to Caroline Gordon, 28 April 1963, McKeldin. In "A Defense of Circe" Porter observes that "Odysseus was wise in his mortal wisdom. He knew that men cannot live as the gods do. His universal fate: birth, death, and the larger disasters, are from the gods; but within that circle he must work out his personal fate with or without their help" (CE, 139).

Chapter Six. Style and Theme

1. "Introduction," *Katherine Anne Porter: A Collection of Critical Essays*, 14.
2. "Recent Southern Fiction: A Panel Discussion," 4.
3. Warren has summarized the similarities between Faulkner and Porter in the introduction to *Katherine Anne Porter: A Collection of Critical Essays*, 15.
4. "The Lady and the Temple," *College English*, 14 (April 1953): pp. 386–91.
5. See, for example, Robert B. Heilman, "*Ship of Fools*: Notes on Style," *Four Quarters*, 12 (November 1962): 46–55; and Beverly Gross, "The Poetic Narrative: A Reading of 'Flowering Judas,'" *Style*, 2 (1968): 129–39.
6. KAP to Gay Porter Holloway, 6 June 1933, McKeldin.
7. KAP to William Harlan Hale, 8 July 1932, photocopy in the Beinecke.
8. Ibid.
9. Ibid.
10. KAP to Caroline Gordon, 28 April 1963, McKeldin.

Bibliography

Porter Bibliographies

Bixby, George, comp. "Katherine Anne Porter: A Bibliographical Checklist." *American Book Collector* 1, no. 6 (1980): 19–33.

Givner, Joan, Jane DeMouy, and Ruth M. Alvarez. "Katherine Anne Porter," *American Women Writers: A Critical Reference Guide from Colonial Times to the Present*, edited by Lina Mainiero. New York: Frederick Ungar, 1979.

Kiernan, Robert F., comp. *Katherine Anne Porter and Carson McCullers: A Reference Guide*. Reference Guide in Literature, no. 9. Boston: G. K. Hall, 1976.

Schwartz, Edward, comp. *Katherine Anne Porter: A Critical Bibliography*. New York: New York Public Library, 1953.

Sylvester, William A., comp. "A Selected and Critical Bibliography of the Uncollected Works of Katherine Anne Porter." *Bulletin of Bibliography* 19 (January 1947): 36.

Waldrip, Louise and Shirley Ann Bauer, comps. A *Bibliography of the Works of Katherine Anne Porter* and A *Bibliography of the Criticism of the Works of Katherine Anne Porter*. Metuchen, N.J.: Scarecrow Press, 1969.

Primary Works

Stories: First Publication

"The Circus," *Southern Review*, o.s., 1 (Summer 1935): 36–41.

"The Cracked Looking-Glass," *Scribner's Magazine*, 91 (May 1932): 271–76, 313–20.

"A Day's Work," *Nation*, 150 (February 10, 1940): 205–207.
"The Downward Path to Wisdom," *Harper's Bazaar* (December 1939): 72–73ff.
"The Fig Tree," *Harper's Magazine*, 220 (June 1960): 55–59.
"Flowering Judas," *Hound and Horn*, 3 (Spring 1930): 316–31.
"The Grave," *Virginia Quarterly Review*, 11 (April 1935): 177–83.
"Hacienda," *Virginia Quarterly Review*, 8 (October 1932): 556–69.
"He," *New Masses*, 3 (October 1927): 13–15.
"Holiday," *Atlantic Monthly*, 206 (December 1960): 44–56.
"The Jilting of Granny Weatherall," *transition*, 15 (February 1929): 129–46.
"The Leaning Tower," *Southern Review*, o.s., 7 (Autumn 1941): 219–79.
"Magic," *transition*, 8 (Summer 1928): 229–31.
"María Concepción," *Century*, 105 (December 1922): 224–39.
"The Martyr," *Century*, 106 (July 1923): 410–13.
"Noon Wine," *Story*, 10 (June 1937): 71–103.
"Old Mortality," *Southern Review*, o.s., 2 (Spring 1937): 686–735.
"The Old Order," *Southern Review*, o.s., 1 (Winter 1936): 495–509. This title was later used by Porter for *The Old Order*, a collection of Southern stories published in 1955 by Harcourt, Brace & World. The short story was then retitled "The Journey."
"Pale Horse, Pale Rider," *Southern Review*, o.s., 3 (Winter 1938): 417–66.
"Rope," *The Second American Caravan*. Edited by A. Kreymborg. New York: Macauley, 1928.
"The Source," *Accent*, 1 (Spring 1941): 144–47.
"That Tree," *Virginia Quarterly Review*, 10 (July 1934): 351–61.
"Theft," *Gyroscope* (November 1929): 21–25.
"Two Plantation Portraits" ("The Witness" and "The Last Leaf"), *Virginia Quarterly Review*, 11 (January 1935): 85–92.
"Virgin Violeta," *Century*, 109 (December 1924): 261–68. Reprinted as "Violeta" in *Redbook*, December 1964.

Books

A Christmas Story. New York: Seymour Lawrence, 1967.
The Collected Essays and Occasional Writings of Katherine Anne Porter. New York: Delacorte Press, 1970. Contents: All of *The Days Before*; "A Wreath for the Gamekeeper," "On Christopher Sykes," "Max Beerbohm," "Eleanor Clark," "The Winged Skull," "On Modern Fiction," "A Little Incident in

the Rue de l'Odéon," "A Letter to Sylvia Beach," "Letters to a Nephew," "Dylan Thomas," "A Defense of Circe," "Pull Dick, Pull Devil," "A Note on Pierre-Joseph Redouté," "A Letter to the Editor of *The Village Voice*," "A Letter to the Editor of *The Nation*," "On Communism in Hollywood," "A Letter to the Editor of *The Saturday Review of Literature*," "Opening Speech at Paris Conference, 1952," "Remarks on the Agenda," "A Letter to the Editor of *The Yale Review*," "A Letter to the Editor of the *Washington Post*," "Speech of Acceptance"; "Ole Woman River," "A Sprig of Mint for Allen," "On First Meeting T. S. Eliot," "Flannery O'Connor at Home," "From the Notebooks: Yeats, Joyce, Eliot, Pound," "Romany Marie, Joe Gould—Two Legends Come to Life," "Jacqueline Kennedy," "Miss Porter Adds a Comment," "The Fiesta of Guadalupe," "My First Speech," "Notes on Writing," "On Writing," " 'Noon Wine': The Sources"; Poems: "Enchanted," "Two Songs from Mexico," "Little Requiem," "Winter Burial," "Anniversary in a Country Cemetery," "November in Windham," "After a Long Journey," "Measures for Song and Dance."

The Days Before. New York: Harcourt, Brace, 1952. Contents: "The Days Before," "On a Criticism of Thomas Hardy," "Gertrude Stein: Three Views," "Reflections on Willa Cather," " 'It Is Hard to Stand in the Middle,' " "The Art of Katherine Mansfield," "Orpheus in Purgatory," "The Laughing Heat of the Sun," "Eudora Welty and *A Curtain of Green*," "Homage to Ford Madox Ford," "Virginia Woolf," "E. M. Forster," "Three Statements about Writing," "No Plot, My Dear, No Story," "The Flower of Flowers," "Portrait: Old South," "Audubon's Happy Land," "A House of My Own," "The Necessary Enemy," " 'Marriage Is Belonging,' " "American Statement: 4 July 1942," "The Future Is Now," "Notes on the Life and Death of a Hero," "Why I Write about Mexico," "Leaving the Petate," "The Mexican Trinity," "La Conquistadora," "Quetzalcoatl," "The Charmed Life."

A Defense of Circe. New York: Harcourt, Brace, 1955.

Flowering Judas and Other Stories. New York: Harcourt, Brace, 1930. Contents: "María Concepción," "Magic," "Rope," "He," "The Jilting of Granny Weatherall," "Flowering Judas." Reprinted by Harcourt Brace & Company, 1935, with four new stories: "Theft," "That Tree," "The Cracked Looking-Glass," and "Hacienda." 1935 edition reprinted by Modern Library in 1940.

Hacienda. [New York:] Harrison of Paris, 1934.

The Leaning Tower and Other Stories. New York: Harcourt, Brace, 1944.

Contents: "The Source," "The Witness," "The Circus," "The Old Order," "The Last Leaf," "The Grave," "The Downward Path to Wisdom," "A Day's Work," and "The Leaning Tower."

[M. T. F.] *My Chinese Marriage*. New York: Asia Publishing Company, 1922.

The Never-Ending Wrong. Boston: Little, Brown, 1977.

Noon Wine. Detroit: Schuman's, 1937.

Outline of Mexican Popular Arts and Crafts. Los Angeles: Young and Mc-Callister, 1922.

Pale Horse, Pale Rider: Three Short Novels. New York: Harcourt, Brace, 1939. Contents: "Old Mortality," "Noon Wine," and "Pale Horse, Pale Rider." Reprinted by Modern Library in 1949.

Ship of Fools. Boston: Atlantic-Little, Brown, 1962. Parts of *Ship of Fools* were published separately as follows: "Embarkation," *Sewanee Review*, 55 (1947): 1–23; "The Exile," *Harper's*, 201 (November 1950): 70–78; "The High Sea," *Partisan Review*, 12 (1945): 514–49; "Kein Haus, Keine Heimat," *Sewanee Review*, 52 (1944): 465–82; "The Prisoner," *Harper's*, 201 (October 1950): 89–96; "Seducers," *Harper's*, 207 (November 1953): 33–38; "Ship of Fools," *Atlantic*, 197 (March and April 1956): 33–38, 56–63; "Ship of Fools," *Mademoiselle*, 47 (July 1958): 26–43; "Ship of Fools," *Texas Quarterly*, 2 (1959): 97–151; "The Strangers," *Accent*, 6 (1946): 211–29; "Under Weigh," *Harper's*, 201 (November 1950): 80–88.

Selected Uncollected Works

"Ay, Que Chamaco." *New Republic*, 23 December 1925, pp. 141–42.

"Children and Art." *Nation* 2 (March 1927): 233–34.

"From a Mexican Painter's Notebook." *Arts* 7 (January 1925): 21.

"The Guild Spirit in Mexican Art." *Survey* 56 (1 May 1924): 174–78.

"History on the Wing." *New Republic*, 18 November 1936, p. 82.

Introduction to *What Price Marriage*, edited by Hamblen Sears, pp. 7–13. New York: J. H. Sears and Company, 1927.

"Mexico." *New York Herald Tribune Books*, 2 November 1924, p. 9.

"Mexico's Thirty Long Years of Revolution." *New York Herald Tribune Books*, 30 May 1943, pp. 1–2.

"Mr. George on the Woman Problem." *New York Herald Tribune Books*, 29 November 1925, p. 11.

"Paternalism and the Mexican Problem." *New York Herald Tribune Books*, 27 March 1927, p. 12.

"Rivera's Personal Revolution in Mexico." *New York Herald Tribune Books,* 21 March 1937, p. 7.

"Theatregoers Like to Shiver Over Sins of Stage Heroes." *Rocky Mountain News,* 23 February 1919.

"These Pictures Must Be Seen." *New York Herald Tribune Books,* 22 December 1929, p. 5.

"They Lived with the Enemy in the House." *New York Herald Tribune Weekly Book Review,* 4 March 1945, p. 1.

"Why She Selected 'Flowering Judas.'" In *This Is My Best,* edited by Whit Burnett, pp. 539–40. New York: Dial Press, 1942.

Interviews and Discussions

Doblier, Maurice. "I've Had a Good Run for My Money." *New York Herald Tribune Books,* 1 April 1962, pp. 3, 11.

Dorsey, John. "Katherine Anne Porter on . . ." *Baltimore Sun Magazine,* 26 October 1969, pp. 16ff.

Espejo, Beatrice. "Entrevista con Katherine Anne Porter." *Sabado,* 11 October 1981, p. 6.

From *Invitation to Learning,* a series of radio broadcasts: "Alice in Wonderland," in *The New Invitation to Learning,* edited by Mark Van Doren. New York: New Home Library, 1942. A discussion with Bertrand Russell and Van Doren.

"*Moll Flanders,*" in *The Invitation to Learning,* edited by Huntington Cairns, Allen Tate, and Mark Van Doren. New York: New Home Library, 1942. With the editors.

"*Tom Jones,*" in *The New Invitation to Learning,* edited by Mark Van Doren. With Tate and Van Doren.

"*The Turn of the Screw,*" in *The New Invitation to Learning,* edited by Mark Van Doren. With Tate and Van Doren.

Janeway, Elizabeth. "For Katherine Anne Porter, *Ship of Fools* Was a Lively Twenty-Two Year Voyage," *New York Times Book Review,* 1 April 1962, pp. 4–5.

Lopez, Hank. "A Country and Some People I Love." *Harper's,* 231 (September 1965): 58, 62, 65, 68.

Newquist, Roy. "An Interview with Katherine Anne Porter." *McCall's* 92 (August 1965): 88–89, 137–43.

"Recent Southern Fiction: A Panel Discussion." *Bulletin of Wesleyan College* 41 (January 1961): 1–16.

Ruoff, James. "Katherine Anne Porter Comes to Kansas," *Midwest Quarterly*, 4 (1963): 205–34.

Ruoff, James and Del Smith. "Katherine Anne Porter on *Ship of Fools*," *College English*, 24 (1963): 396–97.

Thompson, Barbara. "The Art of Fiction XXIX—Katherine Anne Porter: An Interview." *Paris Review*, No. 29 (1963): 87–114. Reprinted in *Writers at Work: "The Paris Review" Interviews* (New York: Viking Press, 1963), 137–63.

Winston, Archer. "The Portrait of an Artist." *New York Post*, 6 May 1937, p. 17.

Biographies

Givner, Joan. *Katherine Anne Porter: A Life*. New York: Simon & Schuster, 1982.

Lopez, Enrique Hank. *Conversations with Katherine Anne Porter: Refugee from Indian Creek*. Boston: Little, Brown, 1981.

Secondary Works Cited

Allen, Charles A. "Katherine Anne Porter: Psychology as Art." *Southwest Review* 41 (1956): 226.

Aristotle. *The Basic Works of Aristotle*. Edited by Richard McKeon. Oxford translation. New York: Random House, 1941.

Atwater, Donald. *The Penguin Dictionary of Saints*. Baltimore: Penguin Books, 1965.

Augustine, St. *City of God*. Translated by Marcus Dods. New York: Modern Library, 1950.

Baird, Peggy. "The Last Days of Hart Crane." *Venture* 4 (1961): 36–38.

Batres, Leopold. *A Historic Guide to Mexico City*. Mexico: Imprenta Mundial, 1935.

Beals, Carleton. *Glass Houses: Ten Years of Free-Lancing*. Philadelphia: J. B. Lippincott, 1938.

———. *The Great Circle: Further Adventures in Free-Lancing*. Philadelphia: J. B. Lippincott, 1940.

———. *Mexico: An Interpretation*. Philadelphia: J. B. Lippincott, 1923.

Bogan, Louise. "Flowering Judas." *New Republic* 64 (22 October 1930): 277.

Brenner, Anita. *The Wind That Swept Mexico: The History of the Mexican Revolution, 1910–1942.* Austin: University of Texas Press, 1971.

Brooks, Cleanth. "On 'The Grave.'" *Yale Review* 55 (1966): 275–79.

Browne, Thomas. *The Works of Sir Thomas Browne.* Edited by Geoffrey Keynes. 4 vols. Chicago: University of Chicago Press, 1964.

Burchwood, Katherine Tyler. *The Origin and Legacy of Mexican Art.* South Brunswick and New York: A. S. Barnes, 1971.

Bynner, Witter. *Journey with Genius: Recollections and Reflections Concerning the D. H. Lawrences.* New York: John Day, 1951.

Core, George. "The Best Residuum of Truth." *Georgia Review* 20 (Fall 1966): 278–91.

Curley, Daniel. "Katherine Anne Porter: The Larger Plan." *Kenyon Review* 25 (1963): 671–95.

DeMouy, Jane. *Katherine Anne Porter's Women: The Eye of Her Fiction.* Austin: University of Texas Press, 1983.

Dodd, William George. "The System of Courtly Love." In *Courtly Love in Chaucer and Gower,* pp. 1–20. Harvard Studies in English, vol. 1. Boston: Ginn, 1913.

Dulles, John W. F. *Yesterday in Mexico.* Austin: University of Texas Press, 1961.

Emmons, Winifred S. *Katherine Anne Porter: The Regional Stories.* Austin: Steck-Vaughn, 1967.

Fernández, Justino. *A Guide to Mexican Art; From Its Beginnings to the Present.* Translated by Joshua C. Taylor. Chicago: University of Chicago Press, 1969.

Geijerstam, Claes af. *Popular Music in Mexico.* Albuquerque: University of New Mexico Press, 1976.

Givner, Joan. "A Re-reading of Katherine Anne Porter's 'Theft.'" *Studies in Short Fiction* 6 (Summer 1969): 463–65.

Gordon, Caroline. "Katherine Anne Porter and the ICM." *Harper's* 229 (November 1964): 146–48.

Gunn, Drewey Wayne. "The American and British Author in Mexico, 1911–1941." Unpublished doctoral dissertation, University of North Carolina, Chapel Hill, 1968.

———. *American and British Writers in Mexico, 1556–1973.* Austin: University of Texas Press, 1973.

Hale, William Harlan. *Challenge to Defeat; Modern Man in Goethe's World and Spengler's Century.* New York: Harcourt, Brace, 1932.

Hanna, Paul. "Mexico—1921; I. Introductory—The House Set in Order." *Nation* 112 (30 March 1921): 471–72.

———. "Mexico—1921; II. A Labor Republic." *Nation* 112 (6 April 1921): 503–505.

———. "Mexico—1921; III. Restoring the Land to the People." *Nation* 112 (13 April 1921): 532–34.

———. "Mexico—1921; IV. Culture and the Intellectuals." *Nation* 112 (20 April 1921): 585–87.

———. "Mexico—1921; V. Relations with the United States." *Nation* 112, (27 April 1921): 614–17.

———. "Reply to Kellogg's 'Oil and Mexico.'" *Nation* 112 (8 June 1921): 816–18.

Hardy, Edward. *Katherine Anne Porter.* New York: Frederick Ungar, 1973.

Hartley, Lodwick. "Dark Voyagers: A Study of Katherine Anne Porter's *Ship of Fools.*" *University of Kansas City Review* 30 (Winter 1963): 83–94.

———. "Katherine Anne Porter." *Sewanee Review* 48 (April 1940): 206–16.

———. "The Lady and the Temple." *College English* 14 (April 1953): 386–91.

Hartley, Lodwick, and George Core, eds. *Katherine Anne Porter: A Critical Symposium.* Athens: University of Georgia Press, 1969.

Heilman, Robert B. "*Ship of Fools:* Notes on Style." *Four Quarters* 12 (November 1962): 46–55.

Hendrick, George. *Katherine Anne Porter.* New York: Twayne, 1965.

Hertz, Robert N. "Sebastian Brant and Porter's *Ship of Fools.*" *Midwest Quarterly* 6 (1965): 389–401.

Hoffman, Frederick J. *The Art of Southern Fiction: A Study of Some Modern Novelists.* Carbondale and Edwardsville: Southern Illinois University Press, 1967.

Isherwood, Christopher. Review of *Pale Horse, Pale Rider: Three Short Novels. New Republic* 98 (19 April 1939): 312–13.

Johnson, James William. "Another Look at Katherine Anne Porter." *Virginia Quarterly Review* 36 (Autumn 1960): 598–613.

Joselyn, M. "Animal Imagery in Katherine Anne Porter's Fiction." In *Myth and Symbol,* edited by Bernice Slote, pp. 101–15. Lincoln: University of Nebraska Press, 1963.

Kepler, D. F. *The Literature of the Second Self.* Tucson: University of Arizona Press, 1972.

Krishnamurthi, M. G. *Katherine Anne Porter: A Study.* Mysore, India: Rao and Raghaven, 1971.

Liberman, M. M. *Katherine Anne Porter's Fiction*. Detroit: Wayne State University Press, 1971.

————. "The Responsibility of the Novelist and the Critical Reception of *Ship of Fools*." *Criticism* 8 (1966): 377–88.

Lugg, Bonelyn. "Mexican Influences on the Work of Katherine Anne Porter." Unpublished doctoral dissertation, Pennsylvania State University, 1976.

Mooney, Harry John, Jr. *The Fiction and Criticism of Katherine Anne Porter*. Pittsburgh: University of Pittsburgh Press, 1957; rev. 1962.

Nance, William L., S.M. *Katherine Anne Porter and the Art of Rejection*. Chapel Hill: University of North Carolina Press, 1964.

Niven, William. *Novedades arqueologicas*. With Ramón Mena. Mexico, 1921.

————. "Ometlan: A Prehistoric City in Mexico." *American Antiquarian* 19 (1897): 187–90.

————. *Prehistoric Ruins in Mexico: Interesting Discoveries by Professor Niven*. Boston, 1900.

Painter, Sidney. *French Chivalry*. Baltimore: Johns Hopkins University Press, 1940.

Perry, Robert L. "Porter's 'Hacienda' and the Theme of Change." *Midwest Quarterly* 6 (Summer 1965): 403–15.

Plato. *The Works of Plato*. Edited by Irwin Edman. Translated by Benjamin Jowett. New York: Modern Library, 1956.

Prager, Leonard. "Getting and Spending: Porter's 'Theft.'" *Perspective* 11 (Winter 1960): 230–34.

Prescott, Orville. Review of *The Leaning Tower and Other Stories*. *Yale Review* 34 (Autumn 1944): 190.

"Professor Niven Dead; Archaeologist, 86." *New York Times*, 4 June 1937, p. 23, col. 1.

Quirk, Robert E. *Mexico*. Englewood Cliffs, N.J.: Prentice-Hall, 1971.

Railo, Eino. *The Haunted Castle: A Study of the Elements of English Romanticism*. New York: E. P. Dutton, 1927.

Rank, Otto. *The Double: A Psychoanalytic Study* (1914). Translated by Harry Tucker. Chapel Hill: University of North Carolina Press, 1971.

Reed, Alma. *The Mexican Muralists*. New York: Crown, 1960.

Rice, P. B. "The Art of Katherine Anne Porter." *Nation* 148 (15 April 1939): 442.

Richardson, E. R. Review of *Flowering Judas and Other Stories*. *Bookman* 72 (October 1930): 172.

Schmidt, Henry C. "The American Intellectual Discovery of Mexico in the 1920's." *South Atlantic Quarterly* 77 (Summer 1978): 335–51.

Seton, Marie. *Sergei M. Eisenstein: A Biography.* 1952; rpt. New York: Grove Press, 1960.

"Shall We Go to the Theatre, Dearie . . . ?" *Mexican Life*, January 1925, p. 12.

Stein, William Bysshe. " 'Theft': Porter's Politics of Modern Love." *Perspective* 11 (1960): 223–28.

Stern, Carol Simpson. " 'A Flaw in Katherine Anne Porter's "Theft": The Teacher Taught'—A Reply." *CEA Critic* 39 (May 1977): 4–8.

Sullivan, Richard. "More Distinguished Prose from a Fascinating Mind." *Chicago Sunday Tribune Magazine of Books*, 26 October 1952, p. 4.

Tannenbaum, Frank. *Peace by Revolution: An Interpretation of Mexico.* New York: Columbia University Press, 1933.

Tate, Allen. "A New Star." *Nation* 131 (October 1930): 352–53.

Tomkins, Peter. *Mysteries of the Mexican Pyramids.* New York: Harper & Row, 1976.

Unrue, Darlene Harbour. "Henry James and the Grotesque." *Arizona Quarterly* 32 (Winter 1976): 293–300.

Walsh, Thomas F. "Deep Similarities in 'Noon Wine.' " *Mosaic* 9 (1975): 83–91.

———. "Identifying a Sketch by Katherine Anne Porter." *Journal of Modern Literature* 7 (1979): 551–61.

———. "Xochitl: Katherine Anne Porter's Changing Goddess." *American Literature* 52 (May 1980): 183–93.

Warren, Robert Penn. Introduction to *Katherine Anne Porter: A Collection of Critical Essays.* Edited by Robert Penn Warren. Englewood Cliffs, N.J.: Prentice-Hall, 1979.

———. Introduction to *Katherine Anne Porter: A Critical Bibliography*, by Edward Schwartz. New York Public Library, 1953.

———. "Katherine Anne Porter (Irony with a Center)." *Kenyon Review* 4 (1942): 29–42.

Wescott, Glenway. "Katherine Anne Porter Personally." In *Images of Truth*, pp. 25–58. New York: Harper & Row, 1962.

West, Ray B., Jr. *Katherine Anne Porter.* Minneapolis: University of Minnesota Press, 1963.

———. "Katherine Anne Porter: Symbol and Theme in 'Flowering Judas.' " *Accent* 7 (Spring 1947): 182–87.

Weston, Edward. *The Daybooks*. Vol. 1: *Mexico*. Edited by Nancy Newhall. Rochester: George Eastman, 1961.

Wiesenfarth, Joseph. "Illusion and Allusion: Reflections in 'The Cracked Looking-Glass.'" *Four Quarters* 12 (1962): 30–37.

———. "Negatives of Hope: A Reading of Katherine Anne Porter." *Renascence* 25 (1973): 85–94.

———. "The Structure of Katherine Anne Porter's 'Theft.'" *Cithara* 10 (May 1971): 64–71.

Wilson, Edmund. "Katherine Anne Porter." *New Yorker* 20 (30 September 1944): 64–66; reprinted in *Classics and Commercials: A Literary Chronicle of the Forties*, pp. 219–23. New York: Farrar, Straus, 1950.

Wolfe, Bertram. *The Fabulous Life of Diego Rivera*. New York: Stein and Day, 1963.

Index

Adams, Henry, 62, 213
Aguilera, Francisco, 228 (n. 47)
Alexandrov, Grigori, 27
Anderson, Sherwood, 242 (n. 38)
Angel, Abraham, 234 (n. 55)
Anti-American Activities Committee, 83
Archer, Isabel (*The Portrait of a Lady*), 203
Aristotle, 152, 228 (n. 47)
Atl, Dr., 224 (n. 13)
Augustine, Saint, 40, 69, 153
Aztecs, 13, 15, 25, 61

Bancroft, H. H., 224 (n. 13)
Bandolier, Adolph, 224 (n. 13)
Baron, Rosa, 233 (n. 43)
"Bartleby the Scrivener" (Melville), 42
Batres, Leopoldo, 15
Beals, Carleton, 35, 107, 133, 169, 229 (n. 58); Lillian Beals and, as models for journalist and Miriam in "That Tree," 134–35
Best-Maugard, Adolfo, 25, 27, 71, 233 (n. 52); Porter's meeting of, 13; system of design of, 13; method of painting of, 14; as model for Betancourt in "Hacienda," 90

Blake, William, 227 (n. 43)
Blanchard, Katrina, 231 (n. 15)
Brant, Sebastian, 162
Brenner, Anita, 134, 165
Browne, Sir Thomas, 128
Bullock, William, 15
Burnett, Whit, 3, 80

Calvin, John, 234 (n. 59)
Calderón de la Barca, Madame, 224 (n. 13)
Calles, Plutarco Elías, 14, 223 (n. 7)
Cárdenas, Lázaro, 14, 223 (n. 7)
Carranza, Venustiano, 14, 58, 134
Charnay, Joseph Desire, 15
Chaucer, Geoffrey, 9
Chekhov, Anton, 89
Chichen Itza, excavations at, 15
Chrétien de Troyes, 200
Christianity, Augustinian, 7
Circe, 13
Clement VII, Pope, 61
Confessions (Saint Augustine), 153, 231 (n. 19)
Cooper, James Fenimore, 148
Core, George, 2
Cortés, Hernando, 61

Covarrubias, Miguel, 236 (n. 16); as model for Ramón in "The Martyr," 113
Cowley, Malcolm, 95, 225 (n. 23)
Cowley, Peggy, 82
"Creation" (Rivera), 115
Cronstadt (*Tropic of Cancer*), 242 (n. 37)
Cymbeline (Shakespeare), 156

Dante Alighieri, 9, 69, 169, 219
Darwin, Charles, 149
Das Kapital (Marx), 71
Das Narrenschiff (Brant), 162
Dekker, Albert, 83
DeMouy, Jane, 2, 5
Díaz, Porfirio, 15; as symbol in "Hacienda," 92, 93
The Divine Comedy (Dante), 69
Doherty, Mary, 52, 109, 116, 232 (n. 39), 233 (n. 43), 235 (n. 13); as model for Laura in "Flowering Judas," 80
Dos Passos, John, 134
Dylan (Michaels), 94

Eisenstein, Sergei M., 26–27, 225 (n. 23)
Eleanor of Aquitaine, 200
Eliot, T. S., 9
Emerson, Ralph Waldo, 7, 148
Emmons, Winifred S., 2
"An Encounter" (Joyce), 31
Encyclopedists, 12
Erasmus, Desiderius, 231 (n. 19)
Erskine, Albert Russell, 70, 213
Evans, Ernestine, 84, 85, 108
Evans, Rosalie Caden, 174

The Faerie Queen (Spenser), 69
Faulkner, William, 10, 58, 89, 149, 218
Finn, Huck (*The Adventures of Huckleberry Finn*), 139

Firmin, Geoffrey (*Under the Volcano*), 70
Flaubert, Gustave, 219
Forster, E. M., 8, 9, 83, 171
Francis of Assisi, Saint, 231 (n. 19)
The Frescoes of Diego Rivera, 108

Gamio, Manuel, 15, 16, 224 (n. 13)
Gay, Annie and Thomas, as models for Amy and Gabriel in "Old Mortality," 124
Gay, Miranda. *See* Miranda
Gemelli, Giovanni Francesco, 15
George, W. L., 116
Gil, Emilio Portes, 223 (n. 7)
Givner, Joan, 3, 56, 122, 164, 169, 178, 209
Glass Houses (Beals), 107, 134
Goethe, Johann Wolfgang von, 196
Gordon, Caroline, 4, 47, 62, 151, 172, 216, 220, 222 (n. 9 and n. 11)
Gothic fiction, 32
Green, Julian, 178
Gruening, Ernest, 134
Guerrero, Xavier, 234 (n. 55)
Gunn, Drewey, 3
Guzmán, Soledad, 94

Haberman, Robert and Thorberg, 73
Hale, William Harlan, 86, 220
Hanna, Paul, 74–75, 81, 82
Hardy, Edward, 2
Hartley, Lodwick, 1–2, 24, 219
Hawthorne, Nathaniel, 7, 178, 179, 219
Hearst, William Randolph, 72–73
Hendrick, George, 2, 128
Herbst, Josephine, 29, 163, 178, 233 (n. 43)
Hergesheimer, Joseph, 229 (n. 58)
Hermann, John, 114

Herring, Hubert, 85
Hillendahl, Kuno, as source for name Kuno Hillentafel in "The Leaning Tower," 238 (n. 64)
Holloway, Gay Porter (sister of KAP), 58, 64, 72, 219
Holloway, Mary Alice (niece of KAP), 64
Homer, 9, 151
Huerta, Adolfo de la, 223 (n. 7)
Humboldt, Alexander von, 15, 224 (n. 13)
"Hydriotaphia" (Browne), 237 (n. 46)

Inferno (Dante), 70
International Congress of Writers, 83
Ishmael (*Moby-Dick*), 159, 165

James, Henry, 30, 32, 33, 144, 149, 172, 178, 179, 219, 222 (n. 20); child-characters of, 36; style of in "That Tree," 139; villains of, 179
Johns, Erna Schlemmer, 169, 231 (n. 19)
Johnson, James William, 5–6
"The Jolly Corner" (James), 30
Jones, Madison, 151
Joyce, James, 219
Juárez, Benito Pablo, 93

Kahlo, Frida, 108
Kant, Immanuel, 196
Keats, John, 151
Kesey, Ken, 149
Kimbrough, Hunter, 27
Koontz, J. H., 242 (n. 35)
Krishnamurthi, M. G., 2

"The Last of the Valerii" (James), 33
Lavery, Emmet, 83

Lawrence, D. H., 13, 121, 134, 178, 208
Leon, Nicholas, 224 (n. 13)
Le Plongeon, Augustus and Alice, 15
Liberman, M. M., 2, 52
Lopez, Enrique Hank, 3, 16, 107, 117, 224 (n. 12)
Lowenfels, Walter, as model for Julius Löwenthal in *Ship of Fools*, 242 (n. 37)
Lowry, Malcolm, 70
Lugg, Bonelyn, 3

McAlmon, Robert, 107
Madero, Francisco, 14, 15, 84, 93
Magner, James, 62
Mansfield, Katherine, 163
Marie of Champagne, 200
Marin, Guadalupe, as model for Isabel in "The Martyr," 109
Mather, Cotton, 62
Maximilian (Emperor of Mexico), 15
Mayahuel, 229 (n. 53)
Mayans, 13, 61
Melville, Herman, 7, 42
Men of Mexico (Magner), 62
Mena, Licenciado Ramón, 224 (n. 13)
Metaphysics (Aristotle), 228 (n. 47)
Mexican Constitution of 1917, 14, 58
Mexican Feminist Council (La Liga Feminista Obrera), 116, 117
Mexican Revolution (1910–1942), 13, 27–28, 29, 30, 58–59, 61, 194; coalition between primitive art and politics in, 14; indigenism as part of, 15, 22; feminism as part of, 22; socialism as part of, 22; failure of, 28, 107; muralists' role in, 14, 75, 107; as background in "Flowering Judas," 52, 179; as background in "Hacienda," 93; relation of, to European

Mexican Revolution (*cont'd*)
movements, 108; abdication of artists
in, 113; as inspiration for "The
Martyr," 113; Rivera's importance to,
115; as background in *Ship of Fools*
and "That Tree," 167
Mexico: archaeological ruins in, 14, 15,
18; Conquest of, 14, 15; Indians in,
14, 25, 61, 75, 84; *indigenista*
movement in, 14; pre-Columbian
past of, 14; pyramids in valley of, 15;
archaeologists in, 19; Roman Catholic
Church in, 28, 61, 76; Porter in
during the 1920s, 29, 59; petroleum
industry in, 58; Land, Oil, and the
Church as forces in, 59; Mayans in,
61; National University in, 72;
feminist movement in, 79, 116;
Escuelas de Bellas Artes in, 85;
idealized in "That Tree," 131;
expatriate community in, 134, 139; as
ideal in "The Leaning Tower," 142;
National Revolutionary party in, 223
(n. 7)
Mexico City: Porter's arrival in, 58;
Institute of Social Sciences in, 72;
Escuela Preparatoria in, 107; as
represented in *Ship of Fools*, 188;
Chapultepec Park in, 232 (n. 37)
Miller, Henry, 242 (n. 37)
Miranda (Miranda Gay), 220;
relationship to Shakespeare's
Miranda, 49; quest of, 153; source of
name of, 228 (n. 47)
Miranda stories: as early category of
Porter's stories, 4, 5, 48; cycle of, 36,
53, 56, 59, 147, 218
Moby-Dick (Melville), 165
Modotti, Tina, 134
Montherlant, Henry de, 178
Mooney, Harry John, Jr., 2, 83
More, Sir Thomas, 127, 231 (n. 19)

Morones, Luis N., 82
Morrow, Dwight, 84
"The Mysterious Stranger" (Twain),
43

Nance, William L., 2, 4–5, 222 (n. 11)
"Nature" (Emerson), 7
New Masses, 82, 233 (n. 43)
Nietzsche, Friedrich, 196
Niven, William, 16, 224 (n. 15), 224
(n. 16); shop of, 16; as model for
Givens in "María Concepción," 18; as
collaborator with Porter on OMPAC,
18
"A Noiseless Patient Spider" (Whitman),
148
"La Norteña," 233–34 (n. 53)

Obregón, Alvaro, 14, 16, 58, 223 (n. 7);
reforms of, 14; regime of, 14
O'Connor, Flannery, 151
Odilia, Saint, 148
Odyssey (Homer), 216
O'Gorman, Juan, 92
Old Mortality (Scott), 128
Orozco, José Clemente, 236 (n. 16)
Osmond, Gilbert (*The Portrait of a
Lady*), 203

Padilla, Castro, 233 (n. 53)
Palacio, Vicente Riva, 224 (n. 13)
Pauline pattern, 69
Pavlova, Anna, 13, 25
Pilgrim's Progress (Bunyan), 162
Plato, 12, 49, 85, 228 (n. 47)
Poe, Edgar Allan, 127, 129
Porter, Gay. *See* Holloway, Gay Porter
Porter, Harrison Boone (father of KAP),
7, 59, 70, 227 (n. 40); religious views
of, 229–30 (n. 4); as inspiration for
Thompsons in "Noon Wine," 230 (n.
11)

Porter, Harrison Paul (nephew of KAP), 70, 106, 120, 227 (n. 40)

Porter, Harry Ray [Harrison Paul] (brother of KAP), 59, 116

Porter, Katherine Anne: life of, as inspiration for art, 3; canonical plan of, 4, 6, 7, 46, 161, 201, 222 (n. 8); as artistically preoccupied with truth, 6; world view of, 7, 219; reasons for going to Mexico, 13; scapegoat theme in fiction of, 23–24, 28, 29; interest of, in primitivism, 24; departure from Mexico in 1931, 29; experiences in Mexican revolution, 35, 71, 107, 130, 209; Miranda cycle in works of, 53, 56, 59, 218; disdain for capitalists, 72; leftist sympathies of, 72, 82; plans to teach dancing in Mexico, 72; idealistic view of mother, 124; meaning of Germany to, 169, 242 (n. 36); heritage of, 218; settings in stories of, 218; as avoider of dogma, 219; style of, as symbol of aesthetic integrity, 219–20; as artist, 220; source for religious symbols of, 230 (n. 12), 231 (n. 17); appreciation of, for corrido, 234 (n. 54)

—Books:

The Collected Stories of Katherine Anne Porter, 225 (n. 30)

The Days Before, 1

Flowering Judas and Other Stories, 1, 4, 24

The Leaning Tower and Other Stories, 1

My Chinese Marriage, 17, 116

Outline of Mexican Popular Arts and Crafts, 16, 18, 130

Pale Horse, Pale Rider: Three Short Novels, 1

Ship of Fools, 5, 33, 70, 139, 145; critical controversy of, 1; as final stage of thematic and stylistic evolution, 161, archetypal quest in, 161, 162, 170; genesis of, 161; stylistic techniques in, 161; early titles for, 162–63; voyage symbolism in, 162, 208, 213; Bremerhaven in, 163, 185, 213; composition of, 163–64; Veracruz in, 163, 165, 166–70, 184, 185, 202, 213; structure of, 164–65; symbolism in, 164–65; opening frame of, 165–72; themes of, 165; crucifixion symbolism in, 166–70; class stratification in, 167, 185, 186; revolutionary background of, 167; animal imagery in, 168, 171, 176, 213; multiple viewpoints in, 168; allegorical context of, 169; illusion in, 169, 198; the Vera in, 169, 172; Dr. Schumann in, 170–71, 177, 178, 179, 180, 181, 183–84, 190, 192, 196–97, 198–99, 201, 203, 204–205, 206, 207–208, 211, 212, 214, 216; truth in, 170; identity as theme in, 171; David Scott in, 172, 173, 179, 185, 186, 189, 190, 191, 201, 203, 204, 211, 214, 215; death in, 172, 181, 182–84, 213–14, 216; Germany represented in, 172, 187; instinct in, 172; Jenny Brown in, 172, 173, 179, 185, 189, 190, 191, 193, 201, 202–203, 204, 205, 208, 210–11, 212, 213, 214, 216–17; La Condesa in, 172, 176, 177, 179, 180–81, 192, 197, 203, 205, 207, 212; love in, 172, 201, 202, 208–12, 216; Captain Thiele in, 172, 186, 187, 194–95, 199, 211; Wilibald Graf in, 172, 175, 183, 192, 196, 203, 208, 209; Zarzuela troupe in, 172, 173, 174–75, 176,

Katherine Anne Porter
—Books (cont'd)
    177, 178, 179, 187, 193, 199, 203,
    213; dream-vision in, 173, 198,
    207–208; Mary Treadwell in, 173–
    75, 181, 182, 183, 184, 186, 189,
    192, 193, 197, 201, 202, 203, 208,
    212; bloodlust in, 174; sexuality in,
    174; William Denny in, 174, 175,
    179, 186, 189, 215, 242 (n. 35);
    Ric and Rac in, 175, 176, 177,
    208, 211, 213; Wilhelm Freytag in,
    175, 187, 188, 189, 191, 200–201,
    202–203, 204, 205, 215; cruelty
    in, 178; religious perspectives in,
    178, 185, 190, 193; good and evil
    in, 177, 179–81, 184, 196, 216;
    Karl Glocken in, 179, 213, 214,
    215; Julius Löwenthal in, 179, 187,
    188, 189, 190, 242 (n. 37);
    isolation as theme in, 184; stranger
    as metaphor in, 184; nationalism
    in, 185, 186–87; regionalism in,
    185; sexism in, 185, 190–93; anti-
    Semitism in, 187, 188, 190; Mary
    Champagne in, 187, 188, 197,
    200–201, 202, 215; Nazism in,
    187, 188, 189, 194, 195, 199, 233
    (n. 43); order in, 193, 199; politics
    in, 193; social decorum in, 193,
    197; systems in, 193, 195; socialism
    in, 194; the past in, 196; place as
    ideal in, 197–99; myth in, 198,
    209; canonical design apparent in,
    201; primitive art in, 201; antilife
    imagery in, 213–15; false hopes in,
    215; conclusion of, 216; reviews of,
    216
—Essays and miscellaneous pieces:
    "The Charmed Life," 18
    "The Children of Xochitl," 25, 28,
    107; María Santísima in, 29

"The Fiesta of Guadalupe," 26
"The Flower of Flowers," 57, 64,
    120, 122
"From a Mexican Painter's
    Notebook," 108, 114
"The Historical Present" (unfinished
    novel), 130
Introduction to What Price Marriage,
    236 (n. 25)
"The Man in the Tree" (unfinished
    story), 225 (n. 27)
"Marriage Is Belonging," 36, 39
"Measures for Song and Dance"
    (poem), 22
"The Mexican Trinity," 59, 62, 74,
    107, 110
"The Necessary Enemy," 35, 39
"The Never-Ending Wrong"
    (unfinished story), 225 (n. 27)
" 'Noon Wine': The Sources," 3, 51, 94
"On a Criticism of Thomas Hardy,"
    149
"St. Augustine and the Bullfight," 6,
    8, 39–40, 152
"Why She Selected 'Flowering
    Judas,' " 3
"Xochimilco," 25
—Short fiction:
    "The Circus," 5, 52, 59, 149;
    analyzed, 30–33; bloodlust in, 31;
    cruelty in, 31, 33; death in, 31, 33,
    48; love, profane, in, 31, 33;
    Miranda in, 31, 32, 33, 39, 40, 45,
    118, 146, 182; symbolism of circus
    in, 31; grotesque as character in,
    33; female principle in, 48
    "The Cracked Looking-Glass," 2, 6,
    62, 97, 122–24; Rosaleen O'Toole
    in, 63, 97, 122–24, 202; analyzed,
    122–24; illusion in, 122; "St.
    Martin's Summer," early title for,
    122

"A Day's Work," 6, 63, 98, 146; social decorum in, 98
"The Downward Path to Wisdom," 5, 33, 50, 59, 146, 177; analyzed, 36–39; animal imagery in, 36–37; Stephen in, 36–39, 177, 220; cruelty and hate in, 37
"The Fig Tree," 5, 29, 52, 56, 59; primitivism in, 29–30; analyzed, 45–48; Great-Aunt Eliza in, 45, 46, 48, 149; Cedar Grove in, 46–47; Grandmother in, 46–48; Miranda in, 46–47, 55, 146; Aunt Nannie in, 47–48; symbolism of fig tree in, 47, 48, 213; Adam and Eve myth in, 48; death in, 48; female principle in, 48; elemental truths in, 149; science in, 149
"Flowering Judas," 2, 6, 60, 63, 70, 75–82, 93, 113, 116, 117, 146, 173, 174, 181, 206, 215–16; analyzed, 52–59; Laura in, 52–57, 59, 60, 76–81, 84–85, 93, 139, 146, 173, 174, 206, 208, 220; revolution in, 52, 66, 79, 167; West's interpretation of, 52; Braggioni in, 53–54, 57, 68, 76–81, 106, 110; Eugenio in, 53–55, 78–80, 206; love in, 53, 77–78; primitivism in, 53; sexual imagery in, 53; flower symbolism and imagery in, 55–59; symbolism of Judas tree in, 55–56; female principle in, 56, 59, 80; machine imagery and symbolism in, 57, 59, 86; biblical imagery in, 66, 76–77; religious structure of, 69; Catholicism in, 76; Mrs. Braggioni in, 77, 79–81, 106, 117; feminism in, 79; genesis of, 80–81; self-love in, 80, 106; betrayal in, 101; use of historical present tense in, 130;

expatriated woman in, 139; dream-vision in, 146, 181, 206
"The Grave," 5, 45, 52–53, 56, 59, 147, 170; analyzed, 48–53; dove symbolism in, 49–51, 151; social decorum in, 49; Miranda in, 49–53, 149, 181; Paul in, 49–51, 149, 152, 159–60; rabbit symbolism in, 49–51; death in, 50; female principle in, 52, 150; allusion to Eden in, 52; truth about luxury in, 128; elemental truths in, 149–53; mortality in, 150; symbolism of grave in, 150–51; symbolism of ring in, 151; structure of, 152, 159–60
"Hacienda," 30, 59, 60, 75, 113; primitivism in, 25, 26, 27; analyzed, 26–29, 85–93; revision of, 26–27, 85, 86, 87; Tetlapajac hacienda as model for hacienda in, 26; Indians in, 27; myth in, 27; Andreyev in, 28, 87, 88, 91–92, 233 (n. 51); Carlos Montaña in, 28, 60, 90–91, 146; *corrido* in, 28, 91, 233 (n. 51); homosexuality in, 28; machine and oil metaphors in, 57; Betancourt in, 60, 87, 89, 90, 91, 92; Kennerly in, 62, 90, 92; as thematically related to "Flowering Judas," 83; revolution in, 84, 93, 167; unnamed narrator of, 84, 86, 91, 93, 139, 146, 159; change as theme in, 86–88, 92–93; train and automobile symbolism in, 86; illusion in, 87; baby imagery in, 89; love in, 91; Díaz as symbol in, 92; light symbolism in, 92; changing of orders in, 93; use of historical present tense in, 130; as extension of "Flowering Judas," 139
"He," 6, 39, 59, 95, 97, 104, 146,

Katherine Anne Porter
—Short Fiction (*cont'd*)
220; analyzed, 33–35; setting of,
40; class consciousness in, 95;
fundamentalists as models for
characters in, 95
"Holiday," 33, 35, 39, 59, 70, 71,
101, 147, 148, 199; animal
imagery in, 50–51, 104; religious
structure of, 69; atheism in, 71;
Marxism in, 71; order as theme in,
101–102, 104, 148; setting of,
101–102; Ottilie Müller in, 102–
104, 147, 148, 213; unnamed
narrator of, 102–104, 147, 148,
149; love in, 103, 122; analyzed,
147–49; death in, 148; composition
of, 225 (n. 30)
"The Jilting of Granny Weatherall,"
6, 63, 71, 104, 142, 146, 183, 199,
220; Catholicism in, 63; truth in,
63; light symbolism in, 64, 99;
religious structure of, 69; analyzed,
98–101; patterns in, 98–99; color
imagery in, 100; betrayal as theme
in, 101; biblical allusion in, 101;
dream-vision in, 101; deification of
humans as theme in, 106
"The Journey," 30; as background for
"The Fig Tree," 149
"The Last Leaf," 29; Aunt Nannie in,
29–30
"The Leaning Tower," 5, 6, 60, 198,
199; analyzed, 139–45; Germans
in, 139; Germany as setting for,
139; relationship of, to *Ship of
Fools*, 139; illusion of ideals in,
140, 144, 145; Kuno in, 140, 144;
place as ideal in, 140–42, 144;
Charles Upton in, 140–45, 146,
169; pig imagery in, 141; leaning
tower as symbol of ideal in, 142;

Rosa Reichl in, 142–45;
subjectivity of ideals in, 143; death
in, 145; Germany as symbol of false
hopes in, 145; title of, 238 (n. 61)
"Magic," 6, 64–65, 146; religious
structure of, 69; model for Madame
Blanchard in, 231 (n. 15)
"María Concepción," 6, 17, 19, 26,
27, 28, 29, 30, 35, 59, 61, 75,
107, 113, 146, 197; analyzed, 16–
25; as Porter's first published story,
16–17; source of, 16; Indians in,
17, 19, 21; Juan Villegas in, 17,
19–24, 33, 61, 68; María
Concepción in, 17, 18, 19–23;
María Rosa in, 17, 19–24, 197;
Givens in, 18, 19, 22–23;
indigenista movement represented
in, 19; Lupe in, 19, 33; Porter's
later style evident in, 19;
Catholicism in, 20–21; racial myth
in, 20; relationship between
primitive and civilized in, 20, 21;
Adam and Eve myth in, 21; instinct
in, 21; feminism in, 22; scapegoat
myth in, 23–24, 28; Allen Tate on,
24; Lodwick Hartley on, 24;
religion in, 60–61; religious
structure of, 69; revolution in, 83;
biblical imagery and allusion in,
166; setting of, 224–25 (n. 18)
"The Martyr," 146; Rubén in, 60,
107, 109, 110, 112, 114, 214;
religious structure of, 69;
deification of humans in, 106, 109;
analyzed, 107–15; Isabel in, 109,
110, 112, 114; love in, 110, 111,
112; Ramón in, 111, 112, 113;
doctor in, 112, 195; perversion of
art in, 112; Guadalupe Marin as
model for Isabel in, 112–13; the
Mexican revolution as inspiration

for, 113; *Monotes* as model for café in, 113; number symbolism in, 115; reasons Porter did not include in early collections, 115

"Noon Wine," 2, 5, 35, 59, 62, 90, 95, 96, 172, 184; analyzed, 40–45; Ellie Thompson in, 40–45, 62, 63, 95, 97, 104, 180; evil in, 40; Homer T. Hatch in, 40–45, 63, 90, 96; Olaf Helton in, 40–44, 63; Royal Earle Thompson in, 40–45, 59, 63, 94, 96, 97, 104, 220, 227 (n. 40); title of, 41–42; rabbit imagery and symbolism in, 44–45; animal imagery in, 50; light and sight symbolism in, 63–64; religion in, 63; religious structure of, 69; class consciousness in, 95; fundamentalists as models for characters in, 95; social decorum in, 95; stranger as metaphor in, 184

"Old Mortality," 2, 6, 70; Amy in, 124–27; Amy-Gabriel legend in, 124–25, 127; analyzed, 124–31; Gabriel in, 124, 125–29; Miranda in, 124–31, 146, 153, 158; past as ideal in, 124, 127, 129; romantic love in, 124, 125–26; art in, 127; truth about victory in, 128; integration of past and present in, 130; duality as theme in, 131; "That Book of Amy," early working title of, 131

"The Old Order" (series of seven stories), 5, 30, 31, 45, 59; Miranda in, 30, 149, 153, 158; Uncle Jimbilly in, 128

"Pale Horse, Pale Rider," 6, 45, 59, 147, 172; religious structure of, 69; analyzed, 153–60; death as theme in, 153–55; imagery and symbolism in, 153–58; Miranda in,

153–60, 181, 182, 183, 184, 216; narrative style in, 153; Adam in, 154–55, 157–60, 234–35 (n. 1); journey motif in, 154–57; reconciling power of love in, 157; illusion as theme in, 159; narrative structure of, 159–60; title of, 159; inspiration for, 240 (n. 12)

"The Prisoner," 202

"Rope," 6, 35, 59, 146, 172; composition of, 226 (n. 32)

"The Source," 30; as background for "The Fig Tree," 149

"The Strangers," 184

"That Tree," 6, 60, 146; Miriam in, 62, 131–38; analyzed, 131–39; unnamed journalist in, 131–38; expatriate community in, 133; narrative viewpoint of, 135–37; American bourgeoise ideal in, 137; meaning of title of, 137–38; symbolism of tree in, 137–38; symbolism of chalk line in, 138; as Porter's comment on Anglo-American expatriates in Mexico, 139; as transitional story, 139; James's style in, 139; revolutionary background of, 167

"Theft," 6, 181; analyzed, 65–70; Christian imagery in, 66–70; unnamed protagonist of, 66–70, 146; alcohol as sacrament in, 68; wasteland theme in, 68; water symbolism in, 68; inferno images in, 69, 231 (n. 18); religious structure of, 69

"Virgin Violeta," 33, 59, 146, 202; religious structure of, 69; feminism in, 115; inspired by Mexican revolution, 115; analyzed, 117–20; Carlos in, 117, 118–20; sexuality in, 118, 120; unrequited love in,

Katherine Anne Porter
—Short Fiction (cont'd)
  118; lust in, 119, 120; the Catholic
  church in, 120; romantic love in,
  120
  "The Witness," 30; as background for
  "The Fig Tree," 149
—Views and opinions:
  Apathy, 66, 70, 180
  Art: as shaper of order, 8; as
    inspiration, 9; unnatural, 9; as way
    to truth, 60; greatness in, 114
  Artist: mission of, 8, 60, 220; dangers
    to, 71; plague of, 178; public
    interest in, 178; as affiliated with
    evil, 179
  Bloodlust, 39, 40
  Catholicism, Roman, 61–63, 230 (n.
    7); in Mexico, 62, 116, 117
  Change, 86
  Children, 13, 36
  Class stratification, 94
  Communism, 82, 83
  Death, 39, 51
  Evil, 7, 10, 12, 40, 57, 64, 172, 175;
    as assisted by apathy, 70, 180;
    psychological causes of, 175
  Feminism, 116
  God, 7, 9–10, 11, 230 (n. 4)
  Governments, 10
  Hate, 35–36, 38
  Love, 10, 11, 106, 120, 121, 122
  Middle class virtue, 95
  Past, 10, 86
  Primitivism, 13, 16, 21, 24, 28, 29,
    134
  Religion, 10, 26, 60, 62, 64, 71, 190;
    as shaper of sense of order, 8; values
    and dangers of, 9
  Revolution: Mexican, 24, 71–75;
    Russian, 75
  Self-righteousness, 62
  Sexism, 116

Spiritualism, 64
Symbolism, 55, 163, 240 (n. 6)
Truth, 6, 7, 9, 13, 60, 70, 113, 145,
  219
Witchcraft, 64
Porter, Mary Alice [Breckenridge] (sister
  of KAP), 50, 57, 210
Porter, Mary Alice Jones (mother of
  KAP), 124, 209
Portrait of Mexico (Wolfe), 108
Prescott, William Hickling, 224 (n. 13)
Pressly, Eugene, 56–57, 139, 163, 233
  (n. 43)
Prynne, Hester (The Scarlet Letter), 139

Que Viva Mexico, 26, 93, 225 (n. 23)

Redencion, 116
Reed, John, 134
Retinger, Joseph Hieronim, 235 (n. 13),
  239 (n. 66), 243 (n. 43)
Reville, Albert, 224 (n. 13)
Rhetoric (Aristotle), 152
Rilke, Rainer Maria, 242 (n. 36)
Rivera, Diego, 75, 84, 92–93, 107–
  109, 112, 113, 115, 235 (n. 14); as
  model for Rubén in "The Martyr,"
  109; "Monkeys" of, as symbolic of
  aesthetic ideal, 113
Robles, Eduardo Vigil y, 234 (n. 53)
Rodríguez, Abelardo, 14, 223 (n. 7)
Royas, Avelina, 116–17
Rubin, Louis D., Jr., 151

Sahagún, Bernardino de, 15
Saints and Strangers (Willison), 231 (n.
  9)
Saldívar, don Julio, 27
Sanctuary (Faulkner), 58
"La Sandunga," 233 (n. 51)
Schlemmer, Erna. See Johns, Erna
  Schlemmer
Schopenhauer, Arthur, 196

Selva, Salomon de la, 117
Shakespeare, William, 9, 127, 196
Siqueiros, David, 92, 107, 109, 234 (n. 55)
Simpson, Lesley Byrd, 134
"Song of Myself" (Whitman), 151
Sophocles, 9
The Sound and the Fury (Faulkner), 10, 58
Spenser, Edmund, 69, 127
Spratling, William, 84
"Spring and Fall: To a Young Child" (Hopkins), 51
Steffens, Lincoln, 73, 138
Stevens, Wallace, 8, 9
The Story of Women (George), 116
Sutherland, Donald, 6, 8

Taggard, Genevieve, 231 (n. 19)
Tannenbaum, Frank, 61, 85, 134
Tate, Allen, 24
Tenenbaum, Jean Thompson, 228 (n. 47)
Tenney, Jack, 83
Tetlapajac, Hacienda, as model for Genaro hacienda in "Hacienda," 26
Texcoco, archaeological digs near, 18
Theaetetus (Plato), 228 (n. 47)
Thomas, Dylan, 94, 134
Thomas Aquinas, Saint, 180, 231 (n. 19)
Thomas School, as model for convent school in "Old Mortality," 237 (n. 43)
Thompson, Barbara, 8, 13, 75, 80, 105, 164, 184, 222 (n. 10), 240 (n. 12)
Thoreau, Henry David, 7, 214
Tissé, Eduard, 27
Tlalnepantla, archaeological digs near, 18
Teotihuacán, ruins of, 15, 16
Torres, Elena, 116
"Town Meeting of the Air," 82

Transcendentalists, 7, 9
Traven, B., 229 (n. 53)
Tropic of Cancer (Miller), 242 (n. 37)
Tula, excavations at, 15
Two Cheers for Democracy (Forster), 83

Under the Volcano (Lowry), 70
"Urne-Burial" (Browne), 128

Vasconcelos, José, 107
Villa, Pancho, 73
Vita Nuova (Dante), 127

War and Peace (Tolstoy), 231 (n. 19)
Warren, Robert Penn, 3, 10, 37, 155–56, 218, 222 (n. 10), 228 (n. 49), 233 (n. 43); as early critic of Porter's fiction, 2
Waugh, Evelyn, 229 (n. 58)
Wescott, Glenway, 163
West, Ray B., 2, 52
Weston, Edward, 134
Wheeler, Monroe, 13, 178
Whitman, Walt, 7, 9, 148, 213
Williams, William Carlos, 8, 242 (n. 38)
Willison, George F., 230 (n. 9)
Wilson, Edmund, 4, 222 (n. 10)
Winston, Archer, 185
Wolfe, Bertram, 108, 113
Wolfe, Thomas, 218
Woolf, Virginia, 238 (n. 61)

Xochimilco, 13, 25, 52
Xochitl, 25, 55, 209, 229 (n. 53)

Yaddo, 161, 163
Yeats, William Butler, 10, 152
Yúdico, Samuel, 80–81, 232 (n. 39), 235 (n. 13)

Zanoni (Bulwer-Lytton), 32